Literacy Activities for Classic and Contemporary Texts 7–14

English teachers are always keen to explore new ways of motivating their pupils to engage with reading, both for learning and for pleasure. *Literacy Activities for Classic and Contemporary Texts 7–14* is a practical, friendly book which uses the 'Whoosh' to cover some of our best known classic and contemporary texts and offers a thoroughly enjoyable way for pupils to become part of the story, rather than just passive recipients of it. As an innovative and active learning strategy, the Whoosh technique allows all students, regardless of gender, age, ability, learning need or command of language, to partake on an equal footing.

For younger pupils, the activities in this book provide an ideal way to internalise structure and key elements in storytelling through physical response. For older students, they provide an enjoyable way to engage with challenging texts as well as facilitating the analysis of themes, issues, characterisation and setting. Students themselves become the story as its characters, sounds and even objects and, once they are familiar with whooshing, many students will want to write and produce a Whoosh of their own.

Classic authors and texts covered by this book include:

- Aesop's fables, Greek myths and legends;
- 'Beowulf', 'Sir Gawain and the Green Knight';
- Shakespeare ('The Tempest', 'Twelfth Night', 'Hamlet', 'A Midsummer Night's Dream' and more);
- Charlotte Brontë, Charles Dickens, George Eliot, Robert Louis Stevenson, Mary Shelley, Oscar Wilde, George Bernard Shaw;
- Andrew Norriss, Frank Cottrell Boyce, Nina Bawden, Michelle Magorian and many more...

You can use a Whoosh to introduce a new text, to examine conflict, dilemma, plot, setting or characterisation, whoosh a controversial section of text to provoke discussion, or overcome reluctance to engage with archaic language by whooshing key sections of a story. Discussion starters, lesson objectives and follow-up activities are included throughout the text alongside the Whooshes, and scripts enabling pupils to deliver dialogue are provided on the book's eResources website.

This book is an invaluable resource, providing Whooshes across a wide range of genres to meet the learning needs of children from 7 to 14, for both practising primary and lower secondary teachers.

Gill Robins is a former deputy head in the primary sector, managing English for several years. She received the UKLA John Downing Award in 2010. Until 2011 she chaired the English Association Editorial Board for the *English 4–11* journal.

Laura-Jane Evans-Jones is a secondary school English teacher who also sat on the TES English Teaching panel from 2010 to 2011.

They are authors of *The Essential Charles Dickens School Resource*.

Literacy Activities for Classic and Contemporary Texts 7–14

The Whoosh Book

Gill Robins and
Laura-Jane Evans-Jones

Routledge
Taylor & Francis Group

LONDON AND NEW YORK

First published 2013
by Routledge
2 Park Square, Milton Park, Abingdon, Oxon OX14 4RN

Simultaneously published in the USA and Canada
by Routledge
711 Third Avenue, New York, NY 10017

Routledge is an imprint of the Taylor & Francis Group, an informa business

British Library Cataloguing in Publication Data
A catalogue record for this book is available from the British Library

Library of Congress Cataloging in Publication Data
Robins, Gill.
Literacy activities for classic and contemporary texts 7-14 : the whoosh
book / Gill Robins and Laura-Jane Evans-Jones.
    pages cm
Includes index.
1. Language arts (Elementary) – Activity programs. 2. Reading
(Elementary). 3. Literature – Study and teaching (Elementary).
I. Evans-Jones, Laura-Jane. II. Title.
LB1576.R625 2013
372.6´044–dc23   2012047504

ISBN: 978-0-415-81178-1 (pbk)

Typeset in Helvetica
by HWA Text and Data Management, London

MIX
Paper from
responsible sources
FSC
www.fsc.org   FSC® C013604

Printed and bound by CPI Group (UK) Ltd, Croydon, CR0 4YY

Contents

Resources

Acknowledgements

We would like to thank Professor Joseph Winston of the University of Warwick for permission to use his original concept of a Whoosh.

The following are reproduced by permission of Penguin Books Ltd, London, UK:
    Chapter 1 of *The Touchstone* by Andrew Norriss (2004)
    Chapter 1 of *Carrie's War* by Nina Bawden (1974)
    Chapter 15 of *Goodnight Mister Tom* by Michelle Magorian (Kestrel 1981)
    pp 93–132 of *Stone Cold* by Robert Swindells (1993).

The Vomit Comet (pp161–172) from *Cosmic* by Frank Cottrell Boyce is reproduced by permission of Macmillan Children's Books, London, UK.

Extracts from chapters 1–6 of *Holes* by Louis Sachar (2000) are reproduced by permission of Bloomsbury Publishing plc.

Extracts from *Kensuke's Kingdom* by Michael Morpurgo are reproduced by permission of David Higham Associates on behalf of Michael Morpurgo.

Extracts from *An Inspector Calls* are reprinted by permission of United Agents on behalf of the Estate of J B Priestley.

Acts I and II of *Pygmalion* are reproduced by permission of the Society of Authors on behalf of the Bernard Shaw Estate.

Extracts from *The Hound of the Baskervilles* by Sir Arthur Conan Doyle are reproduced by permission of Jonathan Clowes Ltd on behalf of Andrea Plunkett.

Introduction

This book introduces the Whoosh; the following information explains what a Whoosh is and suggests how and when it can be used. It is a powerful means of engaging all pupils, regardless of gender, age or language maturity, in a multimodal learning experience that brings texts alive.

The origin of the Whoosh

Whoosh is a drama activity created by Joe Winston, Professor of Drama and Arts Education at the University of Warwick. It was first described in his 2008 book *Beginning Drama 4–11*. The activity, which he explains as 'acting out the story' was then incorporated into the Royal Shakespeare Company's education programme. The term 'Whoosh' was inspired by a sound which formed an integral part of the original activity.

Who can Whoosh

Because of its versatility, it can be used with any pupils. It requires no specific experience, just a willingness to participate in a circle activity. There is no limit on the age or ability of students who will enjoy and learn from a Whoosh. The teacher acts as the storyteller and directs pupils' entry to, and exit from, the action. This directing role could also be taken by a student.

How to Whoosh

Stand or seat pupils in a circle which is big enough to provide a performance space. Start reading the Whoosh. When a character, object, place or event is mentioned, the first pupil, or group of pupils, should move into the circle to enact this by creating a pose rather like a still image. For example, pupils could create the shape of a window or pillar, or pose to portray a key character. Mime, action, interaction or dialogue can be improvised as the Whoosh progresses.

Sound effects can be added by single students, a small group or, if appropriate, by everyone. They also give an opportunity to explore vocal sounds and body percussion – a significant musical skill which younger children need to develop. The important thing is to improvise and explore possibilities.

The complete group can also become a setting, for example a wood or an abandoned village. Props can be included and pupils' creative ideas incorporated as the action progresses. As the story unfolds, more pupils step into the circle to act out the story and a scene is built up.

When a scene is complete, the leader says, 'Whoosh' and everyone returns to their original place in the circle, ready for the next section of the story. With young children, a special sound can be substituted for the word 'Whoosh'. The original activity used a stick and it is the magical sound which accompanied the stick from which the activity derives its name. Whatever your agreed signal to end the action, rehearse its use and ensure that everyone understands what to do when the signal is given – it can also be used at any time if the performance space becomes too crowded or pupils are losing focus.

Before commencing a Whoosh, ensure that pupils are familiar with the use of body language and other forms of non-verbal communication. Use a warm-up game to refresh skills at the start of a session. It can also be advantageous to video the Whoosh. This provides students with the opportunity to revisit the Whoosh, reminding themselves of details which they may have missed or forgotten. A video also provides pupils with an opportunity to evaluate their own learning.

Why Whoosh

By being part of the action, pupils become part of the story, rather than just passive recipients of it. Participants are able to step outside of their personal experience, consider issues from perspectives other than their own and develop empathy with characters. It provides a safe medium within which to suspend disbelief while exploring new ideas and experimenting with new roles. Because roles are changed frequently, everyone has a chance to act out different characters in a shared context. As a circle activity, all participants in the group are equal, regardless of age, ability, command of language or gender – this also strengthens social cohesion.

The improvisatory nature of a Whoosh provides ample opportunity to develop creativity. It supports students' development of spatial awareness and self-confidence in the use of their voices when speaking and their bodies when considering facial expression, gesture and posture as modes of communication. It also contributes to the development of language skills; a more extensive vocabulary is used for speaking than writing.

A Whoosh can be embarked upon without prior knowledge of the text, motivating students to engage with complex stories which may not relate directly to their individual social or cultural contexts. Once students own the story through active learning, they are more likely to embark willingly on a study of the text, even one which involves archaic language, complex sentence structures or dense narrative. A Whoosh will enhance understanding, build skills in inference and deduction and lay the seedbed for response activities.

Alongside the wide range of whooshed texts provided in this book, there are suggestions for the possible application of each Whoosh within a unit of work. There are ideas about learning outcomes, possible follow up activities, discussion points and core skill development. Whooshes provide a powerful interactive learning experience at every level for pupils who engage in them.

The Whoosh book structure

The book is divided into six sections. Parts 1 and 2 use complete stories and are designed primarily for 7–9 year olds. This supports the development of understanding of story structure, storytelling skills and vocabulary enrichment, and it also offers scaffolds for creative writing. Some of the Whooshes focus on specific language objectives; this feature is not included for older students where language study needs to be confined to consideration of the author's original text.

Part 3 focuses on plays, in particular those Shakespeare plays most often studied by the 7–14 age group. Most use Shakespeare's original language in dialogue but *Hamlet* is transcribed. Part 4 offers a range of classic texts, Part 5 contains some popular modern novels and Part 6 demonstrates how to write an effective Whoosh.

The texts which form the basis of the Whooshes, together with the follow-up activities, have been specifically chosen to offer coverage of a balanced English curriculum. They include speaking and listening (talking to and with others and talking within role play), text meaning (understanding text structure and organisation; identifying authorial viewpoint and purpose; describing, inferring and deducing meaning and relating texts to historical, cultural and social settings), and creative and analytical writing.

There are opportunities to challenge all learning competencies, with activities ranging from recall and understanding to analysis and evaluation. A few activities offer ways for students to create new texts. Suggested questions range from straightforward fact retrieval to questions which develop the higher-order thinking: skills of hypothesis, analysis and synthesis.

Using the book

Each Whoosh uses a common format. The list of characters, objects and sounds which follows the objective gives an idea of how many people are needed and what props and sound effects could be sourced. The bold text shows where a character should perform an action, an object should be present in the performance space or a sound should be performed. These are suggestions – as you and your students become more confident, you will create other ideas.

Speech, where it is integral to the narrative, is also bolded. For younger pupils, this is limited to words or short phrases which can be echoed after the leader has read them. There are also opportunities for choral speaking of short phrases at key points in the story. More confident pupils can improvise dialogue where the text suggests; the Whooshes for older students contain more speech – in this case provide scripts for the actors.

We hope that you enjoy whooshing with your students and that it provides an exciting and engaging way of approaching texts. We also hope that you go beyond using the book, both to write your own Whooshes and encourage your students to write and produce their own Whooshes, too.

Gill Robins
Laura-Jane Evans-Jones
October 2012

1 Legends, myths and fables

1 Aesop's fables: *The Lion and the Mouse*

A fable is a short story which aims to teach children a particular moral point. Usually, fables are anthropomorphic, using animals as the central characters and giving them human characteristics. This structure is common to many cultures and is valued as a means of engaging children in stories whilst also teaching important lessons. Fables demonstrate one of the reasons why we tell stories – to pass wisdom and knowledge from generation to generation in a memorable and entertaining form.

Aesop is one of the most famous creators of fables. He was a slave and renowned story teller, who probably lived in ancient Greece in the fifth century BC. More than 650 fables are attributed to Aesop and although modern scholars question whether he actually created all of these tales himself, they are now famous and much-loved across the world.

Because fables are short, they are ideal for young children to act out in one session. The following Whoosh focuses on story structure.

Objective

- to consider story structure.

Characters	Objects	Sounds
Lion Mouse hunters other animals	sky sun rays from the sun grasses rope tree	swishing breathing roaring shouting

One afternoon, drowsy **Lion** fell fast asleep, with his head resting peacefully on his huge, soft paws. High up in a cloudless blue **sky** the burning **sun** shimmered, its **rays** reaching down to warm Lion's fur as he slept. The long **grasses** swayed in the breeze, gently **swishing** in time with Lion's steady **breathing**. **Mouse**, who was busily running up and down through the **grass**, grew bold and scuttled across **Lion**'s nose. Feeling a tickle, **Lion** opened one eye and stretched out a huge paw to catch **Mouse** and swallow him. '*Forgive me*,' squeaked **Mouse**. '*Please don't hurt me. Let me go and one day I might be able to help you in return*.' **Lion** found this idea so funny that he lifted up his paw and let **Mouse** run away, before drifting back to sleep.

WHOOSH

A few weeks later, **Lion** was stalking proudly through the **grass** when he felt the tug of a **rope** around his feet. **Lion** twisted this way and that way, but the more he struggled, the tighter the **rope** became. As a group of **hunters** surrounded him, he **roared** with all of his might. The **other animals** shook with fear at the terrible sound, but the **hunters** just laughed as they tied **Lion** firmly to a **tree**. '*We will keep this fine beast alive and take him to the King*,' they all agreed and they went off **shouting** in triumph to find a cart big enough to carry **Lion**.

WHOOSH

Mouse, who had heard the roars, found **Lion** struggling to break free from the **ropes** that bound him so tightly to the **tree**. With his little sharp teeth, **Mouse** soon nibbled right through the **ropes** and **Lion** found himself free. '*I laughed at you, little Mouse*' boomed **Lion**, '*because I didn't think such a tiny creature could help someone so strong and brave as me. But you have saved my life.*' And so, that day, **Lion** learned that even little friends can turn out to be great friends.

WHOOSH

Follow-up activities

- If you are introducing the concept of story structure for the first time, draw a simple story frame with three consecutive sections labelled beginning, middle and end and explain the terms. Through shared discussion, recall together the key facts of the story, recording contributions in the correct box in word or picture form to show the sequence of events. A template is provided as Resource 1.
- If pupils have prior knowledge of story structure, use shared discussion to define the beginning, middle and end of the story, noting the content in each section. Paired discussion can be useful to assist recall of key facts. You could also use story tennis: a pair of pupils alternate to recall one fact from the story, expressing it in a single sentence.
- Provide confident or able pupils with a blank sheet of paper and challenge them to devise a three-section story plan with the key facts of each section of the story written or drawn in sequence.
- Using the outcome of these discussions, model the planning of a new fable in picture or word form. Discuss what needs to be created (characters, a plot and a meaning) and brainstorm ideas. Then ask pupils to do the same, individually, in pairs or in groups. Pupils could use Resource 1 as the planning format, recording their story plan and key vocabulary.
- If appropriate to age and ability, model the writing of a fable before asking pupils to write their own fable, either in words or pictures.

2 The Panchatantra: *The Blue Jackal*

This collection of Indian animal fables, some in verse and some in prose, probably dates back to the third century BC. In addition to becoming part of Hindu folklore, there are now many variations of the stories in other countries around the world. 'Panchatantra' is a Sanskrit word meaning 'five principles' and more than 80 stories are organised into five books, each of which centres on a different theme.

During this Whoosh, capture the action by taking digital pictures to use in the follow up activity. Take one image of each section of the Whoosh to use as an overview of the section, together with several other images which provide further detail. These images will then be used for sequencing, teaching paragraphing and internal paragraph structure.

Objective

- to analyse how the sequencing of a story creates coherence
- to develop an awareness of text cohesion through the use of paragraphs.

Characters	Objects	Sounds
Blue Jackal	desert	barking
dogs	village	splash
monkeys	houses	forest
lions	dye pot	howling
tigers	forest	
wolves	tree stump	
Lion King	food	
jackals	forest entrance	

Resource 1 Story structure

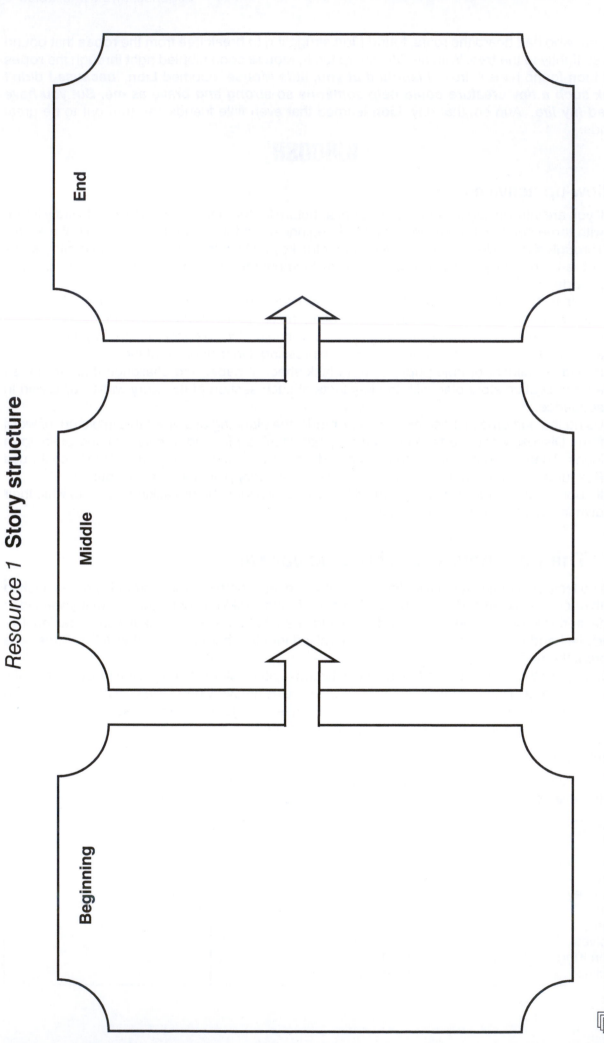

Beginning

Middle

End

One day, a tired, lonely **jackal** was wandering through the hot **desert** looking for his friends. He was desperately hungry, so as he drew near to a **village** he decided to search for food. He prowled quietly around the **houses** so that nobody would know that he was there. Suddenly, he heard the sound of **barking** – first one **dog**, then **several**. Scared of being caught, the **jackal** started to run. He was so determined to escape from the **village** that he did not notice the huge, round **pot of blue dye** that one of the villagers had left. He tried to stop, but it was too late. There was a loud **splash**, and in he fell.

WHOOSH

He lifted himself out of the **dye pot** only to find that he was completely blue. Getting hungrier with every step, **Blue Jackal** left the **village** and walked on until he stumbled into a **forest**. He looked around for his friends – he could see **monkeys**, **lions**, **tigers** and **wolves**, but no jackals. The **animals** were not sure what to make of this blue creature, so they all gathered in a clearing in the **forest**. When he realised that they were all a little frightened of him, **Blue Jackal** saw a chance to make himself important. So he walked right into the middle of the **animals** and declared, '***Don't be afraid of me. I am your new King. I have been sent to rule over you and to keep you safe***.'

WHOOSH

The **Lion King**, realising that he was no longer important, walked sadly away. He sat outside the group of **animals** and watched. **Blue Jackal** was given his special **tree stump** to sit on and the **animals** brought him the best **food**. There was fruit, nuts, and meat from the hunt, all piled high on leaf-plates. He banished all other jackals from the forest, appointing the **wolves** to guard the **forest entrance**.

WHOOSH

For a while, everything went well. The **forest** was peaceful, everyone had enough to eat, and only the **Lion King** seemed to be unhappy. But then one day, they suddenly heard the sound of a skulk of **jackals howling** outside of the **forest**. Thrilled by the sound of his own friends, **Blue Jackal** forgot who he was pretending to be and he **howled** back in answer. Realising that they had been tricked, the **animals** drove **Blue Jackal** out of the forest for ever.

WHOOSH

Follow-up activities

- To explore sequencing, print some of the key digital images which were taken during the Whoosh and attach them to a board in random order. Through shared discussion, decide on the correct sequence of images to tell the story. Then divide pupils into groups, providing a set of images for each group. Ask pupils to order the images and write a sentence under each image to retell the story. Title the story.
- For older or able pupils, print a larger set of images from the Whoosh and attach them to a board in random order. Demonstrate to pupils how to sort them into the four sections of the Whoosh and then put them in order within each section. Show how these sections form four separate paragraphs which mirror the sections of the original story. Repeat this as a group activity, asking pupils to write a sentence for each image.
- Next, through shared discussion, decide how paragraphs are linked with connectives. Can pupils then select appropriate connectives to link each of the paragraphs in their group writing?
- As an extension activity, ask pupils to choose one image from each paragraph which summarises the content of that section. Then place this image first, arranging the remaining pictures in a line below it. Through modelling, demonstrate how a sentence to describe the first image acts as a topic or focal sentence for the following detail in the paragraph: use the remaining images to provide the detail.
- Complete the activity by asking pupils to write their own version of *The Blue Jackal*, focusing on the correct sequence of events. For younger pupils, this could be in the form of captioned pictures. For older pupils, the story should be paragraphed, with connectives linking each paragraph and if appropriate, a focal sentence used to introduce the content of each section.

3   Rudyard Kipling: *Just So Stories: The Elephant's Child*

The *Just So Stories for Children* were published by the British author Rudyard Kipling in 1902. Many of the stories recount how animals acquired their unique features, for example how the leopard got his spots and the camel got his hump. They are rich in detail and laced with humour so they are ideal stories for younger children to enjoy.

Objective

* to identify key elements of a story: characters, settings, problem and resolution.

Characters	Objects	Sounds
elephants Elephant's Child Ostrich Giraffe Hippopotamus Baboon other animals Kolokolo Bird Python Crocodile fly Elephant's Child's brothers	food water burning sun thorn bush bananas sugar cane melons melon skins Limpopo River fever trees rock Crocodile's mouth nose mud Limpopo river bank trunk	Choral speaking,' Go away, Elephant's Child.' rustling squawk splashing squelching water bubbles

Once upon a time, a very long time ago, herds of **elephants** plodded across the African savannah on their wide padded feet in search of **food** and **water**. They flapped their huge ears to cool themselves down in the **burning sun** and wallowed in mud whenever they found **water**. But these **elephants** did not have trunks. Instead, they had noses like big, black boots. They could wrinkle them and wriggle them, but they were not long enough to pick anything up.

WHOOSH

But then, one day, a new, little **Elephant** was born. Unlike his parents, **Elephant's Child** was really, really curious. He never stopped asking questions and often his curiosity would get him into trouble. One day, he asked his aunt **Ostrich** why her tail feathers grew so long and he asked his uncle **Giraffe** what made his skin so spotty. '*Go away, Elephant's Child*,' they grumbled. Another day he asked his big aunt **Hippopotamus** why her eyes were so red and his hairy uncle **Baboon** why melons tasted like they did. '*GO AWAY, Elephant's Child*,' they shouted. Nobody would ever answer his questions.

WHOOSH

He asked the other **animals** questions about everything that he saw, everything that he touched, everything that he smelt and everything that he felt. But the answer was always the same. '*Go away, Elephant's Child*'. But then one day he asked a new question. And nobody told him to go away. In fact, nobody answered him at all. There was just silence.

   '*What does the Crocodile have for lunch?*' asked **Elephant's Child** again. But still they refused to answer. Only the **Kolokolo Bird** called out from his **thorn bush**, '*Go to the banks of the great grey-green, greasy Limpopo River, all set about with fever trees, and you will find out*.'

WHOOSH

So saying goodbye to his **family**, off went **Elephant's Child**. He took plenty of the little red **bananas** that he liked, some **sugar cane** to chew and lots of juicy **melons**. As he walked, he ate the **melons**, dropping the **skins** on the ground. Eventually he came to the banks of the great, grey-green, greasy **Limpopo River** all set about with **rustling fever trees**, and he found a **Python** curled up on a **rock**, basking in the **hot sun**.

WHOOSH

'*Excuse me*,' said **Elephant's Child** politely to the **Python**, '*but have you seen a Crocodile around these parts? And if you have, could you kindly tell me what he eats for lunch?*' But **Python** did not answer. Instead, he uncurled himself from the **rock** and flicked **Elephant's Child** with his long tail. So **Elephant's Child** kept walking. After a while, he trod on something. At first, he thought it was a log, but when it moved he realised it was an animal and he said, very politely, '*Excuse me, but have you seen a Crocodile around these parts? And if you have, could you kindly tell me what he eats for lunch?*'

'*Come closer, little one*,' said the grinning **animal**, '*because I am Crocodile. I will tell you what I eat for lunch, but I will whisper it in your ear.*' So **Elephant's Child** crept close and put his head right down to **Crocodile's mouth**. In a flash, **Crocodile** grabbed him by the **nose** and with a **squawk**, **Elephant's Child** suddenly realised that he was about to be lunch.

He pulled and pulled with all of his might, but he could not get free. Instead, his **nose** just started to stretch and stretch. The more he pulled, the longer his **nose** became. Even **Python** joined in, wrapping himself around **Elephant Child's** legs and pulling with all of his might, too. They pulled and they pulled and they pulled. Then they pulled some more and eventually **Crocodile** let go. **Elephant's Child** fell backwards into the **Limpopo River** with a **huge splashing** of **water** and **squelching** of thick, oozing **mud**.

WHOOSH

For three days **Elephant's Child** sat on the banks of the **river** waiting for his nose to shrink. But it never did. And then on the third day a **fly** landed on his shoulder. **Elephant's Child** swatted the **fly** with his new **nose** and decided that it was rather useful after all. When he felt too hot, he scooped up **mud** from the **bank** of the great, grey-green, greasy **Limpopo River** to cool himself down. Eventually he decided to keep the new **trunk** and he set off home, flicking it proudly from side to side.

On the way, he picked up all the **melon skins** that he had dropped. And when he got home, he did not bother at all when his family thought that his trunk was ugly. Because he uncurled it and knocked his **brothers** over. He picked up grumpy **Baboon** and threw him into the air. He pulled out proud **Ostrich's** tail feathers, dragged lofty **Giraffe** through a **thorn bush** and blew **water bubbles** in **Hippopotamus's** ear. He had great fun and that is why, from that day to this, all elephants have trunks.

WHOOSH

Follow-up activities

Text mapping has a range of definitions and applications, depending on the genre of the text being mapped and the intended outcome of the activity. Writing frames are a form of mapping which are often used for non-fiction writing. The use of images to plot paragraphs and build cohesive text suggested above for *The Blue Jackal* is also a form of mapping. The activity for *The Elephant's Child* involves a pictorial representation of the story, almost as a geographical map.

- Demonstrate this in sketch form before asking pupils to work independently. The left hand side of the page should show the savannah with elephants, ostriches, giraffes and a mud hole for the hippo. Leading away from this should be a route to the Limpopo River which should be placed in the middle of the sheet of paper. From this, on the right hand side of the sheet of paper, should flow the route home and the savannah after Elephant's Child returns.
- Use any facts that pupils recall during this discussion (for example, how will Elephant Child's nose differ at the right hand side of the picture?) to sketch onto your map. Also note colours.
- Next, ask pupils to draw their own coloured maps, including as much detail as they can recall from the Whoosh.
- When maps are complete, pupils should use them to retell the story to a peer partner. You can use the maps for formative assessment as they will show how much each pupil understood about the structure of the story and the details of characterisation.
- If you want pupils to write their own story, they could approach this through the use of a picture map as a planning format.

4   Native American legends: *How the Butterflies Came To Be*

There are many hundreds of legends told by Native American people. Oral storytelling is part of their heritage, showing reverence for the Earth and the place of humans on it. The stories, passed from generation to generation, teach important values of respect and honour. Common to many of the stories are explanations about the creation of the world. But each Native American tribe also has its own distinct culture and stories often reflect the natural world of the mountains or lakes where each tribe lives. This Whoosh is based on a story told by the Papago or Tohono O'odham people, who live in a dry desert area of Arizona.

Objective

*   to explore how figurative and expressive language creates images in the mind of the reader.

Characters	Objects	Sounds
Earth Maker Elder Brother children mothers people	world sun stones pine needles flowers birds sky leaves trees day night bag cornmeal spots of sunlight hair butterflies	giggles rustling songs

One day, soon after the **Earth Maker** had finished shaping our **world**, **Elder Brother** was sitting in the warm midday **sun** watching the **children** play. He saw their happy smiles and heard their infectious **giggles** and he was content. He watched their kneeling **mothers**, busy grinding cornmeal between firm, round **stones**. He shielded his eyes from the sunlight as it reflected from their glossy black hair. The fresh, woody smell of crushed **pine needles** mingled with the sweet scent of the **gold-poppies** and **desert marigold**. Song **birds** soared into a cloudless blue **sky**. It was a perfect day.

WHOOSH

And yet, **Elder Brother** felt sad. For he knew that one day this would change. The **children** would stop playing and grow old. Glossy black hair would become streaked with grey. The **leaves** would stop **rustling** on the **trees** and would fall to the ground, wrinkled and dead. The **flowers** would droop and fade, **days** would grow short and **nights** would grow long and cold. And as he watched the **mothers** grind their cornmeal, he decided that he must do something to capture this moment of beauty for ever. So **Elder Brother** took out his **bag**.

WHOOSH

Reaching into the **sky**, **Elder Brother** grasped a pinch of blue. Reaching to the **cornmeal** on the ground, he plucked a handful of white. Some **spots of sunlight**, shimmering like diamonds, were gathered into the **bag**, together with a splash of ebony black from the ladies' **hair**. Quickly pulling together red, silver, purple, yellow, blue and pink from the desert **flowers**, he added them to his collection. He collected sweet-tasting nectar and he even seized russet and gold from the falling **leaves** and vibrant green from the **pine needles**. Finally, he removed the songs of the **birds** and let them fall gently into the **bag**.

WHOOSH

Then **Elder Brother** called the **children** to him, telling them that the **bag** contained a surprise. And as they opened **Elder Brother's bag** out fluttered hundreds of beautiful **butterflies**, each one splashed with different colours. **They** wheeled and circled in the air. **They** danced around the **children**, settling on their hands and quivering on their heads. The **children** and their **mothers** were thrilled – they had never before seen such beauty. And as they flew, the **butterflies** began to sing. Their **songs** sounded like liquid gold.

WHOOSH

But the **birds** were not happy. They asked **Elder Brother** why he had given their songs to these **butterflies**. Were their exotic colours not enough? Why should they have the birds' songs too? And **Elder Brother** agreed, because he remembered that he had given to each **bird** their own special song. And so he decided that the **butterflies** should be silent and their rainbow beauty should brighten every day. And so it was. But even though **butterflies** are silent, many **people** sing in their hearts when they see such exquisite and fragile beauty.

WHOOSH

Follow-up activities

- Descriptive writing is given power by the quality of the words which the author chooses. *How the Butterflies Came To Be* is an excellent example of a story which calls on all of the senses. Use Resource 2 with younger listeners to list the sensory elements of the story.
- With older pupils, re-read the story, asking pupils to listen for examples of noun phrases (an adjective plus a noun), expanded noun phrases (two adjectives plus a noun) and powerful verbs. For example, how many different verbs are used instead of 'took' or 'got' in section three of the Whoosh? Read the section aloud, replacing all of the powerful verbs with routine verbs. What effect does this have on the picture created in the mind of the listener?
- With older pupils, this can be extended to consider the effect of alliteration, simile, metaphor, onomatopoeia and personification, all of which are included in the Whoosh. Divide the class into five groups, giving each group one section of the Whoosh script to analyse. What examples of figurative and expressive language can they find? Ask each group to re-write their given section with routine words. Read it aloud. What difference does it make?
- Explore the use of a thesaurus as a resource for selecting rich vocabulary.

5 Greek myths: *King Midas*

Greek mythology comprises a large body of stories about gods, the world and heroic characters. The most famous stories are contained in Homer's two poems *Iliad* and *Odyssey*. Many of the epic narratives were also told on pot and vase paintings. The stories give insight into the religious beliefs of the ancient Greeks. They describe great wars, courageous acts and gallant behaviour, even in the face of capricious and manipulative gods.

Objective

- to understand how setting and characterisation are used to create interesting narrative.

Characters	Objects		Sounds
King Midas	castle	violets and parsley	whispering grass
daughter	chairs	counting room	clinking and chinking
guards	pictures and frames	gold coins	coins
Silenus	pots and plates	message	scream
Dinoysius	gardens	desk	splashing water
servants	olive, cypress and	food and wine	
	fruit trees	tears	
	vines and grapes	pillar	
	meadows	river	

Resource 2 **What can you …**

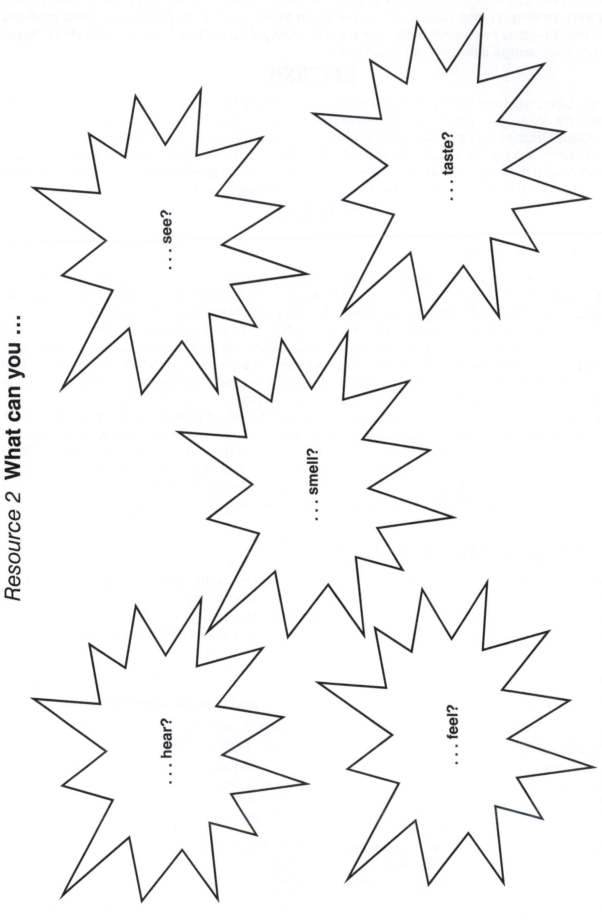

… see?

… taste?

… smell?

… hear?

… feel?

Once upon a time, in an ancient country called Greece, there was a very rich King called **Midas**. He lived comfortably in a huge **castle** full of beautiful **chairs**, elegant **pictures** in golden **frames** and decorated golden **pots** and **plates** which he had collected from all around the world. His palace **gardens** were full of many kinds of bent, gnarled **olive trees** and tall, straight, sweet smelling **cypress trees**. **Pear**, **apple** and **pomegranate trees** filled the palace with the smell of their blossom and the **King** loved to pluck and eat the ripe, juicy **fruits** when he was walking in his **garden**. **Vines** were weighed down by plump, ripe **grapes** and the lush **meadows** around the castle were overflowing with **violets** and **parsley** that grew thickly in the **whispering** grasses.

WHOOSH

King Midas loved his **garden**. And almost more than anything else in the world, he loved his little **daughter**. He laughed with her, played with her and made sure that she was always given the best of everything that he had. But secretly, in his heart, **King Midas** knew that he loved gold even more than he loved his daughter.

One day, he was sitting in his **counting room** letting **gold coins** flow through his open fingers. They **clinked** and **chinked** together as they fell around him. While he was enjoying the feel and sound of his treasure, his **guards** appeared leading the satyr **Silenus** whom they had found sleeping peacefully in the castle **garden**. **King Midas**, knowing that **Silenus** was a great friend of the god **Dionysius**, invited **Silenus** to stay for a few days and enjoy all that his beautiful **castle** had to offer. He sent a **message** to **Dionysius** to let him know where **Silenus** was.

WHOOSH

When **Dionysius** arrived a few days later, he wanted to thank the **King** for being a good friend, so he offered him one gift. He could choose anything he wanted. And **King Midas**, knowing the secret of his heart, asked that everything that he touched should turn to gold. **Dionysius** was anxious and argued with **Midas**, trying to get him to change his mind, but it was to no avail. The god had made a promise and it had to be kept. So **King Midas** got his dearest wish.

He reached out to touch his **desk**. It turned to gold. He touched his **plates**. They turned to solid gold. He touched everything that he could in his **counting room**. And it all turned to gold. Then, feeling hungry after his excitement, he asked his **servants** to bring some **food** and **wine**. But as the **food** touched his lips, it turned to solid gold. And even worse, his precious little **daughter** ran in from the garden to show him the flowers that she had picked for him. Before he could stop her, she had hugged him and turned into a golden statue. His anguished **scream** echoed through the gloomy, golden **castle**.

WHOOSH

It was not long before **King Midas** felt hungry, thirsty, lonely and very, very sad. He realised that his greed had harmed all that he valued in his life. He slumped into his golden **chair** wondering why he had been so foolish. But just then, **Dionysius** stepped out from behind a golden **pillar**. King Midas, crying **tears** that turned into tiny golden droplets as they fell onto his hands, pleaded with the god to take away the terrible gift. And **Dionysius** had mercy on **King Midas**, because he really had learnt his lesson. He told the King to go and immerse himself in the **river** and the gift would be washed away. Not only that, but everything that he had turned to gold would be restored when he touched it again.

Midas could not wait to do as he was told. He jumped and **splashed** and covered himself completely in water. And when he rushed back to the **palace**, dripping wet, the first thing that he did was to hug his little **daughter** and bring her back to life. He was never greedy again, because he had learnt that many things mattered more than money.

WHOOSH

Follow-up activities

- It is important when writing stories to ensure that characters grow and develop but also that they are consistent with their setting. Using Resource 3, find evidence from the story of King Midas that supports the setting. There are two aspects to this – the localised setting of a king's castle and the broader historical setting of ancient Greece within which the story is set.

Resource 3 Setting

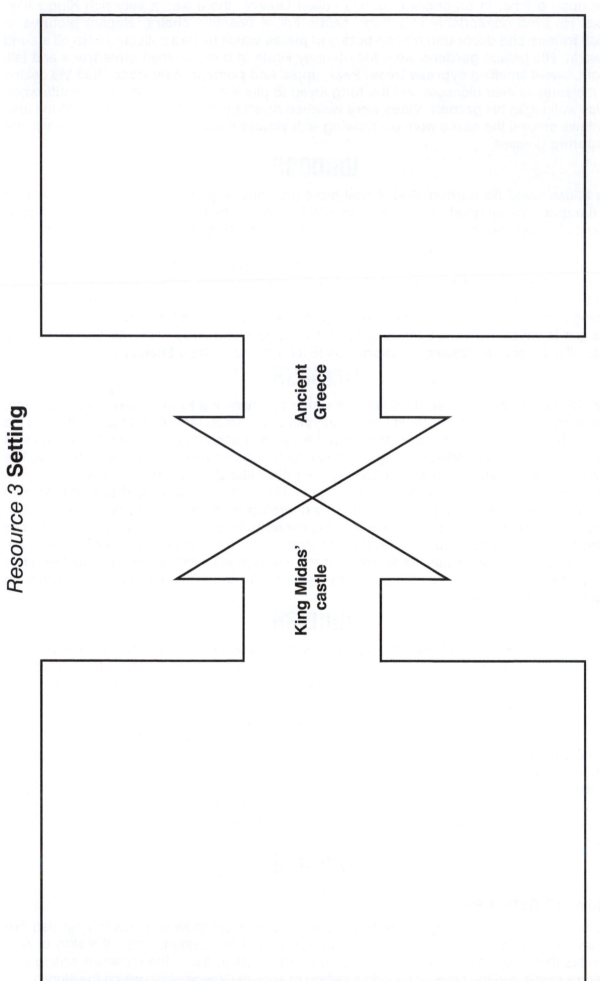

Ancient Greece

King Midas' castle

After finding evidence of setting, discuss how the two elements of the setting are mutually inclusive.

- To consider characterisation, provide pupils with Resource 4, asking them to highlight all the words which apply to Midas at some point in the story. How does the character differ at the end of the story from the beginning?
- Then discuss how the setting supports the character. Would this story work if it was set somewhere cold and gloomy? Why not?
- Challenge pupils to use their understanding of the interaction of character and setting to create a story structure of their own.

6   Greek myths: *Perseus and Medusa*

Objective

- to explore how conflict within a story is created, developed and resolved.

Characters	Objects	Sounds
Perseus	snakes	hissing
Danae	owl	sobbing
Zeus	polished shield	snigger
Polydectes	magic sword	shrieking
Medusa	eye	swishing
Athena	island	thump
Poseidon	bag	screaming
Hermes	winged sandals	screeching
three ugly sisters	helmet of invisibility	yelling
Nymphs of the North	island	clapping
Gorgons	head	cheering
	prison	

Perseus was an unusual young man. **Danae**, the daughter of the King of Argos, was his mother, but **Zeus**, the King of the gods, was his father, so he was half human and half god. He lived peacefully enough with his mother until one day **Polydectes**, the rather nasty king of Seriphos, decided that he was going to marry **Danae**. Although she thought it was a terrible idea, she did not really have much choice. So **Perseus** went to see the **King** to suggest that he should find a different princess to marry. Hoping to get rid of **Perseus** once and for all, the **King** demanded the head of the Gorgon Medusa in exchange for **Danae**'s freedom.

Perseus knew all about **Medusa**. She had once been a woman with beautiful, long coiled hair, but the goddess **Athena** had turned her hair into **hissing, writhing snakes** as a punishment for falling in love with the god **Poseidon**. Nobody escaped from Medusa's island alive. But **Perseus** loved his **mother** very much and even though she pleaded with him not to go, **Perseus** was determined to meet the challenge. Even the sound of her **sobbing** did not change his mind.

WHOOSH

So **Perseus** said goodbye to his distraught **mother** and set out on his journey. **Zeus** had seen all that had happened. Because **Perseus** was his son and he disliked **Polydectes**, he decided to help **Perseus**. As he walked, two **godly figures** appeared in front of him carrying gifts. One had an **owl** on her shoulder and one was wearing **winged sandals**. '*Hail, Perseus*,' said **Athena**, giving him a **polished shield** which shone brightly in the sun. '*Hail, Perseus*,' said **Hermes**, giving him a **magic sword**. '*To kill the Gorgon, you will need three more magical gifts*,' he added, '*but they are kept by the Nymphs of the North and the only people who know where to find them are Medusa's ugly old sisters.*' And to his surprise, **Hermes** took **Perseus** by the hand and together they flew off to find them.

Resource 4 Characterisation

Brave	Kind	Thoughtful
Selfish	Greedy	Spiteful
Foolish	Caring	Cowardly
Generous	Thoughtless	Sensible
Loving	Happy	Excited
Lazy	Cruel	Unpleasant
Wise	Cheerful	Sad
Content	Gloomy	Miserable

WHOOSH

As he arrived at the lair of the **sisters**, **Perseus** could hear a terrible argument. '*It's my turn today*,' said the first one, holding something in her hand. '*No, it was your turn yesterday*,' shrieked the second sister. And while they were screeching, '*It's my turn*,' at each other, the third sister sneaked up and, with a nasty **snigger**, snatched something out of the hand of her sister. **Perseus** knew that these horrible women had just one **eye** between them and they had to take it in turns to wear it. So, as quick as a flash, before the third sister could put the **eye** in, **Perseus** wrenched it away from her. '*You can have it back when you tell me where to find the Nymphs of the North*,' he shouted. Desperate for their **eye**, they soon told him. Then throwing it on the ground, **Perseus** flew away, smiling at their **shrieking** as they blindly groped around, bumping into each other in their desperation to be the first to find the **eye**.

WHOOSH

The **Nymphs of the North** gave **Perseus** a warm welcome. Their gifts were a **magic bag**, **winged sandals** and a **helmet** of invisibility. But they warned him that killing Medusa would not be easy because anyone who looked at her would instantly be turned to stone. '*Use your shield as a mirror*,' advised the **Nymphs**, '*and use her reflection to find her and kill her*.' So on flew **Perseus**, spurred on by the adventure and thoughts of the danger that his **mother** was in back on Seriphos.

WHOOSH

Perseus flew for many hours before he saw the **island** below. Three ugly **Gorgons**, the **snakes** on their heads writhing and twisting as they slept, were lying on the beach. It was easy to work out which one was **Medusa**, because her human face was still beautiful even though her head was so revolting. Before any of them could wake, **Perseus** put on his **helmet**, set his **shield** to see **Medusa**'s reflection and swooped down, his **sword** slicing off her head as it **swished** through the air. The **head** landed with a thump on the sand. As the other **Gorgons** awoke and started **screaming**, **Perseus** stuffed the **head** into his **bag** and took off. Down on the **island**, the **Gorgons screeched** and **yelled** in helpless fury because they could not turn an invisible person to stone.

WHOOSH

With Medusa's **head** safely in the magic **bag**, **Perseus** started on the long flight home. He arrived not a moment too soon. **Danae**, who was still refusing to marry the **King**, had been thrown into **prison**. **Perseus** was so angry that he stormed into the **King**'s rooms, pulling Medusa's **head** from the bag as he strode towards the **King**. Medusa's **snakes** still writhed and **hissed**. '*I've brought you the head of Medusa*,' **Perseus** laughed triumphantly. And as **Polydectes** looked in disbelief, he was instantly turned to stone. Everybody **clapped** and **cheered**. **Perseus** ruled Seriphos as a just and fair king for many years and the island and its people prospered.

Follow-up activities

A good story not only has a clear beginning, middle and end, it also has a dilemma or problem which is built up and then resolved. The story of Perseus is a good example of a story where conflict is created and resolved.

- Use a story mountain (Resource 5) to analyse rising tension and to track the feelings of the protagonist, Perseus, as the story unfolds. In each box, write a key fact and record Perseus' feelings at that point. The first box is completed as an example. Further facts are:
  - the help Perseus received from Athena and Hermes
  - the visit to Medusa's sisters
  - the Nymphs of the North
  - killing Medusa
  - arriving home
  - defeating Polydectes.

Resource 5 **Story mountain**

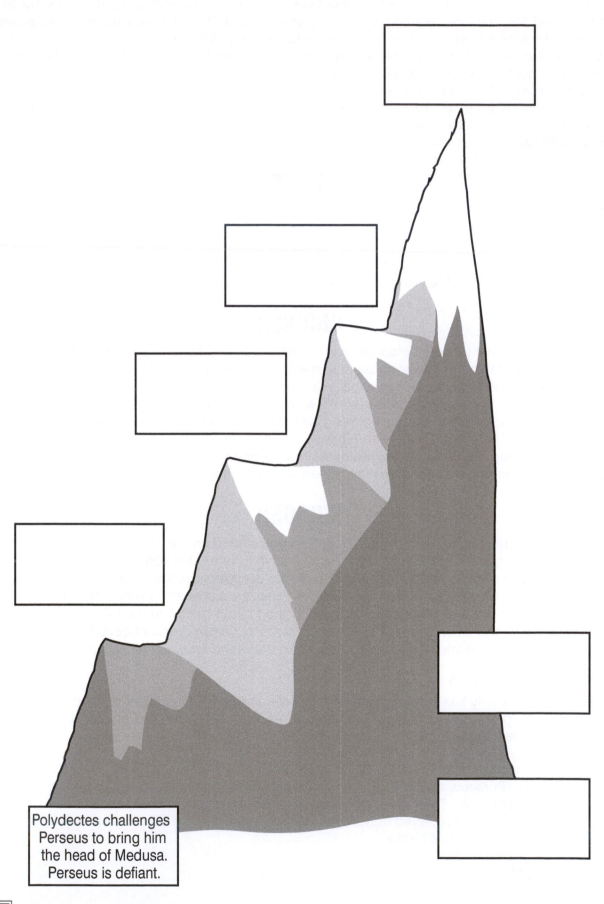

Polydectes challenges Perseus to bring him the head of Medusa. Perseus is defiant.

7   Legends across cultures: *The Hero of Haarlem*

The story of Peter, the Hero of Haarlem, is an example of how stories travel around the world or can even be falsely attributed to a country's folklore. In 1865, the American writer Mary Mapes Dodge published a children's book called *Hans Brinker; or, the Silver Skates: A Story of Life in Holland*. The novel is set in the Netherlands but although she researched the book thoroughly in addition to using first hand information from neighbouring Dutch immigrants, Dodge never actually visited the country.

The story of Peter is a nested narrative within the book; its actual origins are unknown. Versions of it appeared in English and American publications from about 1850 onwards and it seems to be better known in America than in its supposed country of origin. In 1950, a statue was placed at Spaarndam in Holland bearing the inscription, 'Dedicated to our youth, to honor the boy who symbolizes the perpetual struggle of Holland against the water' but this was probably erected for tourist purposes. There is little evidence of this story within the Dutch oral tradition of storytelling.

Objective

* to explore how setting can influence plot.

Characters	Objects	Sounds
Peter Peter's father, the sluicer Peter's mother a blind friend a man walking on the canal path a crowd of workmen	cottage canal huge wooden gates water fields homes sunshine biscuits walls and banks flat country falling rain a friend's house sunset canal path a hole in the bank water canal bursting its banks flood village night canal bank	creaking and groaning gates trickling water rushing water lapping water heavy rainfall crunchy biscuits spurting water shouting and whistling chattering teeth angry water calls for help cheering people

Many years ago, in a city in Holland called Haarlem, there lived a boy called **Peter**. He was just eight years old and he lived with his **parents** in a **cottage** near the **canal**. His **father** was a sluicer, the person who had to open **huge wooden gates** on the **canal** that let the **water** flow through. Every morning, the **gates** would **creak** and **groan** as he slowly pulled them open. **Peter** loved to hear the **trickle** of water become a **steady rush** as the gap between the gates got wider. And at night, he had to close them again, so that the **water** would not rush through and flood the **fields** around the **canal** and the **homes in the town**. They would **creak** and **groan** just as much when they were closed. Then the **water** would **lap gently** behind the **closed gates** and **Peter** would feel safe.

WHOOSH

One autumn afternoon, **Peter's mother** decided to bake some **biscuits**. When they had cooked and cooled and **Peter** had munched a couple, he offered to take some to the blind friend that he often visited. As he walked along, enjoying the late **sunshine**, he started to think about the **walls** and **banks** that criss-crossed the countryside. **Peter** knew, as all Dutch children did, that their **country** was very **flat** and without these **walls** the country could flood. It had **rained hard** recently, and the water in the **canals** was quite high. Peter was glad that his **father** and all the other sluicers were able to keep people safe.

But he thought no more of it as he arrived at his **friend's house**. They chatted as they nibbled the biscuits, with **Peter** enjoying the **crunch** every time he took a bite. Eventually he got up to go, suddenly realising that it was nearly **sunset**. His **parents** would be getting worried. But as he started to run along the **canal path**, he heard a strange sound. There was **water trickling** somewhere but there were no gates nearby. Looking around, **Peter** suddenly saw **water spurting** through a **hole in the bank**. He knew that if it was left, the **water** would wash a bigger and bigger **hole** until the **swollen canal** burst through in all its fury, drowning his **friend** and his **parents**. Even if he ran for help, he could be too late. So **Peter** climbed onto the **bank** and pushed his finger into the hole, stopping the water from trickling through.

WHOOSH

Peter started to **shout** and **whistle**, but the **path** was lonely and very few people walked along it, especially after dark. As the **sun** set, **Peter** began to feel very cold. His teeth started to **chatter** and his body started to shake. All through the long, dark **night**, he kept his finger in the **bank**, knowing that the **water** was building up and that if he moved, the **angry waters** would cause a **terrible flood**.

Eventually **he** stopped **calling for help** and decided that he would have to stay there until the morning. He must have dozed off, because the next thing he knew, a **man** was scrambling across the **bank** towards him, asking him what he was doing. **Peter** was so cold that he could hardly move. But it seemed that in no time at all, help arrived. **Several men** from the **village**, his **father** among them, soon **repaired** the **bank** and **Peter** was carried home on the **men's shoulders**. **Everyone** cheered. He was a hero. He had saved Haarlem from a terrible flood.

WHOOSH

Follow-up activities

- Through shared discussion, define the themes of this story – water and the heroism of the central character. Water plays a central part in the story, which has been emphasised in the Whoosh by the use of sound, from rain to the raging torrent of a burst bank.
- Discuss the setting – what makes this setting unique? How does the setting influence the plot? Could this story work in any other country than Holland?
- Working in groups, ask pupils to brainstorm the defining features of their own environment, for example the buildings, roads and traffic in a city or the fields and open spaces in the country.
- Then challenge pupils to think of something in this environment that could harm the people living there. How could they then create a hero/heroine who will see the danger and save the people around them?
- Finally, create a story. A storyboard template is available as Resource 6. Encourage detailed pictures as this will inform the descriptive detail in the story.

8   The Anansi stories: *Anansi and the Sky God*

These stories are part of the folklore of West Africa. They have travelled widely and are also now part of the storytelling culture of Jamaica. They originate from a mythical time when gods, humans and animals could all communicate with each other. Anansi, also known as the Spider Man, is a trickster, who uses cunning to trick people and animals in order to try and get what he wants for himself. Each tale teaches the listener a different moral point.

There are similarities between the Anansi stories and those told in other areas of Africa. They also share some characteristics with the Brer Rabbit stories, probably because the stories travelled to America with slaves and then became woven into the emerging folklore of a new nation. The stories are full of dramatic action; they lend themselves well to active storytelling and their simple structures and plot lines are ideal for scaffolding children's creative storytelling.

The first Whoosh explains how Anansi became the keeper of the stories which he then gave to his people. The second Whoosh is an example of a typical Anansi story, designed to amuse,

Resource 6 **Storyboard**

	_____ is the central character in the story.	The story is set _____.
	_____ realises that something is wrong and people are in danger.	_____ solves the problem until help arrives.
	One day, _____ goes out to _____.	Everyone welcomes _____ home as a hero/ heroine.

© 2013, *Literacy Activities for Classic and Contemporary Texts 7–14*, Gill Robins and Laura-Jane Evans-Jones, Routledge entertain and instruct. Using drum patterns and African percussion instruments such as seed rattles, *caxixi* (woven rattles) and *shekere* (gourd rattle) during the breaks in the story or to accompany relevant parts of the story would add to the atmosphere.

Objective

• to develop empathy through reflecting on the key events in a story.

Characters	Objects	Sounds
people Nyame Anansi Aso Snake Leopard Hornets Mmoatia Mmoatia's sister	sky golden box spider thread snake leopard hornets invisible fairy vine stick stream Snake's home grasslands sun hole rocks branches home gourd banana leaf tree hornets' nest small bowl doll	bubbling stream swishing and whispering grass clanging spade roaring leopard swishing banana leaf falling rain hornets buzzing and droning angry hornets buzzing

Long, long ago, **people** were sad because they had no stories. The god **Nyame**, who lived high up in the **sky**, kept their stories locked in a **golden box** which he always kept beside him. Nobody had been able to get the stories, although **many people** had tried. So the **people** with no stories became more and more sad.

But one day **Anansi**, the Spider Man, decided to try and help. So, spinning a sticky **spider thread** so long that it reached the heavens, **Anansi** climbed up to **Nyame**. '*May we have our stories back, please?*' asked **Anansi**, bowing low. At first, the **sky god** just laughed at him. But because he could see that **Anansi** was so determined, **Nyame** decided to set him four challenges. **He** promised **Anansi** that he could have the **story box** in exchange for a **snake** that could eat people, a **leopard** with teeth like spears, some stinging **hornets** and Mmoatia, the **invisible fairy**. The challenges were so hard, that **Nyame** was sure that he would be able to keep the stories to himself.

As **he** climbed slowly back down his sticky **thread**, **Anansi** felt very sad. He knew that if he tried to get what Nyame wanted, he would probably be eaten whole, stung to death or killed by the leopard long before he captured any of them. But when he shared what had happened with his wife **Aso**, she thought of a plan.

WHOOSH

The next morning, **Anansi** took his knife, cut a strong **vine** and a long **stick**, and went to the **stream** where Snake lived. As **he** walked along, listening to the stream **bubbling**, he muttered to himself, '*It is longer. No it isn't. Yes it is.*' He kept this up until **Snake**, wondering what **Anansi** was talking about, slithered out of his **home**. When he asked **Anansi** what he was muttering about, **Anansi** explained that he and Aso had been arguing about whether **Snake** was longer than the **stick** he was holding. **Snake**, knowing that he was a huge snake, pulled himself out to his full length. Next he asked **Anansi** to put the **stick** next to him, to solve the argument once and for all. So **Anansi** did as **Snake** suggested, tying him to the **stick** with the **vine** as he went, just to keep him straight. Then, before he could protest or wriggle free, **Anansi** gave **Snake** to **Nyame**. The **sky god** was surprised, but all he said was, '*Where are the other three?*'

WHOOSH

'*Now for the next challenge*,' thought **Anansi** to himself. He had no idea how he was going to catch a leopard with teeth as sharp as a spear. But **Aso** had another plan which she whispered to **Anansi** …

He went out into the **grasslands** and stood under the scorching **sun**. He listened to the grass **swish** and **whisper** in the breeze as he dug a big **hole**. It took a long time and a lot of effort, digging into the dry, baked earth, with his spade **clanging** on stones and **rocks** as he dug. But eventually he stood back, satisfied with his work. He dragged **branches** over the **hole**, then went **home** and enjoyed his dinner.

The next morning, sure enough, **Leopard** had fallen into the hole and **he** was **roaring** and clawing at the sides of the **hole**. It took just a few minutes for **Anansi** to tie **Leopard** to a long **stick** with his sticky spider **threads**. But when **Anansi** arrived high up in the sky with the growling **Leopard**, **Nyame** just laughed and said, '*What about the other two?*'

WHOOSH

For the third challenge, **Anansi** went to the **bubbling** stream, filled a **gourd** with water and cut a huge banana **leaf**, waving it from side to side with a satisfying **swish**. Then he went to the **tree** where the **hornets** lived and poured some of the water all over their **nest**. Next, **he** put the banana **leaf** over his head and splashed the rest of the water over himself. '*It's raining!*' he called to the **hornets**. '*Stay dry inside my gourd.*' The grateful hornets **buzzed** and **droned** as they swarmed gratefully into the **gourd**. Quick as a flash, **Anansi** popped in a cork. No matter how angrily the hornets **buzzed**, they were trapped as **Anansi** climbed into the heavens to give the gourd to **Nyame**. **He** did not laugh this time. **He** looked quite worried as he said, '*What about the last one?*'

WHOOSH

Aso had a final plan for this challenge, too. **Sh**e mixed some yams and eggs together with palm oil and put it into a small **bowl**. **Anansi**, meanwhile, had covered a carved wooden **doll** with sticky tree sap. Taking the food and the **doll**, **he** placed them carefully beneath the odum **tree** where the fairies liked to play. It wasn't long before **Mmoatia** and her **sister** came along and smelt the food. **They** asked the **doll** if they could have some but when there was no answer, **Mmoatia** got quite cross. '*If you don't answer*,' she said,' *I'm going to slap you.*' And that is exactly what **she** did. Except, of course, that the **doll** was covered in sticky tree sap, so **her** hand got stuck fast. When **she** tried to free one hand, the other one got stuck. too. **She** was trapped and it did not take **Anansi** long to tie **her** up with a vine, climb up to **Nyame** and hand **her** over.

WHOOSH

Although **he** really wanted to keep the stories all for himself, **Nyame** agreed to keep his side of the bargain. **He** gave **Anansi** the **gold box** and watched sadly as **Anansi** climbed back down his sticky **thread** for the very last time. Gathering together **all of the people** in a circle, **Anansi** opened the box and gave **them** back their stories. The **people** were very happy as they turned to tell each other their stories. And that is how **Anansi** the Spider-Man became the Keeper of the Stories.

WHOOSH

Follow-up activities

Listeners to this tale empathise with Anansi from the outset, because he wants to retrieve the stories which have been taken from his people. Respect for him grows as he gradually meets each of the challenges and eventually wins back the golden story box.

- To explore the way a listener to the story develops an empathetic relationship with Anansi, use the freeze frame cards (Resource 7) to reflect on the emotions engendered by the key events of the story.

Resource 7 Freeze frames

Scene 1	Scene 2
The people are sad because their stories have been stolen. Anansi climbs up to Nyame the sky god to ask for them back. Although he bows low and is polite, Nyame laughs and sets some difficult challenges. How does Anansi feel? Why?	Anansi tells the people what has happened. He also tells his wife Aso. Although he is very sad, she has plans that will help him to achieve all of the challenges and get the stories back. How does Anansi feel? Why?
Scene 3	**Scene 4**
Anansi takes a vine and a stick to Snake's home near the stream. He tricks Snake by pretending that he wants to see if he is longer than the stick. Snake realises he is trapped when Anansi ties him to the stick. How does Anansi feel? Why?	Anansi digs a deep hole and covers it in branches. Leopard does not see the trap and falls in. Anansi is able to tie him up and deliver him to the sky god. Nyame laughs at him. How does Anansi feel? Why?
Scene 5	**Scene 6**
Anansi uses a gourd full of water and a big banana leaf to persuade the hornets to leave their nest. They swarm into the gourd away from the rain. He traps them. How does Anansi feel? Why?	Anansi catches Mmoatia by using a sticky doll to trap her hands. Then he ties her up. He has achieved the final challenge. How does Anansi feel? Why?
Scene 7	**Scene 8**
Anansi visits Nyame for the last time. Nyame agrees to give the story box back. Anansi has won. How does Anansi feel? Why?	Anansi gathers the people together and unlocks the golden story box. All of their stories are returned. The people are excited. How does Anansi feel? Why?

- Capture the freeze frames as digital images, using the images to reflect on these feelings. Use focused questions to scaffold thinking, noting pupils' responses. After considering each of the eight scenes, an overview will have been created showing reactions to Anansi.
- Why does a listener empathise with Anansi when he uses trickery to achieve his objective? Do Snake's pride and vanity, Mmoatia's rudeness and the aggressive nature of hornets affect our view of what he does?

9   The Anansi stories: *Anansi and the Turtle*

Objective

- to interpret and debate the moral meaning of a text.

Characters	Objects	Sounds
Anansi Aso Turtle	yams Anansi's home rock sun plates bowls table chairs door Turtle's home sun river sky jacket stones river bank	rattle of plates and bowls chairs being moved knock on the door pots and pans

One day, **Anansi** found some huge **yams** growing near his **house**. **He** tried to imagine how creamy and soft the yams would be inside their tough, brown skins; there was nothing that he liked more than baked **yams**. So **he** dug them up and took them **home**. **Aso** peeled them and baked them, while **Anansi** sat on a **rock** in the **sun**, soaking up the beautiful smells that drifted on the afternoon breeze. Soon, he heard the rattle of **plates** and **bowls** being put on the **table** and **chairs** being moved. The sounds were followed by a delicious smell that was so strong that it could only mean one thing. '*Dinner!*' called **Aso**.

   Anansi and **Aso** were just sitting down at the **table** when there was a **knock** on the **door**. **They** were really looking forward to eating their dinner, so, feeling a little impatient, **Anansi** went to find out who was knocking on his **door**. Standing in the dirt was **Turtle**, looking hot and tired. '*Please let me in*,' said Turtle, '*I am so hungry.*' And there was nothing that **Anansi** could do but invite **Turtle** to join them for dinner because it was a custom in their country to share food with visitors.

WHOOSH

Anansi and **Aso** looked at each other in dismay. **They** had looked forward to this meal all afternoon. **Aso** slowly picked up a **plate** and served **Turtle** with some of the delicious baked **yams** but just as he was about to take his first juicy mouthful, **Anansi** called out, '*Your hands are dirty, Turtle. Go and wash them.*' Anansi was right – as **Turtle** looked at his hands he could see that they were very grubby from walking through the dirt all day. So off **he** went to wash them. As soon as **he** had started to crawl slowly away, **Anansi** crammed huge slices of the yams into his mouth. By the time **Turtle** got back to the table, half of the food was already gone.

   But just as **he** settled down at the **table** for a second time, **Anansi** called out, '*Your hands are dirty again. Go and wash them.*' Anansi was right. **Turtle**'s hands had got dirty just walking back to the table. By the time **he** had washed his hands and crawled back to the table again, all of the food was gone. Sadly, **Turtle** set off for his own **home**, but because he was very polite, he remembered to invite **Anansi** to dinner should he ever be passing that way.

WHOOSH

For a few days, **Anansi** forgot all about **Turtle**. But then one day **he** went out for a walk and **he** found himself walking quite close to Turtle's **home**. Feeling tired and hungry, **Anansi** decided to visit **Turtle** and enjoy a free meal. As he arrived, the **sun** was just falling behind the **river**, setting the **sky** on fire with its bright, flaming colours. While **Anansi** sat on the warm **rocks** to watch the last of the **sunset**, **Turtle** dived down to his river home to prepare dinner. **Anansi** could hear **pots** and **pans** being moved around and the tempting sound of **bowls** and **plates** being put on the **table**. Sure enough, **Turtle** soon called out to Anansi, *'Dinner!'*

Anansi dived excitedly down to Turtle's **home**, but no matter how hard he tried, **Anansi** could not sit down at the **table**. Every time **he** tried, **he** floated straight back up to the surface of the **river** again, while **Turtle** just munched his way through the delicious food. **Anansi** was determined to eat plenty because **he** was getting very hungry. So **he** came up with a plan; **he** filled the pockets of his **jacket** with **stones** to make himself heavy. This time as **he** dived down, **he** found that **he** was finally able to sit at Turtle's **table** without floating away. Now **he** was really looking forward to the meal and **he** rubbed his hands together in anticipation.

WHOOSH

The **table** was already half empty because the food was disappearing fast into **Turtle**'s mouth. But just as **Anansi** was about to taste his first luscious mouthful, **Turtle** said, '*Please take your jacket off, Anansi.*' And **Anansi** had no choice, because he knew that it was bad manners to keep a jacket on at a meal table. He removed his **jacket** and went to put it around the back of his **chair**, but as **he** did, **he** started to float back up to the surface of the river. Then all **he** could do was watch angrily from the **river bank**, staring into the water as **Turtle** finished all of the beautiful meal himself.

As **he** walked hungrily home, **Anansi** thought about his own behaviour when Turtle came to dinner and he remembered what his mother had always told him.

WHOOSH

Follow-up activities

- The moral of this story is not explained at the end so that pupils can work out for themselves what Anansi's mother might have told him. To do this, start by pairing pupils for a Sculptor and Sculpted drama activity. One pupil acts as a sculptor, shaping their partner to create a still image of a character at a particular point in the narrative. Pupils can change roles with each new sculpture. The five scenes are Anansi:
  - sitting outside of his house, smelling the beautiful meal being cooked
  - being interrupted just as he is about to start his meal
  - cramming food into his mouth having tricked Turtle into leaving the table
  - filling his pockets with stones in order to get a free meal
  - having to watch Turtle eat all of the food after he has been tricked into leaving the table.

  Combine this drama activity with Thought Tracking. When each sculpture is complete, ask the sculpted characters to speak their thoughts aloud. This will show where the thoughts and actions of Anansi are contradictory.
- When the five scenes and thought tracks are complete, combine pairs of pupils into larger groups and introduce Resource 8. This provides a thought bubble for each of the scenes. Ask pupils to share their thought tracking comments and agree on a thought to write in each bubble.
- Share outcomes as a whole class before deciding on what to write in the final bubble – the moral of the story. The intended moral is that we should always treat others as we would like to be treated ourselves, but pupils may see other moral meanings in the story.

Resource 8 Thought tracking

In each thought bubble, write what Anansi might have been thinking. Do his thoughts always match his actions?

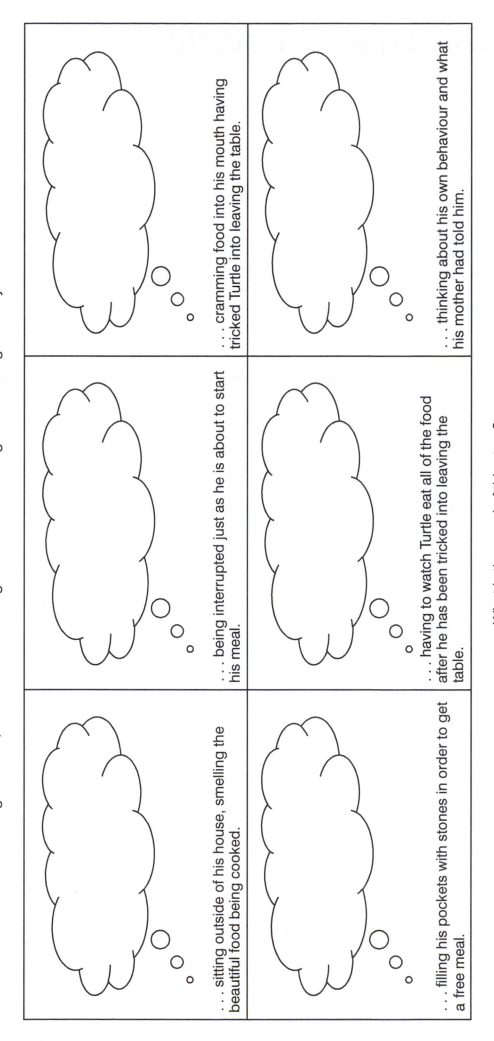

. . . sitting outside of his house, smelling the beautiful food being cooked.

. . . cramming food into his mouth having tricked Turtle into leaving the table.

. . . being interrupted just as he is about to start his meal.

. . . thinking about his own behaviour and what his mother had told him.

. . . filling his pockets with stones in order to get a free meal.

. . . having to watch Turtle eat all of the food after he has been tricked into leaving the table.

What is the moral of this story?

2   Seven short stories

People love stories. Telling stories about ourselves is a way of making sense of our lives and the world around us. So we recount the events of our day, talk on the phone, text or engage in social media interaction. Listening to stories through books, theatre, TV, film, art, opera, music and dance helps us to glimpse other people's lives. We can empathise, imagine, admire, dream of something better, or encounter and confront feelings of fear or sadness within the safety of a story.

Cultures may vary, but the human emotions that give rise to storytelling do not. It has been said that there are only seven basic story plots; rags to riches, journey and return, overcoming the monster, rebirth, quest, tragedy and comedy. Each of these plot types is explored in the following short stories.

1   English folk tales: *Mossycoat*

Mossycoat is one of a number of English folk tales collected in the early years of the twentieth century and published in a collection titled *Folktales of England*. This is a rags to riches story structure which bears a striking resemblance to the better-known *Cinderella*. As with all stories of this type, it gives hope of a brighter future waiting around the corner – a traditional equivalent of winning the Lottery with instant social mobility created by magic. This Whoosh considers how the teller of the story influences the viewpoint of the listener or reader – in this case, how sympathy for the protagonist Mossycoat is developed throughout the story.

Objective

* to examine how a storyteller influences the viewpoint of the listener.

Characters	Objects	Sounds
poor widow daughter (Mossycoat) ugly old pedlar the lady of the house servants pretty girls the young master the lord of the house people at the ball	cottage birds trees in a wood long grass springy moss spinning wheel door white satin dress silk dress silver shoes tattered old bag dawn coat big house kitchen skimmer dance house where the ball was held	bird song swishing grasses laughter whirring clicking loud knock rustling satin door shutting whispering silk silence name calling chatter and laughter snoring

Once upon a time, in **cottage** far away, lived a **poor widow** and her little **daughter**. Life was hard and they were often hungry. Day after day, the mother and child would walk through the **woods**, listening to the **birds** singing in the **trees**. In the summer, they laughed together as they swished through the **long, green grasses**. Every day they would gather huge armfuls of **springy green moss** and carry it back to the **cottage**.

And every day the poor widow would sit for many hours spinning the moss to make thread as fine as silk, her **spinning wheel whirring** and **clicking** as she worked. Year followed year; still the widow spun the delicate mossy thread as her child grew into a fine young woman.

WHOOSH

One day there was a **loud knock** on the **door**. Not many people visited their lonely home and the **daughter** was pleased that she might have someone to talk to. But it was only an **ugly old pedlar** selling something and he looked quite mean and nasty. Sadly, he liked the look of the **daughter** and decided that he wanted to marry her. The **girl** thought this was a terrible idea and rushed to tell her **mother**. But her **mother** just carried on spinning, a little faster than usual, and told her **daughter** to go back to the **door** and tell the **ugly old man** that she needed a **white satin dress** with gold flowers on it before she could get married. And it had to be a perfect fit.

Three days later, he came back with the **dress**, expecting that he could marry **the girl**. **Her mother**, spinning a little faster, told her to say that she also needed a **silk dress** the colour of all the **birds** that flew in the air and **sang** in the **trees**. And it had to fit perfectly. So she took the **white satin dress**, gave him his new instructions and sent the **pedlar** away. Then she tried on her **new dress**. She had never worn anything so beautiful and she **rustled** the dress this way and that way, admiring herself as she glided around the room.

Three days later, the pedlar came back carrying a beautiful **dress** made of silk which glimmered in every colour that she could imagine. She rushed to her mother, crying that she would have to marry him now, but he was so rude and mean. Her mother just started spinning even faster and told her to ask for some **silver shoes**, as she could not possibly get married in her old, worn out working shoes.

As soon as she had given the **pedlar** the new request, she took the **silk dress** and swiftly shut the **door**, pretending not to notice that he was looking quite cross. She rushed to her room to try on the beautiful **dress**. It shone and shimmered as she danced across the floor, the fabric **whispering** gently as she moved. It fitted perfectly, just as she had asked.

But just a couple of days later, back came the mean **old man** with the most beautiful pair of **silver slippers** that she had ever seen. What other excuses could there be to put him off? And now that she had accepted all of his gifts, how could she refuse to marry him?

WHOOSH

Her **mother** spun faster, and told her that the **pedlar** was to return at ten o'clock the next morning for her final answer. The girl packed her beautiful **dresses** and sparkling **slippers** into a **tattered old bag** and went to bed. All night the **spinning wheel whirred**. All night the **girl** lay awake, wondering how she could avoid such a terrible fate. Then, just as **dawn** broke, she realised that the **spinning wheel** had stopped. There was nothing but **silence** for the first time for many days. Creeping downstairs, she found the most beautiful **coat** made from the spun moss, held together with gold thread. Her **mother** wrapped it around her daughter, named her **Mossycoat** and wished her to be gone.

And because there was magic woven into the coat that is exactly what happened. When she was wearing the elegant **coat**, **Mossycoat** could go wherever she wanted to. Finding herself in a **big house**, she asked for work. Because the **lady of the house** was kind and caring, she sent Mossycoat to work in the **kitchen**. The **servants** were horrid to her; they called her names and hit her on the head with a **skimmer**. **Mossycoat** was sad and the harder she worked, the nastier the **servants** were.

WHOOSH

One morning **Mossycoat** found the **kitchen** full of **chatter** and **laughter**. There was to be a big **dance** in a **nearby house** and everyone was very excited. **Mossycoat** longed to go to the **dance**, but the more the **servants** discussed it, the more they teased poor **Mossycoat** about how dirty and bedraggled she was. She said nothing, but on the evening of the **dance** she put the **servants** to sleep. When she could hear them **snoring**, she washed and put on her **white satin dress**. Slipping into her **coat**, she wished herself to be at the **dance**.

Even though there were lots of **pretty girls** at the ball, the **young master** of the house danced with her again and again. When the ball ended, **Mossycoat** returned to her work. Carefully folding away her **dress** she put on her grubby work clothes, went to the **kitchen** and woke the **servants**. Fortunately, they were so worried that Mossycoat would tell the **lady of the house** about them sleeping when they should have been working that they started to tease her less.

WHOOSH

Soon another ball came along. This time, **Mossycoat** wore her **silk dress**. She danced and danced with the **young master** of the house and he ignored all the other **girls** who hoped to dance with him. **He** had obviously fallen deeply in love with **Mossycoat**. As **she** left, **he** tried to catch her but **she** slipped away, leaving one of her shining **slippers** on the floor.

The next day, **he** appeared in the **kitchen** and made all the **servants** try on the **slipper**. But of course, it only fitted **Mossycoat**. When they found out how she had been treated, the **lord and lady of the house** sacked the nasty **servants**. **Mossycoat** wore her **white satin dress** when she married the **young master**. She was always kind to her **servants** and they lived happily ever after.

WHOOSH

Follow-up activities

- Through shared discussion, decide how listeners feel towards Mossycoat. Was this the intention of the storyteller?
- Why are some characters described in great detail whilst others, for example, the lady of the house and the people at the ball, are not described at all? How does this affect what the listener thinks about Mossycoat?
- What evidence is there from the story to support listeners' views?
- Record evidence using the thinking web (Resource 9).
- Listeners are not told what happened when the pedlar returned expecting to marry Mossycoat. Discuss this, offering the opportunity to improvise the conversation between the pedlar and the old widow. Why was this aspect of the story not included in its telling?
- Consider the outcome of the story. Supposing the slipper had fitted more than one person. What might an alternative ending for this story be?
- What might modern equivalents of rags to riches stories be? Can pupils think of any current examples? How do we hear these stories today?
- Using these ideas and Resource 9, ask pupils to create their own contemporary rags to riches stories and tell them to each other. Storytellers should create sympathy for their central character.
- Challenge pupils to include a twist at the end.
- As an extension activity, pupils could whoosh their own stories.

Resource 9 Mossycoat's thinking web

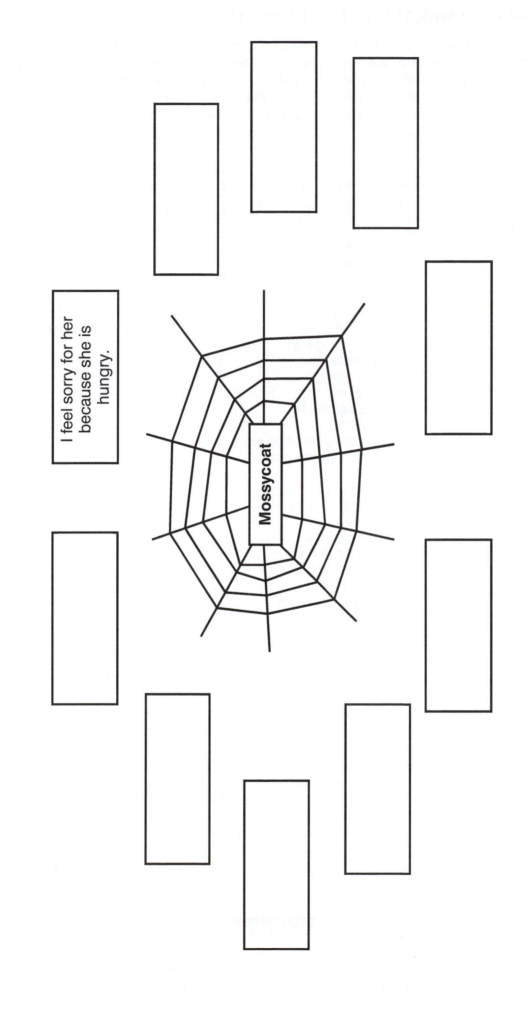

I feel sorry for her because she is hungry.

Mossycoat

2 Russian folk tales: *The Firebird*

The Firebird is a journey and return story which is part of Russian folk lore. The story is told in many forms, but certain key themes remain constant in all forms of the narrative – a Prince's journey to find the beautiful Firebird, challenge, love, death, heroism and ultimate return in triumph. The story inspired Stravinsky's 1910 ballet of the same name and a lavishly illustrated book by Saviour Pirotta and Catherine Hyde, which was published in 2010 to celebrate the one hundredth anniversary of the ballet.

Objective

•   to explore how the pace of a story can be determined by its structure.

Characters	Objects	Sounds
Tsar Vaslav	palace	rustling leaves
Prince Ivan	apple orchard	silence
the Firebird	garden	hooting owl
a grey wolf	golden apple tree	whinnying horse
Evil Wizard	golden apples	squawking crow
Princess Vasilia	leaves	bloodcurdling yell
Baba Yaga	glowing light	screech
crow	tail feather	
two brothers	horse	
	forest	
	open field	
	pillar	
	sunlight/setting sun	
	rich, green grass	
	rock	
	fortress	
	heart of stone	
	hut	
	dark forest	
	golden cord	
	melting heart	
	forest floor	
	fountain of life	
	water	

Once there was a king named **Tsar Vaslav**, who lived in a **palace** in Russia. He had a beautiful **orchard**, full of **apple trees**. In the middle of his **garden** stood one very **special tree**. It was special because it grew **golden apples** that shone and glowed in the sunlight. While he was strolling in the **garden** one evening, admiring the golden fruit, he noticed with alarm that some of the **golden apples** were missing. He was so worried that his youngest son, **Prince Ivan**, offered to sit in the **garden** all night to guard the **tree**.

Sure enough, in the middle of the night, he heard the **rustle** of **leaves** as if someone was climbing the **tree**. **He** could see a strange **light** glowing in the darkness and as **he** walked towards it, the **light** grew brighter and brighter. But just as **he** reached the **tree** and stretched out his arm to catch the thief, a **shining, shimmering bird** flew swiftly away, leaving **Prince Ivan** with just one **tail feather** in his outstretched hand. It was the **Firebird**.

The next morning when **Prince Ivan** went to tell his **father** what had happened, the **feather** was still glittering and glistening like the **golden apples** in the **orchard**. **The Tsar** decided that he wanted the **Firebird** for himself, so he told his **son** to prepare for a long journey. He was not allowed to return home to the **palace** without the Firebird.

WHOOSH

Prince Ivan rode for many long hours, encouraging his **horse** as it stumbled through the **forest**. There was nothing but **silence**, broken only by the occasional **hoot** of an owl. On the third day, the **trees** began to thin out until he came to a broad **open field** with a **pillar** in the middle. **His**

horse whinnied with pleasure at the sight of **sunlight** and stopped to graze on the **rich, green grass**. Curious to know what was written on the **pillar**, the **Prince** rode closer, only to find that he had three choices – **he** could carry on and be cold and hungry. He could turn right but his **horse** would be killed. If he turned left, his **horse** would be fine, but **he** would be killed. Which choice should he make?

After thinking for a while, he turned right, only to be met by a fierce, bloodthirsty **wolf** who killed his **horse**. Feeling very sorry for himself, **he** walked unsteadily on throughout the next day, determined not to fail in his task. As the **sun** began to **set**, he sat down on a **rock** to rest. Suddenly the **wolf** appeared again. But this time, he seemed to be sorry for what he had done and asked **Prince Ivan** where he was going. When the **Prince** explained, the **wolf** promised to help, because he knew where the Firebird lived. So climbing on the wolf's back, Prince Ivan set off on the next stage of his journey to the **fortress** of the **Evil Wizard** where the Firebird lived.

WHOOSH

As **Prince Ivan** stared anxiously at the huge, thick walls of the **fortress**, the **wolf** told him where to find the **Firebird**. But he also warned him that **Princess Vasilia** was being held captive there and her **heart** had been turned to **stone**. If he saw her, he must not look at her, even though she was very beautiful, because if he did, he would fall hopelessly in love with her. So off **Ivan** went. The first person he saw was **Vasilia** and, forgetting all the warnings, he looked at her. Instantly the **Evil Wizard** appeared. He told **Ivan** that the **Firebird** had been stolen by **Baba Yaga**, the terrifying witch who lived in a **hut** on the edge of the **dark forest**. But if he got it back, he could choose between the **Princess** and the **Firebird**.

At first the **wolf** was very angry with **Ivan** for his disobedience, but when he saw how desperate **Ivan** was, he agreed to help him again. So they set off to **Baba Yaga's hut** on the edge of the **dark forest**. When they got there, the **wolf** told **Ivan** where to find the **Firebird**. But he also warned him that she would be tied with a **golden cord** which **Ivan** must not touch. So in **Ivan** went, but he was so overjoyed at finding the **Firebird** that he forgot the warning. Grabbing the **golden cord**, he was about to leave when a **crow** started to **squawk** with all its might. As **Baba Yaga** woke with a **furious, bloodcurdling yell**, **he** managed to escape with both the **Firebird** and his life … just.

WHOOSH

But there was still one challenge to face. How was **Ivan** going to choose between the **Princess** and the **Firebird**? He was pale with worry as he met the **Evil Wizard** again. But just as the **Evil Wizard** raised his arm with a terrible **screech** to turn **Ivan**'s heart to stone, **Princess Vasilia** started to cry. And something strange happened – her **heart melted**. Together **they** escaped. And the **Firebird** – well she was free and she chose to follow **Ivan**. The adventure was almost over. **Ivan** had only to deliver **the Firebird** to his father, **Tsar Vaslav**, then he would be free to marry the love of his life. Suddenly, from behind the **trees** of the forest, jumped his **two** older **brothers**, filled with hatred and jealousy. **Ivan** fought bravely, but he was no match for his **brothers** and soon he lay dead on the **forest floor**.

WHOOSH

But **the Firebird**, who had watched this sadly from the safety of a **tree**, wanted to help **Ivan** because he had given her freedom. Flying swiftly to the **fountain of life**, she scooped up a few drops of the precious **water** in her beak and returned to the **dead Prince**. Carefully she dropped the **liquid** into his open mouth and watched **him** as he gradually revived.

Then **Ivan** and **Vasilia** returned to the Tsar's **palace**. After **Ivan** had recounted his adventures, his murderous **brothers** were banished and **the Firebird** was invited to live in the **golden apple tree**. **Ivan** and **Vasilia** were married and lived happily ever after.

WHOOSH

Follow-up activities

- There are opportunities for discussion built into this story, when the central character has to make choices. In the course of the story, freeze the action and consider Prince Ivan's options when he reaches the pillar and when he returns to the Evil Wizard and has to choose between Princess Vasilia and the Firebird. What are the consequences of each of the choices?

How might each choice affect the actions of other characters in the story and therefore its outcome? What would pupils do?

- Ask pupils to map the story by creating a picture map of the journey. Mark the key points at which Prince Ivan met a challenge. This should include:
  - the palace with the golden apple tree in the garden
  - the forest through which Prince Ivan rode
  - the open field with the pillar and three choices of direction
  - the place where the wolf killed the horse
  - the Evil Wizard's fortress containing the Princess
  - Baba Yaga's hut on the edge of a forest
  - the route of the return journey
  - the place where Prince Ivan was murdered on his way home
  - the fountain of life
- Through shared discussion, consider how the challenges both dictate the structure of the story and also give the narrative pace by creating action. Use this information as a model to create new stories.

3 Anglo-Saxon epic tales: *Beowulf: Grendel the Night-Prowler*

The story of Beowulf is an ancient tale which originates from the Anglo Saxon tradition of oral storytelling as part of community life. It takes the form of an epic poem of over three thousand lines which are rich in alliteration and kennings. It was finally written down somewhere between the eighth and early eleventh centuries using a form of West Saxon English which was spoken in Wessex, particularly in and around the city of Winchester.

According to the story, Beowulf was a strong, brave warrior who lived in Scandinavia. When he heard that Hrothgar, King of the Danes, was threatened by a terrible monster, he hurried to help; Hrothgar and Beowulf's father had been old friends many years before. The following Whoosh retells the first part of the story when Beowulf overcomes the monster which is threatening Hrothgar's people. There are parallels in this plot theme with modern stories such as Doctor Who. We are keen to be scared by monsters in the safe context of a story within which we can face and overcome our own fears. We admire the hero who overcomes the monster, just as the Anglo Saxon listeners did many hundreds of years ago and people have been doing ever since.

Objective

- to explore feelings generated by the use of descriptive language.

Characters	Objects	Sounds
Beowulf	a feast	buzz of conversation
friends and family	fire flames	lapping waves
travellers	Great Hall of the Geats	wind in the sails
sailors	ships	snores
fierce monster (Grendel)	Denmark	cracking twigs
Hrothgar	Great Hall of Hrothgar	whispering, 'Wake up!'
Danish people	tables and benches	creaking door
Beowulf's parents	sea cave	shouting
King of the Geats	shadows	tables crashing
fourteen friends	sword	splintering wood
Hrothgar's servants	door	piercing scream
Queen of Denmark	arm	noisy chatter
	sails	
	flickering fire	

Once, long ago, in the land of the Geats, there lived a young warrior called **Beowulf**. He was known throughout the land for his bravery and strength. At the end of a hard day of hunting there was nothing he enjoyed more than **feasting** with his **friends** and **family**. The Geats were a welcoming people, always happy to include **travellers** in their feasts. They would all enjoy the fine food together as a **buzz of conversation** filled the air, then they would sit contentedly watching the **fire flames** cast shadows on the walls of their **Great Hall** while someone told a story.

WHOOSH

But one night, **Beowulf** heard a story which worried him greatly. **Sailors** told a tale of a **fierce monster** which was tormenting **Hrothgar**, King of the Danes, and his **people**. The **murderous monster** would stalk in the shadows of darkness, seizing innocent **people** and eating them whole. **Hrothgar** had once given refuge to **Beowulf's father** when he was in danger and they had been great friends. Indeed, **Beowulf** had been born while his **parents** were being sheltered by **Hrothgar** and he had lived in the Danish court for the first six years of his life.

Moved with deep distress about his old friend, **Beowulf** begged his **king** to allow him to take help to **Hrothgar**. Although the **king** was reluctant to let his bravest young men go to a certain death, he understood that **Beowulf** had to help such a faithful friend. So **Beowulf** and **fourteen** of his closest, strongest **friends** set sail in their carved wooden **ships** for **Denmark**. As the waves **lapped** against the side of his ship and the wind **whistled** as it filled the billowing sails, **Beowulf** looked back at the disappearing coast of his home. He wondered if he would ever see it again. He wondered what adventures lay ahead.

WHOOSH

It was many years since **Beowulf** had seen his **father's old friend**. He was shocked at how worn and weary **Hrothgar** looked, stooping as he stumbled to greet the **visitors**. There was not much talking or laughter in the **Great Hall** that evening. **People** were silent and scared and the feast was a quiet affair. Early in the evening, **King Hrothgar** decided to go to bed. As his **people** slowly left the safety of their **Hall**, the **servants** moved **tables**, packed away **benches** and laid out straw mattresses for Beowulf and his friends to sleep on. Soon, all was quiet, with just the gentle **snores** of the young **Geats** to disturb the silence.

WHOOSH

Deep from within his **sea cave**, **Grendel**, the fierce and murderous monster, smelt human flesh. For hours he had hidden in the **shadows**, waiting his chance. Only the occasional **cracking** of a **twig** gave away his presence as he crept towards the dark, silent **Hall** where his next feast was sleeping. His thick, green scales glistened in the moonlight and his huge, slimy body cast a threatening **shadow** against the side of the Hall. Inside, **Beowulf** stirred. He had not slept much and the **shadow** told him that danger hovered nearby. He lay his **sword** on the dirt floor, knowing that to win this battle he would have to overcome the monster with his bare hands. But just as he whispered to his **friends** to wake up, the **door creaked** open. Before **Beowulf** had time to move, the ugly **monster** had entered the **Hall** moving more swiftly than his size suggested was possible. Before **Beowulf** could shout any warning, **Grendel** seized one of the **friends** and ate him whole.

The brave **young men**, now fully awake, watched in horror, powerless to save their friend. They watched as **Beowulf** threw himself at **Grendel**, holding and twisting his arm as though he would never let go. The fight went this way and that, knocking over **tables** and **benches** as it went. The **people** of the village, awoken by the **shouting**, stood outside, shaking in fear as they heard the fearful **crashes** and the **splintering** of smashed wood.

WHOOSH

Beowulf did not let go. Armed with their swords, his **companions** thought many times of trying to attack **Grendel** but the fight was so furious that they were afraid they might harm their leader instead. Just once, a huge blow was landed, but the sword slid harmlessly off of **Grendel's** scales without leaving a mark.

Eventually, after what seemed like many hours, there was a **piercing scream** and **Grendel** plunged from the **Great Hall**. Staggering along the cliff edge towards his **sea home**, **he** fell lifeless. In the **Hall**, **Beowulf** stood, exhausted and aching, hold the **arm** of Grendel.

The dead body of the **monster** was soon found. **Tables** and **benches** were replaced, broken wood was swept away and the **people** feasted and celebrated the end of the reign of terror. The **Hall** was full of **noisy chatter** as **Hrothgar** and his **queen** gave **Beowulf** gifts of armour and a payment of gold for the family who had lost their son. As the young **Geats** set their **sails** for home, the story of Beowulf the Brave was already becoming the favourite tale to tell around the **flickering fire** in the **Great Hall** of Hrothgar.

WHOOSH

Follow-up activities

*   Define the key feelings experienced by characters in this narrative – Resource 10 provides a brainstorm sheet with suggestions for linking Beowulf's feelings with the descriptive language which portrays them. Watch a recording of the Whoosh, noting the words or phrases in the story which created the feelings at key points. This can be repeated for other characters in the story.
*   After brainstorming, discussing and sharing ideas, ask pupils to work in groups. Each person in the group should take a different role and describe, in the first person, how they felt. For example, working in role as Beowulf, a pupil might describe how frightened he was when he first saw Grendel, but how elated he felt when he realised that the monster was dead and the people were safe.
*   As an extension activity, pupils could illustrate a character or create their own monster and write kennings to annotate the image. A kenning is a two word description of one item. Anglo-Saxon examples include seal-bath and whale-road for the sea, bone-house for body and sea-garment for sails. This activity starts to develop an awareness of the rhythm and imagery of the original text.

4   Oscar Wilde: *The Selfish Giant*

Although better known for his plays, books and poems for adults, Wilde published a book of fairy stories in 1888 comprised of tales which he told his own children. *The Happy Prince and Other Stories* are part fairy story and part fable, narrated using rich language that both sparks the imagination and takes listeners on an emotional journey. The story of *The Selfish Giant* is an example of a rebirth story, in which a character who was a victim of his own selfishness is reborn as a kind, caring individual.

Objective

*   to track the emotional journey of a character through the course of a story.

Characters	Objects	Sounds
children a Giant Snow Frost North Wind Hail a tiny child	garden flowers grass breeze twelve trees birds gate castle road wall sign window tree branches window panes hole in the wall gold and silver fruit white blossom	rustling grass bird song roaring giant chattering banging 'Trespassers will be prosecuted' screeching whistling drumming hailstones cracking glass breaking tiles music sobbing

There was once a beautiful **garden** where **children** used to play on their way home from school every afternoon. **Flowers** swayed gently and the rich, green **grass rustled** in the **breeze. Twelve** strong, tall **trees** stood proudly in the **garden**. In the spring they were covered in clouds of pink blossom. In the autumn, they carried ripe, luscious peaches. **Birds** perched in the **trees, singing** as the **children** played on the **grass** below. And so they lived for seven happy years.

Resource 10 Beowulf's brainstorm

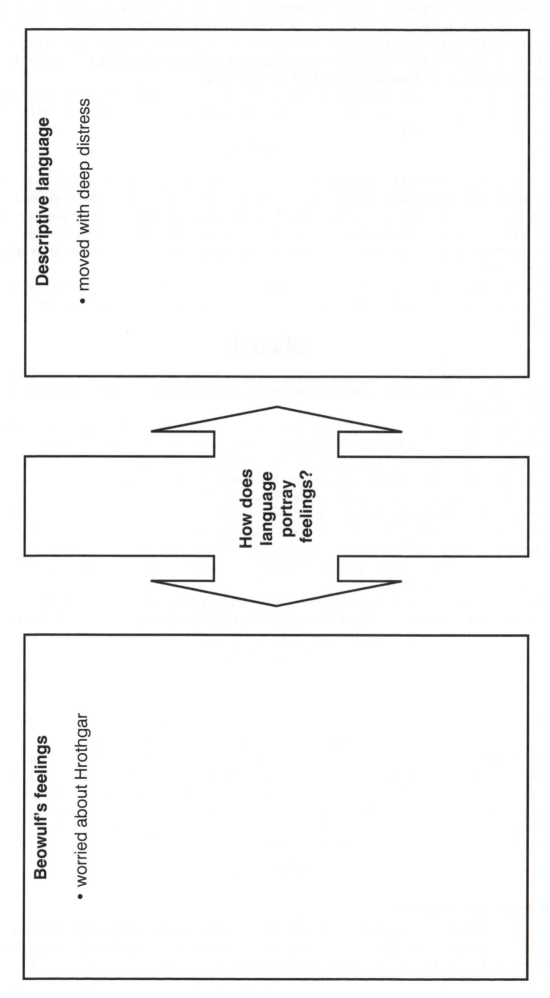

Descriptive language

- moved with deep distress

How does language portray feelings?

Beowulf's feelings

- worried about Hrothgar

But one day the **Giant** who owned the **garden** returned home from a long visit to his friend. As he approached the **gate** of his **castle**, he heard the **children chattering**. As **he** arrived, **he** saw **them** playing. He was so angry that the **children** were frightened and ran away. **They** watched sadly from the **road** as the Giant built a huge, high **wall** around his **garden** and **banged** a sign into the ground. It said, **'Trespassers will be prosecuted.'**

The **children** tried to play in the **road**, but the stones hurt their feet and they used to long for the days when they played in the Giant's beautiful **garden**. Soon spring arrived and the children went to play in other places.

WHOOSH

But as the **Giant** looked out of his **window**, he saw that spring had not arrived in his garden. The **birds** did not sing. **Snow** spread her white cloak over the ground while **Frost** drew delicate silver patterns over the bare **tree branches**. **North Wind** came to visit and stayed, **screeching** around the garden and **whistling** in the cracks of the **castle**. Then **Hail** was invited too. His icy breath **drummed** on the roof and the **window panes** day after day, **cracking glass** and **breaking tiles**.

As the **Giant** looked sadly on his frozen **garden**, he could not understand why spring did not come. But nor did summer. And nor did autumn. Month after freezing month, there was nothing but winter.

WHOOSH

One morning the **Giant** heard some beautiful **music** outside of his bedroom **window**. Hail and North Wind had stopped rushing around his garden and when he opened the **window**, the smell of spring poured in.

And as **he** watched, he saw some **children** creeping into his garden through a **hole** which had been broken into the **wall**. As each **tree** was climbed, it burst into blossom. **Birds** flew between the trees, **singing** with happiness at the return of spring and the **children**. But in the far corner of his garden, there was just one tree which was still in winter's icy grip. On the ground was a **sobbing child**, who was too tiny to climb even the lowest branches.

The **Giant** crept into his garden, but as he did the **children** ran away in fear. All except the one **tiny child**, who was crying too much to hear the **Giant** approaching. Filled with compassion, the **Giant** realised how selfish he had been and he was very sorry. He lifted the **child** gently into the **tree**, then he knocked down the ugly great **wall**, hammer blow after hammer blow falling on the stones until the wall was gone.

Seeing what was happening, the **children** returned and played with the **Giant** all day. When it was time for **them** to leave, the **Giant** realised that the **tiny child** was not there. None of the other children knew who he was – they had never seen him before.

WHOOSH

And so for many years **children** continued to play in the beautiful **garden** on their way home from school. Eventually the **Giant** could no longer play with them because he was too old. He still felt sad that the tiny child had never come back to share his **garden**.

One winter morning, the **Giant** was looking out of his window when, to his delight, he noticed that the **tiny child** had returned to stand underneath his **tree**. **Fruit** of gold and silver hung from the **branches** even though it was the middle of winter. Amazed, the **Giant** went into the **garden**. But when he asked the **child** his name, he just smiled. He said that because the **Giant** had once let him play in the garden, the **Giant** could go with him and play in his garden for ever.

When the **children** ran into the **garden** that afternoon, they found the old **Giant** lying dead under the **tree**. He was covered in **white blossom**.

WHOOSH

Follow-up activities

The emotions tracker in Resource 11 is designed to explore how the central character's feelings change in the course of the story. The horizontal axis contains key events in the story. The vertical axis shows three emotional responses using emoticons.

Resource 11 Tracking the Selfish Giant's emotions

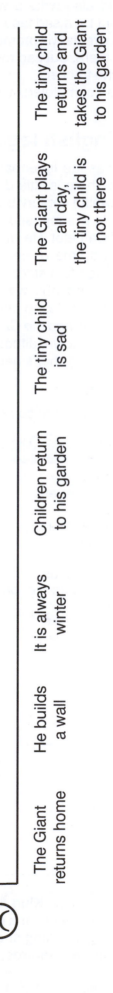

The Giant returns home	He builds a wall	It is always winter	Children return to his garden	The tiny child is sad	The Giant plays all day, the tiny child is not there	The tiny child returns and takes the Giant to his garden

- For each key event in the story, draw the appropriate emoticon above that event. Older pupils could also write a word which summarizes the emotion. For example, the first emoticon would be a sad face, which could be annotated with the word 'angry'.
- The events will prompt discussion – for example, when the children returned he was happy to see them, but sad for the tiny child whose tree was still frozen. How can this be represented on the tracker?
- When completed, it will show the emotional journey of the Giant throughout the story.

5   English legends: *Sir Gawain and the Green Knight*

Arthur was the legendary king who defended Britain against Saxon invasion early in the sixth century. There is little documentary evidence that such a king existed, but folklore which grew from a twelfth century book *History of the Kings of Britain* has built a substantial back story about Arthur. He is supposed to have been born at Tintagel, later marrying Guinevere and basing his court at Camelot. He was owner of Excalibur, the famous sword which he pulled from a rock.

It was a time of deep magic and Merlin the wise magician acted as Arthur's adviser. The knights lived to a strict code of chivalry and were sworn to defend the people of Britain. A seat at Arthur's round table was an honour, the shape of which indicated equality. Because there was no head to the table, no one knight was more important than any other.

Sir Gawain and the Green Knight is a poem which was written in the late fourteenth century. The writer is unknown, although it is written in a dialect which was spoken in the middle of England. Gawain was Arthur's nephew and this narrative represents the quest structure of storytelling.

Objective

- to recall and accurately sequence the events of a story.

Characters	Objects	Sounds

King Arthur
Queen Guinevere
knights
the King's sisters
Sir Gawain
Green Knight
Gawain's friends
people Gawain met on his
   journey
Bertilak
old, wrinkled lady
Lady Bertilak
a servant
	Camelot castle
	tables
	door
	horse
	axe
	head
	melting snow
	trees
	birds
	leaves
	sun
	forest floor
	dawn
	Gryngelot, Gawain's horse
	hills
	rivers
	forest
	turrets
	a castle
	drawbridge
	belt
	path
	stream
	entrance to the Green
	   Chapel
		singing
		trumpet fanfare
		pipe tunes
		drum rhythms
		tapping hooves
		splashing water
		bubbling stream
		cheering
		celebration

It was Christmas. **King Arthur**, **Queen Guinevere** and the **knights** were all gathered at the court at **Camelot castle** for a party. In those days, Christmas lasted for fifteen days, so there was plenty of **feasting**, **dancing** and **singing**. One night there was a special feast because it was New Year's Day. **Trumpet fanfares**, **pipe tunes** and **drum rhythms** announced each course of the meal, until there were so many dishes of food that there was no more room left on the **tables**. **Arthur**, **Guinevere**, the **King's sisters** and **Sir Gawain** were all sitting together at the same **table**.

But as they came to the end of their feast, the great **door** burst open and in came a **Knight**, riding his **horse**. **He** did not wear any armour, and the **Knight** and his clothes were green from head to toe. The mane and tail of his **horse** were braided in green and gold. He carried just a twig of holly and an **axe**. The **Knight** looked like a great hero.

WHOOSH

The **Green Knight** rode slowly around the silent room, the **hooves** of his **horse tapping** rhythmically on the floor as he passed each **table**. He stared at the seated **people**, saying nothing until **Arthur** invited him to join the feast. But he was not there, he explained, to celebrate. He was there with a Christmas challenge. He wanted to know if any one of Arthur's knights was brave enough to kill him with one blow of the **axe**. There was just one condition – any knight who took the challenge would have to seek out the Green Knight one year and one day later when the blow would be returned.

It was silent for just a moment, before **Gawain** stepped forward. Taking the **axe**, he gave a mighty blow to the neck of the kneeling **Green Knight**. His **head** flew off and fell to the floor. But just as **Gawain** turned to walk away, the headless **Knight** stood up, walked across the room, picked up his **head** and climbed back onto his **horse**. He reminded **Gawain** that in one year and one day he must search for the **Knight** of the Green Chapel to play the other part of the game, otherwise he would be known for ever as a coward.

WHOOSH

Snow melted as winter turned to spring. **Trees** budded, **birds** built new nests and **Gawain** tried to forget that time was passing. The bright **sun** warmed his summer, but as the autumn **leaves** slowly drifted from the **trees** onto the **forest floor**, **he** knew that he must prepare for his quest.

The evening before **Gawain** left, **Arthur** held a great feast. The **hall of Camelot** was filled with **people**, but there was none of the dancing and singing that they had all enjoyed nearly a year earlier. **Gawain** was glad when **dawn** arrived. As he strapped on his armour, his **friends** gathered around him to help. As he rode into the sunrise on his faithful **horse** Gryngelot, they felt sad that such a great knight should have to make such a foolish search.

For many days, **Gawain** rode in search of the Knight of the Green Chapel. He climbed **hills**, **splashed** through **rivers** and picked his way slowly through thick **forest**. Whenever he met **someone**, he would ask if they knew where the Green Chapel was. But every time, the person would shake their head. As autumn turned to winter, **Gawain** grew colder and hungrier than he had ever been before. As he began to despair that he would ever find what he was searching for, he saw the **turrets** of a **castle** in the distance. Riding towards it, he hoped that he would be offered food and shelter. He hoped, too, as he rode across the **drawbridge**, that someone might know where the Green Chapel was, because it was nearly New Year's Day.

WHOOSH

He was warmly welcomed into the **castle** by its owner **Bertilak**, who immediately recognised **Sir Gawain** as one of the Knights of the Round Table. For three days he rested and slept while **Bertilak** hunted. Each evening they would feast on the meat that **Bertilak** had brought home from the hunt. And each evening, **Gawain** would talk to **Lady Bertilak**, often watched carefully by an **old, wrinkled lady** who was never far away.

While her husband was out hunting, **Gawain** spent much of his waking time talking to **Lady Bertilak**, who seemed to cheer him up and distract him from thinking about the fate that awaited him. But eventually the time came for him to get ready for his final challenge. **Bertilak** promised to send one of his servants to show **Gawain** the way to the Green Chapel. And privately, just before he left, **Lady Bertilak** unwound a beautiful **belt**, woven in green and gold, from around her waist and gave it to **Gawain**.

Early the next morning, **Gawain** and **Gryngelot** set off with their **guide** to complete his search. They followed a **path** along a **bubbling stream** for a while, until Gawain's **companion** pointed to a rocky opening in the distance. Saying that this was the **entrance** to the **Green Chapel**, **he** turned his horse and headed home.

Gawain moved slowly forward into the **entrance**. The rocks got higher and higher on either side of him and their colour changed until they were completely green. Climbing down from his **horse**, **Gawain** saw the **Green Knight** advancing towards him. Knowing that his quest was ended, **Gawain** knelt to receive the deadly axe blow. He bowed his head, so he could not notice that the **Green Knight** did not intend to kill him. The blow was so light that it only grazed his skin.

Determined that the **Green Knight** should only have one blow as agreed, **Gawain** sprang to his feet, only to find the **Knight** smiling at him. He listened in amazement as the **Green Knight** told his story. He was really **Bertilak**, transformed by the magic of the old, wrinked lady, Morgan le Fey. He had been sent by her to test Gawain. And because **Gawain** had acted towards **Lady Bertilak** with honour as a true knight should, he was not to be killed.

WHOOSH

So Sir **Gawain** turned his **horse** towards **Camelot**. Together they pounded over **fields** and trekked carefully through **forest** dense with trees, hardly resting until they arrived at court. What joy and cheering there was in **Camelot** when he arrived, muddy and exhausted. What a tale he had to tell at the feast that evening. What noise filled the hall as **people celebrated**. And **Arthur** declared that in honour of his brave knight, all the **knights and ladies** of the round table would in future wear belts woven in green and gold.

WHOOSH

Follow-up activities

- Telling a story of any sort requires the speaker to make several quite quick decisions – what to include about each character and then what to emphasise, how to structure and sequence the plot and what to choose from known vocabulary to communicate meaning. To support the development of these skills, ask pupils to work in pairs, taking it in turns to retell the story of Sir Gawain's quest by alternating sentences.
- Then ask pupils to form bigger groups (four per group works well). The purpose is to tell the complete story, dividing it into one section for each storyteller. Video each group and view the videos. What facts of the story are the same as the original? Does the story follow the same sequence? In what ways does each storyteller develop their own content?
- As an extension activity, challenge pupils to create a quest story of their own (possibly in a contemporary or personal setting) and tell the story to a group. Observe to what extent body language, gesture, facial expression, vocal expression and known vocabulary and varied sentence structures are all deployed to engage the audience as the story unfolds.

6   Stories from the sea: *The Flying Dutchman*

The sea is a common setting for stories, from the tales of Joseph Conrad and C.S. Forester to the stories of great ships like the *Titanic* and the fictional *Mary Deare*. It is an ideal setting in many ways, because a ship is a community in miniature with a limited number of characters but a range of different ways of structuring conflict and creating tension. In addition to character interaction, there is the added option of including the role of the elements such as storms, the consequence of shipwreck, abandonment or rescue.

The origins of the tragic story of *The Flying Dutchman* are unclear and there are various versions in both Dutch and German folklore. Some of the stories are traceable in the seventeenth century, with the first written version appearing some 150 years later. Constant in all variations of the narrative is the central fact of a ghost ship which foreshadows the death of anyone who sees it. The story has entered marine superstition to the point that lighthouse keepers and sailors today (King George V among them) still record sightings of *The Flying Dutchman* as portents of impending tragedy. A logical explanation of the phenomenon suggests that it is a mirage caused by the meeting of warm and cold air masses.

In the *Pirates of the Caribbean* movies *Dead Man's Chest* and *At World's End*, *The Flying Dutchman* is given to Davy Jones by Calypso for the purpose of taking the souls of people lost at sea to the afterlife.

The following Whoosh is told in the first person, which gives participants an opportunity to consider viewpoint in storytelling. A first-person story has a fixed viewpoint about others. It raises the question of the reliability of the storyteller because individual viewpoint is always biased by personal interpretation of events.

Objective

- to consider viewpoint.

Characters	Objects	Sounds
Hendrick Hendrick's Mum crew families of other sailors Captain Vanderdecken merchants English sailors	ship crow's nest sea waves Cape of Good Hope sails masts rocks thick black clouds wind ghost ship	firing cannon shouting crashing waves tearing sails splintering masts creaking screaming wind

Let me introduce myself. My name is **Hendrick** and I'm ten years old. This is my first job as a sailor. Well, I'm not a real sailor yet and I won't be until I'm 16. But I joined this **ship** when she set sail with a **crew** of 30 from Amsterdam over a year ago. We were waved off by our **families**. I thought it was really exciting, but my **Mum** just cried and said that lots of ships never came back from where we were going.

It took me a while to get used to the pitching and tossing of the **ship**, but I really enjoy life at **sea**. There are some dangers, of course, apart from the sea. There's this terrible illness called scurvy. Lots of the men get it when they are at sea for a long time but nobody knows what causes it. The food is awful – salted meat and hard, dry biscuits mostly, washed down with weak beer, but I love it when I'm high up in the **crow's nest**, feeling as though I own the world. That's my job, you see, to stand in the crow's nest and warn the **Captain** if there's any danger ahead. Big **waves** rock the ship a lot more when you're high up and sometimes I feel really seasick, but most of the time it's fine.

I mentioned the Captain – **Captain Vanderdecken**. That's him down there, strutting up and down the deck. He works for something called the Dutch East India Company. Seamen sail half way around the world to buy cheap spices and pepper. They fill up their ships then sail home to Holland where **merchants** from the Company sell the cargo for huge amounts of money. It can be quite dangerous – the **English sailors** are violent and they often **fire** at us so that they can drown us and steal our cargo. Some of the **sailors** have worked with **Captain Vanderdecken** for years, but they're still frightened of him. He **shouts** a lot and he never cares how tired his **men** are. He still makes us carry on working.

WHOOSH

We're on our way back from the East Indies now and we're about to sail around the bottom of Africa – it's called the **Cape of Good Hope**. Sometimes, when we have some time, the older **men** tell terrible tales about the weather at the Cape. **Waves** as big as mountains, they say, **crashing** onto the decks, t**earing** the **sails** and **splintering** the **masts**. And all the time, the **waves** are trying to drive **ships** onto the **rocks**. It can be a frightening thing, the **sea**. I think it must be called Good Hope because we all hope that we're going to get round it without being shipwrecked.

The **wind** is beginning to pick up, so I've just **shouted** a warning down. There are **thick black clouds** ahead and I can see the **Cape** in the distance. We just need to sail around it and then we won't be many weeks from home. But if there's a storm brewing, I'm sure the Captain will wait until it blows itself out …

WHOOSH

I can't believe this. Down on deck, the **wind** is blowing so hard that we can't control the **sails** any more. They are starting to **flap** in the wind. The **wave**s are so high I can't see the top of them and they're **crashing** onto the deck with a deafening roar. **We're** all terrified, but the **Captain** says we have to keep going – that the best thing to do with a storm is to sail straight into it. The **masts** are **creaking** and **bending** in the **wind**. I'm sure the **ship** is going to smash apart with the next **wave**. And all the time, we are washing closer and closer to the **rocks**. I'm too small to be of any use and I'm so scared.

In the end, it was all over very quickly. A few huge **waves** smashing into the side of the **ship** one after another; one long, **screaming** gust of **wind** and the **ship** hit the **rocks**. There was no way we could save ourselves. My **family** will wonder what happened to me and I'm a bit sad about that, but it's very peaceful now.

And **Captain Vanderdecken**? Well, for thinking that he was bigger and cleverer than nature, **he** has been condemned to sail the seven seas for ever. They do say that if his **ghost ship** crosses your path, your ship will be wrecked. And if only **one person** on your ship sees The Flying Dutchman that person is sure to die. As for me, I'm glad I can rest now.

WHOOSH

Follow-up activities

- Discuss the issue of bias in the telling of this story. How might Hendrick's viewpoint about the captain be influenced by his age and inexperience? Why, for example, have many of the men continued to work with the same captain for many years? Explore with pupils a retelling of the story from the captain's perspective. Maybe he thought his men were lazy. He was a very experienced captain. How might this have affected his decision to sail into the storm rather than find a safe haven until the storm blew over? Why might he have been in a hurry to get his cargo back to Amsterdam?
- Working in groups, ask pupils to choose a nursery rhyme and retell the story in the first person. Each storyteller can improvise as much detail as they wish. For instance, a pupil storytelling in role as Little Miss Muffet could describe how she looked around to find some springy, green grass to enjoy her picnic. She could describe the spider in detail and explain how she showed her fear, through screaming or throwing her bowl into the air. This activity encourages imaginative storytelling and develops the ability to access, select and organise vocabulary.

7   Uncle Remus tales: *Brer Rabbit and the Tar Baby*

This collection of animal stories is of African American origin. The tales were collected and adapted by Joel Chandler Harris and published in 1881. Although Harris was originally praised for the way he captured the dialect of African plantation slaves in the southern USA, by the mid-twentieth century, this was perceived to be racist and the stories were transcribed to preserve their essential character as didactic tales with a moral. In 1946, the *Uncle Remus Tales* inspired Disney's *Song of the South*.

The following Brer Rabbit tale represents the comic plot. In its purest form, the definition of comedy refers to the comedy inherent in the plot where unlikely complex problems are finally resolved in surprising ways. An example would be where misunderstanding keeps central characters of the story apart – Jane Austen's novels adopt this plot structure whilst also making perceptive comments on the social structure of the time.

In this story, comedy is explored in the form of humour. Brer Fox and Brer Rabbit are drawn in sharp contrast and it is the way the characters' behaviour is determined by their personalities which creates the comedic content of the story.

Objectives

• to consider how characterisation can be used to create humour.

Characters	Objects	Sounds
Brer Rabbit animals Brer Fox	tar baby road bushes fire river bramble patch tree stump	whistling scuttling choral speaking: 'Good morning' evil laugh rustling choral speaking: 'Please don't throw me in the bramble patch' choral speaking: 'I was born in the bramble patch' thump piercing scream silence

Brer Rabbit loved to tease the other **animals** and he often played tricks on them. He always ended up getting the better of the **animals** that he teased and one day, **Brer Fox** decided that enough was enough. It was time to get his own back. So he scratched his head and stroked his chin and came up with a cunning plan. He decided to make a **tar baby**. He got a lump of tar, shaped it into a baby, put some clothes on it and sat it in the middle of the **road**. Then he hid behind some **bushes**.

WHOOSH

It was not long before he heard some **whistling** and **scuttling** and **Brer Fox** smiled, because he knew that it was **Brer Rabbit**. As he reached the **tar baby**, **Brer Rabbit** stopped. He took a good look around, but he could not see anyone. So he hopped forward and said to the **tar baby**, '*Good morning.*' There was no answer. **Brer Rabbit** tried again, a little louder, '*Good morning.*' Still there was no answer. **Brer Rabbit** was not used to being ignored and by now he was getting quite cross. '*GOOD MORNING,*' he shouted, reaching forward to touch the strange person. But, oh dear, the tar was so sticky that **Brer Rabbit's** paw got stuck. As he struggled to pull away, he pushed the **tar baby** with his other paw. That stuck too. So he pushed it with his feet and pushed it some more with his head and all the time, he just became more and more stuck. No matter how much he wriggled and pulled, he could not get away. Then, from behind the **rustling bushes**, he heard **Brer Fox's evil laugh**.

WHOOSH

Brer Fox came out from behind the **bushes**, but he was laughing so much that all he could do was roll around in the **road**. 'You've tricked me for the very last time, Brer Rabbit. What shall I do with you?' he grinned. '*Please don't throw me in the bramble patch,*' pleaded **Brer Rabbit**. 'I could roast you over a **fire** and have you for dinner,' mused **Brer Fox**, 'although that would be too much trouble.'

'*Please don't throw me in the bramble patch,*' begged **Brer Rabbit**.

'Maybe I could drown you in the **river**,' pondered Brer Fox.

'*Please don't throw me in the bramble patch,*' called **Brer Rabbit** again.

'Hm,' said **Brer Fox**, '*the bramble patch. Now there's a good idea. That would be scratchy enough.*' And without thinking any more of it, he picked up the tarry **rabbit** and threw him over his head and into the thick, thorny **bramble patch**.

WHOOSH

There was a **thump** followed by a piercing **scream** that made the hair on the back of **Brer Fox's** neck stand up on end. Then there was nothing. Just **silence**. He put his head on one side to listen for any sound, but there was none. **Brer Fox** was just starting to feel very pleased with himself, when he heard a familiar voice behind him, calling his name. As he turned around, he saw **Brer Rabbit**, sitting on a **tree stump**, just out of reach and pulling lumps of tar out of his fur as if he hadn't a care in the world. '*I was born in the bramble patch. I was born in the bramble patch*,' sang **Brer Rabbit** as he danced away. He turned to wave just once, before disappearing back into the **bramble patch**.

As for **Brer Fox**, he was left alone in the middle of **road**, looking at the **tar baby** and feeling very silly. **Brer Rabbit** had won again!

WHOOSH

Follow-up activities

Inference and deduction are key skills for pupils to develop. From an early age, children infer things about people through body language and tone of voice. Being able to do this with written text is a mature skill, but one which storytelling can help to develop.

- Explain to pupils that you are going to explore the two characters in the story, thinking about why they behaved as they did and how that has made the story funny. List one fact about the character of Brer Rabbit and one fact about Brer Fox on a resource sheet – suggested examples are provided as Resources 12 and 13. Then discuss how you know this by demonstrating evidence from the Whoosh. Some facts are obvious; for example the story says that Brer Rabbit loved teasing animals. But what about the phrase, 'So he scratched his head and stroked his chin,' referring to Brer Fox? What does this tell us about him – what do we infer from the words? Do we sympathise with him or smile about him?
- Divide pupils into groups, providing each group with a resource sheet. Half the groups should discuss and list evidence for Brer Rabbit and half should discuss Brer Fox. After a suitable time, ask one pupil from each group to envoy to another group which has discussed the same character. Repeat this until the envoy has collected additional thoughts from each group. Then ask envoys to return to their groups and share new information. Have views changed in the light of peer thinking?
- Complete the activity by shared discussion. What has been inferred about the two characters? How have their characters been used by the storyteller to create humour?

Character	Evidence
Annoying	Brer Fox is fed up with his teasing

Resource 13 Learning about characterisation
Brer Fox

Character	Evidence
Not very clever	Kept getting tricked by Brer Rabbit

3 Plays

1 William Shakespeare: *The Tempest*

The Tempest is one of Shakespeare's last, and arguably finest, plays. It was written between 1610 and 1611. It tells the story of Prospero, the rightful Duke of Milan, who was deposed by his brother Antonio in alliance with Alonso, King of Naples. Prospero and his three-year-old daughter Miranda were cast adrift at sea in a leaky boat, eventually washing up on an island. Prospero had already learnt magic from his book studies and he used it to take the island from Sycorax, the evil user of magic who owned it; to restore himself as the rightful Duke, and to manipulate a meeting between Miranda and Ferdinand, heir to the throne of Naples. During his twelve-year stay on the island, Caliban (the son of Sycorax) and Ariel, a spirit, became Prospero's servants.

The play is steeped in magic so it is very visual and gives plenty of scope for imaginative interpretation of special effects. In its original performance, the stage would have been bare, with the action and sound effects used to create settings in the minds of the viewers. Suggestions are made for sound and action, but pupils will also develop their own ideas and interpretations as they become familiar with the play.

This Whoosh is designed to introduce the complete story to pupils so in its entirety it is quite lengthy and will require several sessions. There are three plot lines in the play, with action moving between the different scenes. After the initial shipwreck, each group of characters is in a different place on the island, but Ariel and Prospero are able to see and manipulate everyone to facilitate the plot. Each of the three plots is presented in a separate Whoosh section to aid understanding; act and scene references are provided so that the positions of each section can be located in the play. The story opens with a storm which is Prospero's final act of magic and it ends with him leaving the island with relationships restored and Miranda engaged to marry Ferdinand. The intervening scenes serve to explain the back story which has led to Prospero's action and the events of just a few hours between the shipwreck and the final resolution.

Objective

• to understand the complete and complex plot of a play.

Characters		Objects	Sounds
Prospero master boatswain sailors Alonso, King of 　Naples Sebastian, his 　brother Ferdinand, his son Gonzalo, his servant Antonio, Duke of 　Milan Adrian, fellow 　traveller	Francisco, fellow 　traveller Miranda Ariel, a spirit spirits Caliban, a monster Trinculo, a jester Stephano, his friend Iris Juno Ceres nymphs	ship cave banquet	hissing lightning crashing thunder heavy rain waves hitting the ship creaking timbers voices below decks splintering wood gentle music

Shipwreck! (Act I scenes i + ii)

Start this section with Prospero standing on one side of the circle, wearing a magic cloak and conjuring up a storm. Create the sound effects of hissing lightning and crashing thunder to match Prospero's moves.

On the other side of circle, create a freeze frame of sailors pulling sheets and panicked passengers standing on the deck.

The **Master** and **boatswain** pull frantically at the sails. '*Take in the topsail. Tend to the master's whistle,*' yells the **boatswain** to the **sailors**, just as some of the **passengers** try to run towards him across the deck, struggling to stand against the pitching and tossing of the **creaking ship**.

'*Good boatswain, have care. Where's the master?*' shouts **Alonso**.

'*I pray now,*' returns the **boatswain**, '*keep below. You mar our labour: keep your cabins.*'

'*Be patient,*' urges **Gonzalo**, '*yet remember whom thou hast aboard,*' **he** continues, bowing towards King Alonso.

'*You are a counsellor,*' bellows the **boatswain**. '*If you can command these elements to silence, and work the peace of the present, we will not hand a rope more; use your authority: if you cannot, give thanks you have lived so long. Out of our way, I say.*'

The **passengers** leave the deck and go below while the **sailors** continue to try and save the ship which is **creaking** and **groaning** loudly. It is not long before **Sebastian**, **Antonio** and **Gonzalo** return to the deck, shouting at the boatswain, '*A pox on your throat, you bawling, blasphemous incharitable dog.*' The **boatswain** ignores them, shouting to the sailors '*Lay her a-hold, a-hold! Set her two courses off to sea again,*' just as two **sailors** appear on the deck yelling '*All lost! To prayer, to prayer, all lost!*'

As the **ship** starts to roll, **voices** are heard from below decks, '*Mercy on us!*' – '*We split, we split!*' – '*Farewell, my wife and children!*' – '*Farewell, brother!*' – '*We split, we split, we split!*' The **men** try to return to their cabins as, with a massive sound of **splintering**, the ship breaks apart.

Freeze this action and move to Prospero on the opposite side of the circle.

Miranda runs towards Prospero begging, '*If by your art, my dearest father, you have put the wild waters in this roar, allay them. O, I have suffered with those that I saw suffer: a brave vessel dash'd all to pieces. O, the cry did knock against my very heart. Poor souls, they perish'd.*'

Prospero assures her that he has done it for her sake, but instead of explaining this immediately, **he** takes off his magic cloak and sits down with Miranda beside him. '*Wipe thou thine eyes; have comfort,*' **he** says gently. '*The direful spectacle of the wreck I have with such provision in mine art so safely ordered that there is no soul – no, not so much perdition as an hair betide to any creature in the vessel.*' Reassured that nobody has been hurt by her father's storm, **Miranda** settles down to listen attentively as Prospero starts to tell her about their past. He was once Duke of Milan but he was so busy with his books that he did not notice his brother Antonio, in alliance with Alonso the King of Naples, working to depose him. They had sent him to sea in a leaky old boat with the three-year-old Miranda and they had eventually washed up on the island where they had lived for the past twelve years.

Replacing his cloak, **Prospero** sends Miranda to sleep then calls **Ariel**, his spirit servant. '*Has thou, spirit, performed to point the tempest that I bade thee?*' enquires **Prospero**. **Ariel** describes how the men jumped overboard as he appeared to be setting the ship on fire.

'*But are they safe, Ariel?*' urges **Prospero**.

'*Not a hair perish'd and, as thou badest me, in troops I have dispersed them 'bout the isle. The king's son have I landed by himself,*' responds **Ariel**. Content that his plan is working and that the men are all safe on different parts of the island, **Prospero** promises Ariel that he will soon be given his freedom.

WHOOSH

Guilty! (Act II scene i, Act III scene iii)

On another part of the island, Alonso, Sebastian, Antonio, Gonzalo, Adrian and Francisco are sitting, discussing their brush with death. Ariel watches silently from the opposite side of the circle.

'*Beseech you, sir*,' says **Gonzalo** to the King, '*be merry; you have cause, so have we all, of joy; for our escape is much beyond our loss.*' They start to look around them, although **Sebastian** and **Antonio** seem more interested in mocking Adrian behind his back. '*This island seem to be desert*,' muses **Adrian**, oblivious to the mocking, '*uninhabitable and almost inaccessible, yet the air breathes upon us here almost sweetly.*'

'*Our garments*,' wonders **Gonzalo** looking around at their clothes, '*being, as they were, drenched in the sea, hold not withstanding their freshness and glosses, being rather new-dyed than stained with salt water.*' **They** look at the fine clothes which they had worn at the wedding of Alonso's daughter Claribel and which they were still wearing when the ship sank on their journey home.

'*You cram these words into my ears against the stomach of my sense*,' cries **Alonso**. '*Would I had never married my daughter there for coming thence my son is lost.*'

Francisco is quick to try and reassure the king as the mood of the men becomes sombre. '*Sire*,' **he** says, '*I saw him beat the surges under him*,' but **Alonso** will not be comforted. Eventually, worn out by their ordeal, the **men** fall asleep, with the exception of **Sebastian** and **Antonio** who promise to guard the King.

Ariel leaves the circle.

'*My strong imagination sees a crown dropping on thy head*,' whispers **Antonio**. He points out that Ferdinand has drowned, Claribel is safely married to the King of Tunisia and so there is no heir to the throne of Naples. **They** discuss how Antonio secured the Dukedom of Milan and eventually **Sebastian** is persuaded to kill Alonso and declare himself King. '*Thy case, dear friend*,' **he** declares, '*shall be my precedent; as thou got'st Milan, I'll come by Naples. Draw thy sword.*' But just as **they** draw their swords, **Ariel** enters invisibly and wakes **Gonzalo** by singing in his ear.

Antonio and **Sebastian**, caught with their swords drawn, quickly claim, '*Whiles we stood here securing your repose, even now, we heard a hollow burst of bellowing like bulls, or rather lions: did't not wake you? It struck mine ear most terribly.*'

Alonso decides to go and search for his son, but while **Sebastian** and **Antonio** are whispering to each other about murdering the king that night, several **spirits** appear carrying a banquet. They dance around it, inviting the men to eat.

'*Give us kind keepers, heavens! What were these?*' exclaims **Alonso**. But just as **they** are about to start eating, the food disappears in a rush of **thunder** and **lightning**.

As **Ariel** appears in the guise of a harpy and rests on the table, the **men** all draw their swords. '*You three from Milan*,' declares **Ariel**, ignoring the swords, '*did supplant good Prospero; exposed unto the sea, him and his innocent child: for which foul deed the powers, delaying, not forgetting, have incensed the seas and shores against your peace.*' He turns to the King, '*Thee of thy son, Alonso, they have bereft.*'

After exposing their guilt, **Ariel** vanishes in **thunder** and then gentle **music** plays as the **spirits** enter again, dancing around the men as they remove the table. **Alonso** is frozen to the spot, while **Sebastian** and **Antonio** try to run away. '*All three of them are desperate*,' urges **Gonzalo**. '*Follow them swiftly and hinder them from what this ecstasy may now provoke them to.*'

WHOOSH

Caliban (Act I scene ii, Act II scene ii, Act III scene ii, Act IV scene i)

Outside Prospero's cave.

'*Thou poisonous slave, come forth*,' calls **Prospero** as **Caliban**, a green, scaly monster appears, uttering curses. '*This island's mine, by Sycorax my mother*,' whinges **Caliban**, '*which thou takest from me. When thou camest first, thou strokedst me and madest much of me*,' prompts **Caliban**. **Prospero** will have none of it, reminding Caliban of why his attitude had changed, saying, '*I have used thee with human care and lodged thee in mine own cell, till thou didst seek to violate the honour of my child.*' Still uttering curses about being enslaved by Prospero's power, **Caliban** leaves to collect wood for the fire.

Freeze Prospero. Move the action to another part of the circle where Caliban is collecting wood and where Trinculo and Stephano have been shipwrecked.

Caliban, carrying a pile of wood, is still muttering curses. '*All the infections that the sun sucks up from bogs, fens, flats, on Prosper fall,*' he grumbles, suddenly spotting **Trinculo** and mistaking him for a spirit. '*Here comes a spirit of his, and to torment me for bringing wood in slowly. I'll fall flat; perchance he will not mind me,*' he whispers.

Trinculo who has been drinking heavily from a cask of wine which washed up with him, hears **thunder** in the distance. **He** is looking for shelter when he stumbles across Caliban lying on the ground. '*What have we here?*' he wonders. '*A man or a fish? Dead or alive? A fish: he smells like a fish; a very ancient and fish-like smell.*' As another **thunder clap** makes him jump, **he** decides to try and shelter next to Caliban.

Stephano, with a bottle in his hand, walks towards Trinculo, singing. Because **they** are both drunk, it takes them some time to recognise each other and exchange stories about how they swam ashore. **Caliban** watches their drunken exchanges. Bemused by him, **they** offer him some of their wine. Starting to get drunk himself, **Caliban** sees his chance to escape from Prospero and decides to swear allegiance to them. '*I'll show thee every fertile inch o' th' island,*' he promises, '*and I will kiss thy foot: I prithee, be my god.*'

As **they** start walking around the island, **Caliban** explains, '*I am subject to a tyrant, a sorcerer, that by his cunning hath cheated me of the island.*' **Caliban** continues with his version of the story, promising to serve Trinculo and Stephano if they help him kill Prospero while he sleeps during the afternoon. Emboldened by the wine, **they** agree to the plan. '*Monster, I will kill this man: his daughter and I will be king and queen – save our graces! – and Trinculo and thyself shall be viceroys,*' declares **Stephano**.

However, by the time **they** reach Prospero's cave they are very drunk and not feeling quite so brave. When **Prospero** and **Ariel** summon up spirits disguised as terrifying hunting **dogs**, the drunken men flee.

WHOOSH

Love at first sight. (Act I scene ii, Act III scene i, Act IV scene i)

Miranda and Prospero are together near their home having just finished the conversation in which Prospero explains to Miranda how they came to be on the island twelve years earlier.

Ariel is invisible, but his singing is leading **Ferdinand** towards Miranda. '*Where should this music be?*' he wonders aloud. '*I' the air or the earth? This music crept by me upon the waters. Thence I have follow'd it, or it hath drawn me rather.*' **Ferdinand** is engrossed as **Ariel** sings, '*Full fathom five thy father lies; of his bones are coral made.*' **He** fails to notice Prospero and Miranda.

'*What is't? A spirit?*' wonders **Miranda**. '*Lord, how it looks about! Believe me, sir, it carries a brave form. But 'tis a spirit. I might call him a thing divine, for nothing natural I ever saw so noble.*' **Prospero** assures her that he is not a spirit, but one of the shipwrecked men. **Ferdinand** suddenly notices Miranda and falls instantly in love, promising to make her Queen of Naples. To **Miranda**'s surprise, her **father** accuses Ferdinand of being a spy, intent on taking over the island.

'*There's nothing ill can dwell in such a temple,*' pleads **Miranda** but to no avail.

'*Speak not you for him; he's a traitor. Come; I'll manacle thy neck and feet together,*' he barks at Ferdinand.

'*Be of comfort.*' **Miranda** assures Ferdinand, at a loss to explain her father's odd behaviour. '*My father's of a better nature, sir, than he appears by speech: this is unwonted which now came from him.*'

Prospero, secretly pleased that Miranda has fallen in love so suddenly, mutters aside to Ariel, '*Thou hast done well, fine Ariel.*'

Prospero decides to make Ferdinand his servant and orders him to carry logs for the fire. Watched by **Prospero** from a distance, **Miranda** cries and pleads with Ferdinand to let her help but **he** refuses. While **he** works, he talks to Miranda, explaining, '*I am in my condition a prince, Miranda; I do think, a king. The very instant that I saw you, did my heart fly to your service; there resides, to make me slave to it; and for your sake am I this patient log-man.*'

'*Fair encounter of two most rare affections*,' muses **Prospero**, pleased with his work. **Prospero** walks towards Ferdinand, relenting of his harshness. '*If I have too austerely punish'd you, your compensation makes amends*,' he acknowledges. '*Then, as my gift and thine own acquisition worthily purchased take my daughter.*'

While **Ferdinand** and **Miranda** sit and talk together, **Ariel** summons **Ceres**, **Iris** and **Juno** who, together with other **spirits**, celebrate the engagement with dancing.

'*Honour, riches, marriage-blessing,*
Long continuance, and increasing,
Hourly joys be still upon you!' they sing to the happy couple.

'*Let me live here ever; so rare a wonder'd father and a wife makes this place Paradise*,' sighs **Ferdinand** as he gazes at Miranda.

WHOOSH

The resolution. (Act V scene i)

Prospero, in his magic cloak, and Ariel are outside of the cave reviewing their work.

'*How fares the king and's followers?*' asks **Prospero**.

'*Confined together in the same fashion as you gave charge*,' answers **Ariel**, '*just as you left them; all prisoners, sir.*' **Prospero** sends Ariel to fetch the guilty men while he draws a circle on the ground. **Alonso**, helped by **Gonzalo**, seems frantic, as are **Sebastian** and **Antonio**. **Adrian** and **Franciso** are helping them. As they walk into the circle, they become entranced and stand like statues while **Prospero** speaks to them. '*Gonzalo*,' he begins, '*honourable man. O good Gonzalo, my true preserver.*' Next he turns to the king and Antonio. '*Most cruelly didst thou, Alonso, use me and my daughter. You, brother mine, that entertain'd ambition, expell'd remorse and nature; who with Sebastian would here have killed your king, I do forgive thee.*'

Ariel brings Prospero the clothes that were his as Duke of Milan and the **men** in the circle are released from the spell. When **Prospero** welcomes the King as his guest, **Alonso** responds with, '*I do entreat thou pardon me my wrongs*,' begging, '*If thou be'st Prospero, give us particulars of thy preservation; how thou hast met us here, who three hours since were wreck'd upon this shore; where I have lost – how sharp the point of this remembrance is – my dear son Ferdinand.*'

To his amazement, **Ferdinand** and **Miranda** appear, to her exclamation, '*O, wonder! How many goodly creatures are there here! How beauteous mankind is! O brave new world that has such people in't!*' as she has never seen so many people before. **Ferdinand** introduces Miranda to his father and **he** welcomes her as his future daughter.

As **Trinculo**, **Stephano** and **Caliban** appear on one side of the group, the **sailors** and **boatswain** appear on the other side, announcing that the ship has somehow been restored and is at anchor in the bay. '*Sir,*' declaims **Prospero**, '*I invite your highness and your train to my poor cell, where you shall take your rest for this one night and in the morn I'll bring you to your ship and so to Naples where I have hope to see the nuptial of these our dear-beloved solemnized; and thence retire me to my Milan.*'

As the **group** walk away towards the cave, **Prospero** summons Ariel for one last time. '*My Ariel, chick, be free and fare thou well!*' he says sadly, giving Ariel his promised freedom.

WHOOSH

Epilogue

Prospero appears on stage to appeal to the audience.

With his magic staff broken and buried and his relationship with Antonio restored, Prospero asks the audience to release him to return to Milan.

'Now my charms are all o'erthrown,
And what strength I have's mine own,
Which is most faint: now, 'tis true,
I must be here confined by you,
Or sent to Naples. Let me not,
Since I have my dukedom got
And pardon'd the deceiver, dwell
In this bare island by your spell;
But release me from my bands
With the help of your good hands.'

WHOOSH

Follow-up activities

- Through shared discussion, list the characters and what has been learnt about them. Define the plot and the themes (power, sibling rivalry, treachery, revenge and forgiveness) of the play.
- Use this information for further study.
- How might the play be reproduced in a modern idiom, whilst retaining the themes? .

2   William Shakespeare: *Twelfth Night*

Twelfth Night; or *What You Will* was written to be performed as part of the twelfth night celebrations at the end of the Christmas period. It was first performed in 1602 and tells the comic story of a love-sick Duke who repeatedly offers marriage proposals to the beautiful Olivia. Disdainful of his declared love, she herself falls in love with Cesario, his messenger, unaware that Cesario is actually a girl in disguise. Meanwhile Sir Andrew Aguecheek, a friend of her uncle Sir Toby Belch, is in love with her. Her manservant, Malvolio, also worships her, a foible which is used against him to comic effect.

All is resolved when Viola's identical twin, Sebastian turns up and Olivia proposes to him, thinking that he is Cesario. The Duke falls rapidly in love with Viola when he sees her dressed as a woman, which is good news for Viola who has loved him since she first met him. A double wedding ensues, while Mavolio, declared mad, languishes in the cellar. An added layer of humour would have been appreciated by Shakespearean audiences as all roles were played by males, so the role of Viola/Cesario was played by a boy pretending to be a girl disguised as a boy.

The comedy of the play is not only derived from the tangled plot, which at times appears to involve everyone falling in love with the wrong person, but also in the caricatures that Shakespeare creates for some of the characters. Designing comic characters is a tricky business – it is easy to overdraw the characters and present them as fools rather than as parodies of real people. This Whoosh explores Shakespeare's skill as a comic writer by examining some of the characters in detail, to try and understand what makes them humorous.

Sir Andrew Aguecheek and Sir Toby Belch are contrasting comic characters who work as a team, aided and abetted by Olivia's servant, Maria. Count Orsino, in love with the idea of being in love, also cuts a moping and pathetic figure who is nevertheless used to getting his own way. Malvolio, cast as a Puritan, would have been immediately disliked by the audience as Puritans were opposed to play acting, together with most of the other entertainment that the Tudor populace enjoyed.

Objective

- to explore the genre of comedy by examining characterisation.

Characters	Objects	Sounds
Orsino Curio, a friend lords musicians a messenger Cesario, a servant Sir Andrew Aguecheek Sir Toby Belch Maria jester Malvolio Fabian Officers Olivia	palace scene house scene garden scene bushes orchard	music for the Duke jester songs

Duke Orsino (Act I scene i, Act II scene iv)

In the Duke's palace.

The **Duke** enters attended by **lords** and **musicians**. **He** turns to the musicians, asking them to carry on playing, '*If music be the food of love, play on; give me excess of it that surfeiting, the appetite may sicken and so die.*' **He** listens wistfully, looking very sad and hoping that the music will eventually heal him. '*That strain again!*' **he** says, stopping them dolefully, '*It had a dying fall.*' **He** carries on talking as the music plays, bemoaning the pain of being in love.

Trying to cheer him up, **Curio** suggests, '*Will you go hunt, my Lord? The hart.*' Refusing to be cheered up, **Orsino** deliberately twists his friend's meaning, explaining dramatically that since he first saw Olivia, he has become like a hunted deer himself, pursued by the pain of his love.

When a **messenger** returns to tell him that Olivia is in mourning for her brother and will not see anyone, **Orsino** only adores her more. '*O she that hath a heart of that fine frame to pay this debt of love but to a brother,*' **he** laments, thinking only of himself and not of Olivia's distress. If she loved her brother so much, how much more would she love him when he finally won her heart? Becoming cheerful with that thought **he** muses, '*Away before me to sweet beds of flowers: love thoughts lie rich when canopied with bowers.*'

Some time later, in the palace, Orsino, Curio and Cesario are together:

'*Give me some music,*' **Orsino** demands, '*that old and antique song we heard last night: methought it did relieve my passion much,*' **he** continues, still engrossed with the idea of his own distress. **He** sends Curio to find someone to sing, turning to Cesario while he waits and saying, '*if ever thou shalt love, in the sweet pangs of it remember me; for such as I am all true lovers are. How dost thou like this tune?*' **he** sighs as the **music** starts.

They listen to the song for a while, **Orsino** looking melancholy and appreciating the many references to death that it contains. Then as **everyone** else leaves, **Orsino** tells Cesario that he must go to Olivia again to plead Orsino's cause, even though he knows that she is in mourning for her brother. **Cesario**'s suggestion that Olivia might not love him draws a quick retort from Orsino. '*There is no woman's sides can bide the beating of so strong a passion as love doth give my heart,*' **he** firmly assures Cesario – it seems obvious to him that because she is a woman, Olivia is certain to love someone who loves her so much. '*Make no compare between that love a woman can bear me and that I owe Olivia,*' **he** concludes, returning to his mood of self-pity. **He** gives Cesario a jewel for Olivia, asking him not to return with anything other than an acceptance of his proposal. '*Say my love can give no place, bide no denay,*' **he** instructs Cesario.

WHOOSH

Sir Andrew Aguecheek and Sir Toby Belch (Act II scene iii, Act III scene ii, Act III scene iv)

In Olivia's house, late at night

Sir Toby and **Sir Andrew** have been drinking. **They** are discussing the value of staying up after midnight. '*Not to be abed after midnight is to be up betimes,*' says **Sir Toby**, trying to persuade his friend that it is a good idea to stay up after midnight because then you are up early.

'*To be up late is to be up late,*' shrugs **Sir Andrew**, not able to follow the argument too closely. **Sir Toby** thinks this is as bad an idea as an empty glass, but when **Sir Andrew** decides that life really exists of eating and drinking, **Sir Toby** praises him as a scholar and calls for more wine.

Both men are surprised when the **jester** appears instead of Maria with their wine. **Sir Toby** tosses him a coin in exchange for a song. '*Would you have a love-song, or a song of good life?*' asks the **jester**. **Sir Toby** opts for a love song, which the **jester** sings and the two **men** listen to with enjoyment. '*A mellifluous voice, as I am a true knight,*' slurs **Sir Andrew**. '*Very sweet and contagious.*'

Then **they** appear bored with the love song and decide to sing something more upbeat. After a certain amount of drunken singing from the room, **Maria** enters. '*What a caterwauling do you keep here! If my lady have not called up her steward Malvolio and bid him turn you out of doors, never trust me,*' **she** warns. **They** carry on singing snatches and lines of songs regardless of Maria's warning until **Malvolio** appears. '*Farewell, dear heart,*' **Sir Toby** mocks, as **Malvolio** does exactly what Maria said he would.

The following morning, **Sir Andrew** is in a bad mood and he is threatening to go home. '*Thy reason, dear venom,*' urges **Sir Toby**, '*give thy reason.*'

'*I saw your niece do more favours to the count's serving-man than ever she bestowed upon me,*' **he** answers petulantly. **Fabian** tries to persuade Sir Andrew that Olivia was merely trying to make him jealous, while Sir Toby sees an opportunity for more fun. '*Challenge me the count's youth to fight with him; hurt him in eleven places: my niece shall take note of it,*' says **Sir Toby**, suggesting that having seen it, Olivia could not fail to respond to such valour. **Fabian** assures Sir Andrew that there is no alternative to satisfy his honour and win Olivia; **Sir Andrew** though reluctant, is eventually foolish enough to be persuaded to go and write a letter challenging Cesario to a duel.

When **he** returns with his written challenge, **Sir Toby** decides to read it aloud for amusement. '*Youth, whatsoever thou art, thou art but a scurvy fellow,*' **he** begins. '*Thou comest to the lady Olivia, and in my sight she uses thee kindly: but thou liest in thy throat; that is not the matter I challenge thee for.*'

'*Very brief and to exceeding good sense –less,*' mutters **Fabian**.

'*I will waylay thee going home; where if it be thy chance to kill me thou killest me like a rogue and a villain. Fare thee well and God have mercy on one of our souls. Thy friend, as thou usest him, and thy sworn enemy, ANDREW AGUECHEEK,*' concludes **Sir Toby**, keeping the letter and promising to give it to Cesario himself.

Sir Toby sends Sir Andrew off to wait for Cesario at the corner of the orchard, instructing him to draw his sword and swear horribly when Cesario appears. After **Sir Andrew** leaves, Sir Toby sees even greater sport ahead. '*Now will not I deliver his letter,*' **he** jokes with Fabian, '*for the behaviour of the young gentleman gives him out to be of good capacity and breeding therefore this letter, being so excellently ignorant, will breed no terror in the youth: he will find it comes from a clodpole.*' Instead, **Sir Toby** plans to deliver a challenge by word of mouth so that Cesario will take it seriously. '*I will meditate the while upon some horrid message for a challenge,*' **he** says as he sees Olivia approaching and leaves to find Cesario.

'*Thy intercepter, full of despite, bloody as the hunter, attends thee at the orchard-end,*' **Sir Toby** warns Cesario. '*Thy assailant is quick, skilful and deadly,*' **he** continues. '*If you hold your life at any price, betake you to your guard.*' **He** labours the point by describing how Sir Andrew has cut three people to pieces in brawls, thoroughly frightening Cesario (whom he does not realise is a woman).

He leaves Fabian with Cesario while he goes off to find Sir Andrew, assuring him when they meet that Cesario is really angry. '*I'll not meddle with him,*' decides **Sir Andrew**, '*Let him let* *the matter slip, and I'll give him my horse, grey Capilet,'* **he** declares. Promising to plead his case, **Sir Toby** returns to Cesario but instead of trying to make the deal as he promised he insists that the fight must happen. Just as **Sir Andrew** and **Cesario** draw their swords, both unwilling to fight, **Officers** arrive and they both put their swords away with great relief. **Sir Toby**, meanwhile, has thoroughly enjoyed the trick which he has played on his friend Sir Andrew.

WHOOSH

Malvolio (Act II scene iii, scene v, Act III scene iv, Act IV scene ii)

In Olivia's house, where Sir Toby and Sir Andrew are enjoying their drunken revelling.

'**My masters, are you mad? Or what are you? Have ye no wit, manners, nor honesty, but to gabble like tinkers at this time of night?**' hisses **Malvolio** as he comes into the room where **Sir Toby** and **Sir Andrew** are drinking and singing. '**Is there no respect of place, persons, nor time in you?**'

'**We did keep time, sir, in our catches**,' laughs **Sir Toby**, annoying Malvolio by mistaking his meaning.

'**Sir Toby, I must be round with you. My lady bade me tell you, that, though she harbours you as her kinsman, she's nothing allied to your disorders. If you can separate yourself and your misdemeanors, you are welcome to the house; if not, and it would please you to take leave of her, she is very willing to bid you farewell**,' responds **Malvolio** pompously, refusing to see anything funny in the situation.

Sir Toby is so drunk that he carries on making jokes with the **jester** at Malvolio's expense. Exasperated as **Sir Toby** calls, '**A stoup of wine**,' to Maria, **Malvolio** leaves, indignantly threatening to tell Olivia. **Maria**, who has already told Sir Toby that Malvolio has the views of a puritan, suggests that they should not do anything straight away as Olivia is still upset after Cesario's visit earlier that day. Instead, she suggests a way to get their own back. Malvolio is, '**The best persuaded of himself, so crammed, as he thinks, with excellencies**,' **she** says, '**that it is his grounds of faith that all that look on him love him.**' It is this self-love that she plans to use against him. '**I will drop in his way some obscure epistles of love; wherein, by the colour of his beard, the shape of his leg, the manner of his gait, the expressure of his eye, forehead, and complexion, he shall find himself most feelingly personated**,' **she** laughs. '**I can write very like my lady your niece**,' **she** concludes, seeing that Sir Toby might be too drunk to get her meaning.

'**Excellent!**' slurs **Sir Toby**, '**I smell a device.**'

'**I have't in my nose too**,' adds **Sir Andrew** drunkenly, keen not to be outdone. '**He shall think**,' **Sir Toby** shares conspiratorially, '**by the letters that thou wilt drop, that they come from my niece, and that she's in love with him.**' Glad to see that they finally get it, **Maria** leaves them and goes to bed.

The following day, in Olivia's garden

Sir Toby, **Sir Andrew** and **Fabian** are walking in the garden, discussing Malvolio when **Maria** appears and urges them to hide behind the **bushes** as Malvolio is approaching. She throws the letter down and leaves.

As **Malvolio**, preening himself as he struts along the path, comes into earshot, **they** can hear him talking to himself. '**She uses me with a more exalted respect than any one else that follows her**,' **he** muses. '**What should I think on't? To be Count Malvolio.**' Behind the bushes, **Sir Toby** has to restrain Sir Andrew, who is so angry that **he** wants to shoot Malvolio. '**Having been three months married to her, sitting in my state ...**' **he** continues, so deeply immersed in imagining his future that **he** fails to hear **Sir Toby** getting annoyed and wanting to hit him. '**Calling my officers about me, in my branched velvet gown; having come from a day-bed, where I have left Olivia sleeping ... Toby approaches; he courtesies there to me ...** ' **he** goes on, while **Fabian** struggles to contain Sir Toby behind the hedge, urging both men to restrain themselves as they are in constant danger of spoiling the fun by jumping out from behind the bushes to attack Malvolio.

Malvolio is just enacting a speech in which he reprimands Sir Toby for his drunkenness when **he** suddenly sees the letter. **He** starts to read it aloud, '**To the unknown beloved ...**' immediately recognising the writing. '***Thou canst not choose but know who I am. If thou entertainest my love, let it appear in thy smiling; thy smiles become thee well; therefore in my presence still smile***,' **he** continues. '***She did commend my yellow stockings of late***,' **he** remembers, '***she did praise my leg being cross-gartered***,' as **he** rushes off to change his stockings and practise his smiling.

Some time later, in Olivia's house

Sir Toby, **Sir Andrew** and **Fabian** are talking when **Maria** rushes in, hardly able to speak because **she** is breathless from laughing. '***If you desire … to laugh yourself into stitches, follow me. Yond gull Malvolio is turned heathen. He's in yellow stockings … He does obey every point of the letter that I dropped to betray him***.' **They** all follow Maria into the garden, where **Olivia** is looking sad.

Malvolio approaches Olivia with a huge, silly grin on his face. '***Smilest thou?***' asks **Olivia**. '***I sent for thee upon a sad occasion***.'

'***Sad, lady! I could be sad: this does make some obstruction in the blood, this cross-gartering; but what of that?***' **he** chuckles, '***Not black in my mind though yellow in my legs***,' **he** continues, a gruesome smile glued constantly to his face.

'***God comfort thee!***' murmurs **Olivia** in amazement. '***Why dost thou smile so and kiss thy hand so oft?***' **She** is distracted by news that Cesario has returned with another message from Duke Orsino. As **she** leaves, **she** urges '***Good Maria, let this fellow be looked to. Let some of my people have a special care of him***.'

Malvolio continues to strut around the garden, convinced that nothing can come between him and Olivia. **He** is ushered carefully away by **Sir Toby** and is last seen locked in a dark cellar, repeatedly calling, '***They have laid me here in hideous darkness. There never was man thus abused … help me to a candle, and pen, ink and paper … help me to some light and some paper: I tell thee, I am as well in my wits as any man in Illyria … some ink, paper and light; and convey what I will set down to my lady***,' but he is ignored by everyone.

WHOOSH

Follow-up activities

- A character study sheet is provided as Resource 14. Note and discuss the key characteristics of each of the characters listed, providing evidence for decisions.
- One of the strategies sometimes use in comic writing is the choice of names, which create an immediate impression; this is true of *Twelfth Night*. Ague was a word for plague, so a modern version of Sir Andrew Aguecheek's name might be something like Plagueface or Faceache. The meaning of Belch is obvious and reflects the physical effect that regular ale drinking has on the character. Both men are cast as aristocrats, so Shakespeare is satirising the type of knights who would have been familiar to contemporary audiences.
- What sort of people are seen as comic in modern entertainment? Ask pupils to create some modern character names which reflect a comic aspect of a character.
- In addition, Shakespeare uses the name Orsino for the Duke, a central character in the play. At the time of writing, the Spanish Ambassador was named Orsino. Tension between Spain and England rose and fell during the Tudor era, so Shakespeare is also creating political satire. Which politicians in contemporary government would pupils use in a comic play? What characteristics of their chosen politicians would they emphasise for effect?
- Working in pairs or groups, challenge pupils to create a group of characters for a comic play, modelled on Shakespeare's Twelfth Night characters – a pair of friends one of whom enjoys playing practical jokes on his foolish friend, a person who takes his authority too seriously and a politician.
- As an extension activity, ask pupils to work in groups to design a plot into which their characters could be placed to interact.

Resource 14 Character studies
Twelfth Night

Character	Feature	Evidence
Duke Orsino	Self-obsessed	Constantly listening to sad music to draw attention to himself
Sir Andrew Aguecheek		
Sir Toby Belch		
Malvolio		

3   William Shakespeare: *A Midsummer Night's Dream*

Written some time between 1590 and 1596, *A Midsummer Night's Dream* remains one of Shakespeare's most popular plays. The backdrop for the story is the marriage of Theseus, Duke of Athens and Hippolyta, Queen of the Amazons. Four young Athenian lovers (for whom the course of true love does not initially run smooth) and a troop of amateur actors are controlled by a group of fairies who live in the forest in which most of the play is set.

There are three plots which unfold simultaneously and eventually overlap. Hermia and Lysander are in love, but Hermia has been ordered by her father to marry Demetrius. Initially Demetrius is also in love with Hermia, although he is loved by Helena. The situation is complicated further by the meddling of the fairies. In the world of the fairies, Oberon and his wife Titania are locked in an argument, the effects of which pervade the whole play. The troupe of amateur actors includes Nick Bottom, the weaver who thinks himself capable of playing all the parts in the play. His head is turned into that of a donkey, which Titania falls in love with when Puck's magic goes awry.

All the characters are drawn into the forest, where the tangled web is eventually undone and everyone ends up marrying the person whom they really love. Even Oberon and Titania discover that they love each other and put an end to their regular bickering. Eventually the actors are able to perform their play to Theseus.

The purpose of this Whoosh is to help students to understand the plot and become familiar with the main characters, up to the point at which the magic takes effect and confusion reigns in the forest. Where dialogue is included, Shakespeare's original language is retained.

Objective

* to understand the key facts of a plot and become familiar with the characters involved.

Characrters	Objects	Sounds

Theseus, Duke of Athens
Hippolyta, Queen of the
   Amazons
attendants
Egeus, father to Hermia
Hermia
Demetrius
Lysander
Helena
Puck
Fairy
Oberon
Titania
attendants
Quince
Bottom
Four other actors
	a palace scene
	a forest
		music for character entries in
		   the palace
		forest sounds
		a sound to denote when
		   magic is being performed

Act I scene i

The first section of the Whoosh takes place in the palace of Theseus, Duke of Athens, so a lavish scene needs to be created.

Theseus and **Hippolyta** are talking together. Their **attendants** stand at a discreet distance. '***Now, fair Hippolyta, our nuptial hour draws on apace***,' sighs **Theseus**, although also bemoaning the fact that time is passing slowly and there are still another four days until their wedding.

'***Four days will quickly steep themselves in night; four nights will quickly dream away the time***,' reassures **Hippolyta**. **Theseus** is just sending **one** of the attendants off to encourage the young people of Athens to start celebrating when **Egeus** arrives, pulling **Hermia** behind him. **Lysander** and **Demetrius** are also following.

'*What's the news with thee?*' **Theseus** asks Egeus, turning to greet him.

'*Full of vexation come I, with complaint against my child, my daughter Hermia,*' moans **Egeus**. '*Stand forth, Demetrius,*' **he** orders as **Demetrius** bows to the Duke. '*My noble lord,*' continues **Egeus**, '*this man hath my consent to marry her. Stand forth, Lysander,*' **he** orders **Lysander** in turn, '*and my gracious duke, this man hath bewitch'd the bosom of my child.*' **He** goes on to explain with mounting frustration how **Lysander** has serenaded Hermia with songs, given her gifts and stolen her heart.

Under Athenian law, Hermia has to agree to marry the man of her father's choosing or be punished as he sees fit. **Theseus** turns to Hermia, trying to persuade her to agree with her father, but **Hermia** is resolute. '*I beseech your grace that I may know the worst that may befall me in this case, if I refuse to wed Demetrius,*' she says. **Theseus**' answer is very clear, '*Either to die the death or to abjure for ever the society of men. Therefore, fair Hermia, question your desires; know of your youth whether, if you yield not to your father's choice, you can endure the livery of a nun.*' **Theseus** gives her until the next new moon to make her decision, before taking Demetrius and Egeus away with him to discuss some business relating to his wedding. **Hippolyta** follows, leaving Lysander and Hermia alone together.

WHOOSH

Lysander wastes no time in sharing his plan with Hermia as soon as her father has gone. '*Hear me, Hermia. I have a widow aunt, a dowager of great revenue, and she hath no child: from Athens is her house remote seven leagues; and she respects me as her only son. There, gentle Hermia, may I marry thee; and to that place the sharp Athenian law cannot pursue us.*' **He** urges her, '*If thou lovest me then, steal forth thy father's house to-morrow night; and in the wood, a league without the town, where I did meet thee once with Helena, there will I stay for thee.*'

Just as **Hermia** agrees to meet Lysander in the wood and elope with him, **Helena** herself enters. In answer to **Hermia**'s warm greeting, **Helena** moodily replies, '*O, teach me how you look, and with what art you sway the motion of Demetrius' heart,*' bemoaning the fact that Demetrius loves Hermia instead of her.

'*I frown upon him, yet he loves me still,*' asserts **Hermia**. '*The more I hate, the more he follows me.*'

'*The more I love, the more he hateth me,*' complains **Helena**.

Hermia shares her elopement plan with Helena, reassuring her that she will not see Demetrius again, much less agree to marry him. **Lysander** and **Hermia** leave, talking closely about their plans to run away. Left alone, **Helena** ponders for a while about why Demetrius loves Hermia when he should really love her. Then **she** hatches a plan to tell Demetrius about Hermia and Lysander, hoping that he will thank her for alerting him. '*I will go tell him of fair Hermia's flight: then to the wood will he to-morrow night pursue her; and for this intelligence if I have thanks, it is a dear expense,*' she muses aloud.

WHOOSH

Act II scene i

The next sections are set in the forest. Create a scene with dense areas of trees together with a clearing where the action can take place.

Puck and one of the **fairies** enter, talking to each other. **Puck** reminds the fairy to keep an eye on Titania and try to keep her away from Oberon, warning, '*The king doth keep his revels here to-night: take heed the queen come not within his sight; for Oberon is passing fell and wrath,*' because Titania has a favourite servant whom Oberon wants for himself.

The warning comes too late, as **Oberon** and **Titania**, both with a train of attendants, appear and approach each other. The argument starts again as **they** meet and becomes increasingly fierce as **Oberon**'s jealousy of other men irritates Titania and **she** makes accusations of her own. '*Why should Titania cross her Oberon?*' he wheedles eventually. '*I do but beg a little changeling boy to be my henchman.*' But **Titania** explains that the child's mother has died, '*and for her sake do I rear up her boy, and for her sake I will not part with him,*' she says finally, turning to leave.

'*Well, go thy way,*' grumbles **Oberon** to her disappearing back, '*thou shalt not from this grove till I torment thee for this injury.*' **He** calls to Puck and reminds him about a flower which they had once found, the nectar of which caused people to fall in love. **He** asks Puck to find him another flower so that he can pour the nectar into Titania's eyes while she is asleep, as punishment for her stubbornness.

Suddenly, **Demetrius** enters, followed by **Helena**. **Oberon** decides to make himself invisible to watch what happens.

'*I love thee not, therefore pursue me not,*' insists **Demetrius**. '*Where is Lysander and fair Hermia? The one I'll slay, the other slayeth me,*' he continues. '*Hence, get thee gone, and follow me no more.*' But **Helena** will not be so easily deterred. **Demetrius** tries again, insisting, '*Do I entice you? do I speak you fair? Or, rather, do I not in plainest truth tell you, I do not, nor I cannot love you?*'

'*And even for that do I love you the more,*' whimpers **Helena**. '*I am your spaniel.*'

'*Tempt not too much the hatred of my spirit,*' warns **Demetrius**, '*for I am sick when I look on thee.*'

'*And I am sick when I do not look on you,*' sighs **Helena**.

Exasperated, **Demetrius** threatens to abandon her to the mercy of the wild animals in the forest and leaves to find Lysander and Hermia. **Helena** tries to follows him, still swearing her undying love.

Reappearing, **Oberon** is so moved by Helena's plight that when Puck returns with the flower, Oberon asks him to find Demetrius, urging Puck, '*Take thou some of it, and seek through this grove: a sweet Athenian lady is in love with a disdainful youth: anoint his eyes; but do it when the next thing he espies may be the lady. Thou shalt know the man,*' he assures Puck, '*by the Athenian garments he hath on.*'

WHOOSH

Act II scene ii

Titania is sleeping as **Oberon** approaches her. **He** squeezes some drops of nectar from the flower into her eyes, whispering, '*What thou seest when thou dost wake, do it for thy true-love take, love and languish for his sake. In thy eye that shall appear when thou wakest, it is thy dear: wake when some vile thing is near.*' Then **he** disappears, leaving **Titania** to sleep.

Nearby, **Lysander** and **Hermia** are wandering around, having lost their way through the forest. '*We'll rest us, Hermia, if you think it good and tarry for the comfort of the day,*' suggests **Lysander**, noticing that Hermia is looking faint. **She** agrees, so they find a comfortable spot on the ground and settle down. **They** soon fall asleep.

Meanwhile, **Puck** is wandering through the forest, having failed to find the Athenian that he is looking for. **He** suddenly sees Lysander. '*Who is here?*' he wonders. '*Weeds of Athens he doth wear: this is he, my master said despised the Athenian maid, and here the maiden, sleeping sound.*' Pleased to have found the man in Athenian clothes, **he** squeezes some nectar into Lysander's eyes. Because the lady is sleeping next to him, **Puck** decides that this will work out exactly as Oberon intended because she will be the first person the man sees when he wakes. Just as **Puck** leaves, **Demetrius** comes crashing through the trees, searching for Lysander. **Helena** comes wandering a long way behind him, exhausted from chasing Demetrius. **She** stops to rest near Lysander and Hermia, as **Demetrius** disappears.

WHOOSH

Act III scene i

The six amateur **actors** choose a space near to where **Titania** is sleeping to use as their rehearsal space. **Puck** watches curiously from a distance. '*Are we all met?*' asks **Bottom**, before starting to complain to Quince, the director, about the content of the play and his part in it. '*There are things in this comedy that will never please,*' he grumbles, continuing to moan about killing himself with a sword, frightening ladies with an actor as a lion and the content of the prologue.

They start to rehearse, but **Bottom** stops them again to find out if the moon will be shining on the night of the production, calling out, '*A calendar, a calendar! Look in the almanac; find out*

***moonshine, find out moonshine*,**' because the play should take place in moonlight. Finding that it will be a moonlit night, **he** continues to fuss about how the window should be opened to allow the moonlight to shine in.

Quince is very patient with him, correcting lines and explaining what action he wants. However, when **Bottom** starts to discuss the representation of a wall with a chink to speak through as part of the scenery, **Puck** loses his patience. '***What hempen home-spuns have we swaggering here?***' **he** mutters. Then when Bottom leaves the performance briefly, **Puck** mischievously turns his head into that of a donkey. When **Bottom** returns to the rehearsal, the **actors** run away in fear, leaving **Bottom**, unaware of his new appearance, standing near the sleeping **Titania**.

WHOOSH

Follow-up activities

- Working in groups, ask pupils to create a freeze frame of the plot at the point at which the Whoosh finishes. It should include:
  - Demetrius at a distance, looking angry and hunting for Lysander
  - Lysander and Hermia sleeping
  - An exhausted Helena stopping to rest near Lysander and Hermia
  - Titania sleeping
  - Bottom, with the head of a donkey, looking puzzled.
- Remembering that Lysander and Titania have a magic potion in their eyes which will cause them to fall in love with the first person they see when they awake, predict and act out what might happen next.
- Discuss the different scenarios which the freeze frames suggested. What sort of muddle has now been created?
- What are the possible outcomes?
- Through shared discussion, decide how the confusion can be resolved using all of the available characters.
- The Whoosh also provides a starting point to discuss characterisation. What have pupils learnt about the different characters from the Whoosh?

4   William Shakespeare: *Hamlet*

Shakespeare's play *The Tragedy of Hamlet, Prince of Denmark*, is his longest play and it has been widely adapted. It relates the story of Hamlet's father who has recently died. A ghost, seeming to be that of his father, appears to guards and Hamlet's friends on the castle ramparts. Hamlet is taken to meet the ghost, who claims to have been murdered by the new King, Claudius. In order to test the veracity of the information, Hamlet decides to stage a play.

This Whoosh is in two parts – the visit of the ghost to Hamlet and the play within a play, *The Murder of Gonzago*. The two sections of the Whoosh, separated by Act II, echo each other entirely by design. By whooshing both sections consecutively, pupils will be able to see the similarities of scene content more directly. In addition, dramatising the ghost's story will explain Hamlet's decision to instruct the players to perform the pre-show dumb play. At the point when the play within a play is performed, Hamlet is uncertain of the truth – is Claudius a murderer and usurper who must be avenged? Or did King Hamlet die in the way that Claudius claimed, in which case the ghost is a demon?

Objective

• to explore the key facts of the central plot.

Characters	Obejcts	Sounds
Hamlet Marcellus Horatio A ghost King Claudius Queen Gertrude Polonius Ophelia Rosencrantz Guildernstern attendants player king player queen killer player attendants members of the audience prologue actor player Lucius	castle battlements trees in the orchard	cannon firing party music party noise trumpet music for the play

Part One (Act I scenes iv + v):

Hamlet is standing on the castle **battlements** with **Marcellus** and **Horatio**, listening to the **cannon** and the **noise** emanating from the King's party below when **Horatio** cries out, '***Look, sir! Here it comes!***' **Hamlet** steps forward to confront the strange creature in front of them, '***Whether you are good or evil, friend or foe, I want to talk to you. You look like my father – I can call you whatever you want me to, but you must tell us why you have risen from the ground and come to haunt us. You were at peace and now you are here in your armour. What do you want us to do?***' The **ghost** beckons to **Hamlet**. '***Sir,***' says **Horatio**, '***he seems to want you to follow him.***'

'***But you mustn't go,***' chimes in **Marcellus**, '***even though he is asking nicely.***' **Hamlet**, realising that the ghost is not going to speak in front of the others, decides to follow despite the warnings of his friends. '***Think about it – what's the worst that a ghost can do to me?***' he asks.

'***Well,***' answers **Horatio**, '***what if he beckons you into trouble – over a cliff, for example?***' **Hamlet** waves away their worries and moves to follow the ghost. **Horatio** and **Marcellus** physically try to stop him, but **he** threatens to kill anyone who holds him back. Reluctantly, **they** let him go and **he** follows the ghost away.

WHOOSH

Hamlet follows the ghost patiently for a little while but eventually **he** refuses to go further until the ghost tells him who he is and why he is there. The **ghost** explains that his time is nearly up and Hamlet needs to listen carefully. '***Speak then!***' says **Hamlet**, exasperated, but the **ghost** cautions him that once he has heard what the ghost has to say, he will be filled with vengeance.

Hamlet is shocked but listens as the **ghost** explains. '***I am indeed the ghost of your father, cursed to walk this earth at night and confined to purgatory during the day. I need to be released – the things I have seen are enough to haunt your worst nightmares. Alas, those who are still alive are not allowed to hear tales of the afterlife. Listen closely though, if you ever loved your father, you must avenge his death. His murder.***'

'***Murder?***' cries **Hamlet**, shocked.

'***Yes, murder. Murder most foul, the worst you could imagine,***' the **ghost** responds.

'***Tell me everything.***' says **Hamlet**, firmly, '***and the sooner you tell me, the sooner I can have my revenge.***'

'***Good boy,***' the **ghost** replies. '***Now listen. Everyone has been told that I died as a result of a snakebite, which I suppose is true enough, but the snake that killed me is now sat on my throne wearing my crown.***'

'*Uncle Claudius?*' **Hamlet** is angry.

'*Yes, that vile, incestuous adulterer. And not content with killing me, he has now seduced my own wife and made her his queen. I have been betrayed by both of them – she is weak and he is good with his words, and now it is time to sort things out.*' The **ghost** suddenly breaks off and looks around him. '*Quickly! It is nearly sunrise and soon I will have to leave. Now, he killed me by pouring poison into my ear while I slept in the orchard. It curdled my blood and covered my body in a disgusting rash. He has taken my life, my throne and my queen and I want revenge. I am in purgatory because I had no chance to repent of my sins and it is horrible. Now, I must go, but please – leave your mother unharmed. She is weak but innocent in all of this,*' **he** concludes, before disappearing.

WHOOSH

Part Two (Act III scene ii):

King Claudius, **Queen Gertrude**, **Polonius**, **Ophelia**, **Rosencrantz** and **Guildenstern** enter to **trumpet** music. As **they** are settled in place by their attendants and made comfortable to watch the play, **Hamlet** draws **Horatio** to one side and reminds him, '*Watch my uncle closely – see what his reactions are. If he is not moved, then we will know that the ghost was wrong, sent from the devil to cause trouble. Here, the play is starting – we'll talk afterwards.*' **They** split up and join the others to watch the dumb show, a silent version of the play which is to follow.

A **king** and **queen** enter an **orchard**, clearly in love. **He** tries to kiss her but **she** keeps pushing him away. **They** sit down together under some **trees**, laughing and joking. The **king** eventually falls asleep in the **queen**'s lap and after a while **she** gets up gently, lays him down and wanders off. Another **person** comes in, takes the crown from the sleeping King's head and pours something into his ear. **He** leaves swiftly as the **queen** returns, carrying some flowers that she has just picked to give to the king. However, when **she** cannot wake him, **she** becomes hysterical. The anonymous **killer** comes back with some attendants and **he** comforts the queen after directing his attendants to remove the body. The **killer** gives the queen a variety of gifts that **she** initially rejects but eventually starts to accept and **they** walk off as a couple.

WHOOSH

The **audience** is left a little confused but another **actor** soon appears on the stage. **Hamlet** explains, '*This is the prologue – he will tell us what is going on.*'

The **prologue** begins, '*Please be patient as we act – come with us on the journey through our tragedy.*' As the **prologue** exits again, the **audience** is still confused by the shortness of it, although **everyone** sits back quietly as the **actors** playing the king and queen enter. **They** discuss how the king is becoming elderly and that the queen should take another husband when he dies. **The queen** refuses saying, '*I don't care what anyone else thinks – it would be a betrayal of our love to marry anyone else. Some may marry a second time for money but it always betrays the love of the first husband.*'

'*That's a lovely thing to say, but you will change your mind in time. Promises made in the heat of a moment seem unimportant and silly when that moment has passed. You never know what might happen – love and luck are so closely intertwined that you cannot say which influences the other. What we want and what happens to us are not always the same thing. You make these promises now but they will be gone along with me after my death,*' the **king** replies.

'*If I were to do so, I would not eat or drink or sleep – if I betray you in such a way, may I suffer both in this life and the next,*' the **queen** asserts.

'*You are lovely – a wonderful wife. Now, I feel like a nap ... shall I come and find you in while?*' The **queen** leaves as the **king** settles down. As the **queen** exits the stage, **Hamlet** turns to Gertrude asking, '*Do you like it so far, mother?*'

'*Yes, it is good, although the queen protests her love very strongly. Perhaps too much?*' she replies. **Claudius** leans over to the two of them to enquire, '*Is there anything in this play that I will find offensive?*' to which **Hamlet** replies, '*No, not at all – no offence is meant by any of it.*'

'*What is it called?*' inquires **Claudius**, still clearly suspicious.

'*The Mousetrap, sir. It is an ... an illustration, if you will, about a murder in Vienna. Come, let us watch again – here is Lucius, the king's nephew,*' **Hamlet** answers as **Lucius** enters on stage.

WHOOSH

Hamlet watches his uncle closely as, on the stage, **Lucius** pours the poison into the king's ear. '*Oooh, look,*' **Hamlet** whispers loudly to Ophelia, '*he has killed the king to get the throne for himself. It's getting exciting – much better than the original Italian, however beautifully that was written! Now, see if you can spot the point at which Lucius wins the love of the queen and causes her to break her promise to the king.*' **Ophelia** interrupts him, '*Hamlet, look, the king is getting up.*' There is huge concern for the king and **Polonius** orders the play to be stopped. The **actors** stand around confused as **Claudius** shouts, '*Get the lights on and get them out. I am leaving.*' With that, **Claudius** swoops out of the room followed by a very confused **wife** and all of his **advisors**.

WHOOSH

Follow-up activities

* Improvise Hamlet and Horatio's conversation after the king has left, attempting to determine the truth of the Ghost's allegations.
* Working in pairs, ask each pair of pupils to find evidence for either the King's guilt or his innocence. Where possible, support this with textual evidence. Each pair should then join with another pair who have reached the opposite conclusion and exchange evidence.
* Ask pupils to write individual conclusions in preparation for a debate, noting evidence.
* Hold a debate on the motion, 'This house believes that King Claudius is guilty of murder.' Use textual evidence as much as possible.

5 William Shakespeare: *The Merchant of Venice*

Shakespeare probably wrote the romcom *The Merchant of Venice* between 1596 and 1598. It tells the story of Antonio, a rich and generous Venetian merchant and his friends Bassanio, Gratiano and Lorenzo. Antonio agrees to help his best friend Bassanio win the rich heiress, Portia, by lending him enough money to pursue the courtship, but he can only do this by borrowing from the moneylender, Shylock.

Bassanio woos and marries Portia while his friend Gratiano marries Nerissa, Portia's personal servant. When Antonio then defaults on the loan because his ships are reported lost at sea, Portia travels to Venice to repay the money on his behalf. But Shylock refuses, insisting on the strange terms of repayment which were agreed to be a pound of Antonio's flesh.

Unable to overturn the contract any other way, Portia and Nerissa disguise themselves as a judge (Balthazar) and a clerk (Stephano), eventually persuading Shylock to accept the money instead of the pound of flesh which he is demanding. Not recognising their disguises, Bassanio offers the judge a gift. Portia had given her husband a ring and she requests this ring as the gift for saving Antonio. Stephano (Nerissa) immediately makes the same request of Gratiano. After much persuasion, Bassanio and Gratiano break their promises to their wives and part with the rings.

Alongside these courtships Lorenzo, another friend of Antonio and Bassanio, has fallen in love with Shylock's daughter Jessica. This explains Shylock's anger towards Antonio and his friends as Jessica is a Jew but Lorenzo is a Christian. Jessica and Lorenzo run away together, planning to live in Belmont.

Set in the final act of the play, this Whoosh will help to end a unit of work as all the story lines are rapidly resolved. It takes place in the gardens of Portia's mansion in Belmont, indicating statues, bushes and other luxurious garden items. Pupils can create the garden objects throughout the scene; the more content there is to the set, the more the actors have to work with and move around. The actors of Jessica and Lorenzo can be changed in each section of the Whoosh or remain the same throughout. These actors need to remember that both characters are actively involved in each scene even when they do not speak. They will therefore need to react appropriately to the action and dialogue.

An extra level of differentiation can also be added in the first section by challenging pupils to act as statues and freeze frames of the famous lovers which Lorenzo refers to; Troilus and Cressida, Pyramus and Thisbe, and Dido and Aeneas. Jessica and Lorenzo should move around the stage engaging with the statues whilst they are flirting with each other.

Objective

- to consider the resolution of several plot lines at the conclusion of a play.

Characters	Objects	Sounds
Lorenzo (friend of Antonio) Jessica Stephano house servants Launcelot musicians Portia Nerissa Bassanio Antonio Gratiano travelling servants	garden scene statues of classical lovers	footsteps music trumpet

Lorenzo and **Jessica** enter the **garden**, flirting and playing to impress each other. **Lorenzo** begins to describe how, on nights like this in history, other great lovers had sat together. **He** then becomes more serious, reminding Jessica how, '***on such a night, Jessica ran away from her father Shylock, taking his money with her. With her lover Lorenzo, she left Venice for Belmont where they were to live together.***' **Jessica**, clearly wanting to still enjoy the mood of the evening, retorts that, '***on such a night, a man called Lorenzo declared that he loved her and wooed her heart, but not one word he said was true***.' **Lorenzo** responds in kind. '***On a night like this, the pretty girl called Jessica was outrageously rude to her beloved, but he generously forgave her***.' **Jessica** is all ready to retort further when they hear someone approaching on the steps.

WHOOSH

Lorenzo, having something of a guilty conscience over his plans to marry Jessica, gets defensive. '***Who are you, coming so fast under cover of the night?***' he demands. **Stephano** replies calmly, '***A friend.***'

'***A friend?***' queries **Lorenzo**. '***A friend of whom? What is your name, friend?***' **Stephano** introduces himself and says that his mistress will arrive at Belmont before sunrise. **Stephano** asks for his master, but upon learning that he has not returned and that no-one has heard from him, **he** starts to leave. They are interrupted by **Launcelot** the clown, shouting for Lorenzo and generally causing a disturbance. **Lorenzo** hushes him, and asks for the news. Launcelot announces, '***A message has arrived from the master, full of the good news that he will be here in the morning***,' then he stumbles out again.

Lorenzo begins to suggest that they should go in and wait for the imminent arrivals, but then decides it would be nicer to wait outside so **he** sends **Stephano** inside to warn the **servants** to prepare and **asks** for some musicians to be sent to entertain them while they wait. **Lorenzo** returns to his wooing of Jessica, suggesting, '***Let's sit here and listen to the music – it is such a beautiful evening, with a gorgeous moon, just perfect for couples.***' **He** sits, and pulls **Jessica** down to join him, lying back to look at the sky. Pointing, **he** says '***Look how beautiful the sky is – the stars and planets all moving in perfect patterns***.'

WHOOSH

As **they** lie there contemplating the heavens, the **musicians** enter and set up their instruments. **Lorenzo** sits up, commanding them to provide fitting music for the tranquil scene until their mistress Portia returns. **Jessica** confesses that she does not particularly enjoy music, '***There*** *is nothing on the earth that cannot be moved with music of some kind*,' **Lorenzo** suggests. '*People who are unmoved are fit for nothing and cannot be trusted. Listen to the music!*'

As **they** lie back, listening, **Portia** and **Nerissa** enter, deep in conversation. '*Look!*' cries **Portia**, '*that light over there is from my house – we are nearly home! And listen, music!*'

'*Those are your musicians playing, madam. We are nearly there*,' responds **Nerissa**. As **they** walk they discuss how lovely the music sounds in the peace of the night. '*Isn't it curious*,' says **Portia**, '*how things seem better – lovelier, prettier, more perfect – because of when they happen.*'

WHOOSH

The **music** stops as **Lorenzo** jumps to his feet, recognising Portia's voice. **He** welcomes them as **Portia** asks for news of their husbands for whom they have been praying. **Lorenzo** explains that they are due back imminently, and **Portia** sends **Nerissa** inside to check on the servants. '*Make sure they do not talk of our absence, Nerissa – and neither you, Lorenzo, nor you, Jessica. Keep it a secret for now*,' **she** instructs them.

A **trumpet** sounds, announcing the arrival of **Bassanio**, **Antonio**, **Gratiano** and their **travelling servants**. **Nerissa** greets her husband, **Gratiano** while **Portia** welcomes **Bassanio** home with an embrace. **Bassanio** introduces **Antonio**, mentioning his debt in passing, but they are interrupted by **Nerissa** and **Gratiano**'s increasingly loud conversation. '*I swear by that moon that I'm telling the truth! I gave it to the judge's clerk!*' asserts **Gratiano**. **Nerissa** is clearly upset, and **Portia** asks what has happened. **Gratiano** explains, '*She's upset because I've given away a little present she gave me – a ring engraved with a silly poem "Love me and leave me not".*' This makes **Nerissa** even angrier. '*What does it matter how much it was worth or how good the poem was? It was a gift from me to you and you said you would never take it off! Even if you didn't like it, you should have kept it safe because of its sentimental value.*' **She** starts to make threats about the judge's clerk and does not calm down even in the face of **Gratiano**'s explanation that he did not have the heart to say no to the young boy.

WHOOSH

Portia steps in to try to mediate the situation. '*She's not wrong to be upset, Gratiano. After all, it was the first present she ever gave you and you promised that you would cherish it for ever. I gave my husband a similar ring and I know how I would feel if he had given it away so quickly, but he would never do that. I can understand her anger.*' **Gratiano** does not seem much moved by her speech as she turns to comfort **Nerissa**, but **Bassanio** looks panicked as he mutters to Gratiano, '*Do you think she would believe me if I cut off my left hand and said I lost the ring in a fight? Do you think she would still be angry?*' **Gratiano** steps towards the ladies, saying, '*Madam, try to understand – our lord Bassanio gave his ring to the judge, which is why his clerk wanted mine so much – he had worked really hard after all. Nothing else would satisfy them apart from our rings. We had no choice ...*' He is cut off by **Portia** turning to her husband and asking slowly, '*Which ring, my love? Surely not the one I gave you ....*' **Bassanio** responds, slowly holding out his left hand, '*If I thought it would work, I'd lie, but as I cannot – yes, as you can see, I do not have it any longer.*'

'*You too then have lied. Until that ring is back on your finger, you will be sleeping alone.*' **Portia** turns away from her husband as **Nerissa** echoes her words to her own husband.

WHOOSH

The men are devastated and desperately try to explain the situation. '*Darling*,' **Bassanio** starts, '*if you understood whom I gave the ring to and why I gave it away, I swear you wouldn't be so upset ...*' '*and if you understood what that ring symbolises – my worth and your honour – then you wouldn't have let it go so easily*,' **Portia** retorted angrily. '*Who on earth could possible need or want it more than that? I'm tempted to agree with Nerissa – you gave these rings to other women.*' **Bassanio** becomes nearly frantic as **he** tries to explain. '*Well, you're completely wrong about that – I gave it to a judge who had just saved the life of one of my closest friends. He refused money but requested the ring. I initially said no, but eventually I couldn't resist any longer. I couldn't just walk away so rudely. Please forgive me, my love. If you had been there, I guarantee you would have agreed with me.*'

'*No I most certainly would not!*' responds **Portia**. '*If I ever see that lawyer … actually, I'll tell you what. Since you gave him something of yours that was so precious to me, he should come here and I will give him myself, since you claim that I am precious to you. You should keep a close eye on my comings and goings, for as soon as I get my chance …*'

Nerissa again echoes her mistress's threats, but as **Gratiano** begins to respond to his wife with threats of his own, **Antonio**, having watched the whole debacle, steps forward touching **Bassanio** on the arm. '*All these arguments are my fault. I should go,*' **he** murmurs to Bassanio, who immediately replies, '*Don't let it upset you, Antonio. You are welcome here whatever else is happening*.' **He** turns back to **Portia** to beg forgiveness, but **she** throws his promises back in his face claiming that he is two-faced and duplicitous. **She** turns away, and motions for **Nerissa** to follow her.

WHOOSH

As the **ladies** move to leave, **Antonio** steps forward, visibly upset. '*This is all my fault. Please let me use myself as a guarantee for his promises. He saved me and I owe him so much.*' **Portia**, seemingly convinced, hands him a ring. '*I will agree to that. Now, give him this and tell him to look after it better than he did before*.' **Bassanio** is shocked, '*but … but … this is the ring. MY ring. How did you get it from the judge?*'

'*Exactly what I just threatened, as did she,*' **Portia** replied, indicating to **Nerissa**, who also stepped forward to hand **Gratiano** his ring back. **Gratiano** is appalled. '*But why? Why would you cheat on us when we haven't even done anything wrong? Before you had even heard our reasons?*' The **men** are so upset that **Portia** takes pity on them and reveals their ploy, which **Lorenzo** confirms as truth. **Bassanio** and **Gratiano** are incredulous, but when **she** turns to **Antonio** and tells him that his three ships are safely in the harbour, **Antonio**'s surprise prompts the men into action. '*Were you the judge?*' **Bassanio** demands of **Portia**. '*Were you the judge and I didn't recognise you?*'

'*And you were the clerk? The very clerk with whom you were going to cheat?*' mocks **Gratiano**. As the **couples** embrace and the tension eases, **Antonio** expresses his joy that his livelihood has been restored.

WHOOSH

Meanwhile, **Jessica** and **Lorenzo** have been watching the exchanges between the couples with a mixture of amusement and horror and **they** are shocked when the attention suddenly turns to them. **Portia** prompts **Nerissa** to give **Jessica** a letter. As **she** hands it over, **Nerissa** explains, '*This letter is from your father, Jessica, stating that when he dies you will inherit all that he owns.*' **Jessica** is speechless, but **Lorenzo** has enough wits about him to start asking questions about how this has happened. **Portia** suggests that they all go inside to talk properly and as they leave Gratiano drags **Nerissa** off to their servants' quarters, promising that '*Nothing will ever be as important to me again as keeping my wife's ring safe.*'

WHOOSH

Follow-up activities

- Create a plot map for the play, showing how the plot lines interact and are resolved.
- Alternatively, consider this by exploring the idea of disguise and confusion. Assign a hat or other single costume item to each character. Ask characters to present a brief summary of themselves, explaining how they fitted into the plot and the other characters with whom they interacted – some characters will have to wear two hats and some hats will be worn by more than one character.
- As an additional challenge, this activity could be filmed and edited to include appropriate music for each character.

6 William Shakespeare: *The Taming of the Shrew*

Probably written in the early 1590s, *The Taming of the Shrew* uses the device of a play within a play. The main plot involves the headstrong and obstinate Kate Minola, who lives in Padua with her sister Bianca and her father Baptista. Petruchio, a gentleman from Verona, wants to marry Kate and he embarks on a successful courtship and marriage in which he is determined to 'tame' Kate's obstinacy and teach her compliance.

The subplot involves Kate's more popular sister Bianca, who is pursued by three suitors, but their father has forbidden Bianca's marriage until her sister Kate is safely married. Until this happens, their father will only allow tutors into the house, which necessitates considerable disguise and identity change in pursuit of Bianca. She finally marries her choice of husband Lucentio, but only after a traveller is tricked into masquerading as his father Vincentio in order to agree the terms of the marriage with Bianca's father Baptista. Another of her suitors, Hortensio (who is also a friend of Petruchio's) abandons his attempt to marry Bianca and marries a rich widow instead.

The servants Tranio and Biondello are in the centre of the subplot, manipulating characters to Bianca and Lucentio's advantage. They find themselves in trouble when the real Vincentio arrives home and they have no option but to denounce him. Eventually all disguises are removed, the real characters are revealed and the scheming servants are forgiven.

This Whoosh focuses on Acts IV and V, in which Kate finally learns obedience, the confusing subplot is clarified and three newly married couples settle down to their lives together.

Objective

• to understand how complex plot and subplot lines are resolved.

Petruchio	Petruchio's country house	crackling fire
Kate	fire	cooking
Grumio	fireplace	smashing dishes
Curtis	carpets	horses' hooves
servants	table	knocking on the door
Tranio	supper	
Lucentio	horses	
Hortensio	Baptista's house	
Bianca	Tranio's/Lucentio's house	
Baptista	church	
Vincentio/an old man	door	
Biondello		
a traveller		
a tailor		
a priest		
crowd		

Act IV scene i

Petruchio and Kate, together with their servant Grumio, have travelled to Petruchio's country house immediately after their marriage.

Grumio enters the house alone calling for Curtis, the servant. **Grumio** is freezing cold and grumbles, '*Fie, fie on all tired jades, on all mad masters, and all foul ways! Was ever man so beaten? Was ever man so rayed? Was ever man so weary? I am sent before to make a fire, and they are coming after to warm them.*' **Curtis** comes into the room and although he can see that Grumio is freezing, his only interest is in their new mistress. '*Is she so hot a shrew as she's reported?*' **he** asks, while pointing out to Grumio that a **fire** is already burning in the **fireplace**. After satisfying himself that the **carpets** have been laid, the cobwebs have been swept, the **table** has been laid and the **supper** is being cooked, Grumio warms himself by the **fire**, ready to gossip.

'*First, know, my horse is tired; my master and mistress fallen out. Out of their saddles into the dirt.*' **Grumio** recounts their journey, explaining how Kate's horse had stumbled and **Kate** had fallen in the thick mud with the **horse** on top of her. Instead of helping his wife, **Petruchio** had lost his temper and beaten Grumio, blaming him for the accident. **Kate** had waded through the mud, crying and begging Petruchio to leave Grumio alone. Then, to make things worse, the **horses** had run away. '*By this reckoning he is more shrew than she*,' responds **Curtis**, surprised to hear about Petruchio's unusual behaviour. Then, suddenly realizing that their master will soon be arriving, Grumio instructs Curtis to call the servants, '*with their heads sleekly combed, their blue coats brushed, and their garters of an indifferent knit.*' Whilst **Grumio** is still shaking hands with the servants, **Petruchio** and **Kate** arrive home.

WHOOSH

Petruchio is clearly in a terrible mood, shouting, '*You logger-headed and unpolish'd grooms! What, no attendance? no regard? no duty?*' at the servants in general and, '*Where is the foolish knave I sent before? Did I not bid thee meet me in the park, and bring along these rascal knaves with thee?*' at Grumio in particular.

Petruchio sends the **servants** off to fetch dinner, urging his wife to, '*Be merry, good sweet Kate, be merry*,' whilst simultaneously shouting at the **servants** to take off his boots, bring his slippers and provide some water for **Kate** to wash. But when the meal is served, **Petruchio** becomes enraged, shouting, '*Tis burnt, and so is all the meat.*' **Kate** is clearly hungry so she tries to reason with him but **he** refuses to listen and in temper pushes everything off of the **table**.

Petruchio leaves the room with **Kate**, although **he** can still be heard shouting about the burnt food and the state of the bed linen, until, tired as well as hungry, Kate does not know which way to turn. Just as the **servants** finish clearing the dishes and food from the floor, **Petruchio** returns alone. **He** declares his determination to '*curb her mad and headstrong humour*,' likening her to a falcon who needs to be trained to obey her master.

'*She eat no meat to-day, nor none shall eat; last night she slept not, nor to-night she shall not; as with the meat, some undeserved fault I'll find about the making of the bed; and here I'll fling the pillow, there the bolster, this way the coverlet, another way the sheets*' he says, in order to explain his odd behaviour. **He** goes on to say that during the night '*if she chance to nod I'll rail and brawl and with the clamour keep her still awake. This is a way to kill a wife with kindness.*' After making his intentions clear, **he** leaves the room.

WHOOSH

Act IV scene ii

Back in Padua, Tranio (who is still disguised as Lucentio) and Lucentio (who is still disguised as the Latin schoolmaster) are trying to implement their plan to win Bianca for Lucentio. Hortensio (disguised as Licio, a music teacher) is also there.

Tranio and **Hortensio** stand outside of Baptista's **house**, hoping to see Bianca. **Tranio** wonders aloud whether there is any point in carrying on with his plan to win Bianca as she seems to be favouring Lucentio. '*Is't possible, friend Licio, that Mistress Bianca doth fancy any other but Lucentio?*' They watch as **Lucentio** enters with **Bianca**. **He** is reading *The Art to Love* aloud as part of a lesson. **They** are so engrossed in each other that **Hortensio** finally realises that there is no point in hoping to win Bianca for himself. **Tranio**, pretending to be distraught for himself but actually reinforcing the point on behalf of his master, cries '*O despiteful love! Unconstant womankind! I tell thee, Licio, this is wonderful.*'

In his distress at losing Bianca, **Licio** drops the disguise, declaring, '*Here I firmly vow never to woo her no more, but do forswear her, as one unworthy all the former favours that I have fondly flatter'd her withal.*' **Tranio** pretends to join with Hortensio, declaring, '*here I take the unfeigned oath, never to marry with her though she would entreat*.' Deciding that kindness is better than beauty, **Hortensio** leaves Padua to marry a wealthy widow instead.

As soon as he is out of sight, **Tranio** rushes over to Lucentio and Bianca to tell them that they are finally rid of Hortensio who has '*gone unto the taming school*' to learn how to '*tame a shrew and charm her chattering tongue*'. **They** are all delighted that their plan has worked, but there is still one issue to resolve – Lucentio's father, Vincentio, needs to negotiate the financial arrangements of the marriage with Baptista, but he is not in Padua.

Just then, **Biondello** arrives with some good news. '*O master, master, I have watch'd so long that I am dog-weary: but at last I spied an ancient angel coming down the hill, will* *serve the turn.'* No sooner does Tranio hear this than **he** decides to go and meet the traveller, who is en route from Mantua to Rome. To trick him into compliance with their plan, **Tranio** (still disguised as Lucentio) invents a story about the Duke of Padua killing anyone from Mantua. **He** suggests that the traveller should protect himself by disguising himself and masquerading as Vincentio, explaining that, *'my father is here look'd for every day to pass assurance of a dower in marriage'twixt me and one Baptista's daughter here.'* The **traveller** is completely taken in by Tranio and agrees to everything, going to Tranio's **house** with him to disguise himself as Vincentio.

WHOOSH

Act IV scene iii

A room in Petruchio's house

Having eaten little for several days, **Kate**, tired and starving, complains to Grumio, *'What, did he marry me to famish me? Beggars, that come unto my father's door, upon entreaty have a present alms … But I, who never knew how to entreat, nor never needed that I should entreat, am starved for meat, giddy for lack of sleep'.* **She** begs him, *'I prithee go and get me some repast; I care not what, so it be wholesome food'.* Acting on Petruchio's instructions, **he** refuses.

Eventually, **Petruchio** and **Hortensio** bring her some food, but as soon as she finishes, **Petruchio** announces that they are returning to Padua to visit her father. A **tailor** arrives with new clothes for Kate. **She** tries the cap and although Petruchio thinks that *'it is a paltry cap, a custard-coffin, a bauble, a silken pie,'* Kate responds, *'Love me or love me not, I like the cap; and it I will have, or I will have none.'* **He** does the same with an elegant gown, saying to the tailor, *'What's this? a sleeve? 'tis like a demi-cannon: what, up and down, carved like an apple-tart? Here's snip and nip and cut and slish and slash, like to a censer in a barber's shop.'* **Kate** has never seen *'a better-fashion'd gown, more quaint, more pleasing, nor more commendable,'* but **Petruchio** throws the tailor out for bad workmanship.

Secretly, he sends Hortensio after the tailor with the message, *'I'll pay thee for thy gown tomorrow,'* then he decides to set out for Padua in the clothes that they are already wearing. He sends for his servants and his horses but when he tells Kate that they will arrive with her father by midday, she points out, *'I dare assure you, sir, 'tis almost two; and 'twill be supper-time ere you come there.'* Petruchio is angry. *'Look, what I speak, or do, or think to do, you are still crossing it,'* he says, telling her clearly that, *'it shall be what o'clock I say it is.'*

WHOOSH

Act IV scene iv

In Tranio's house in Padua

Tranio (still disguised as Lucentio) and the **traveller**, (disguised as Vincentio), visit Baptista's **house**. **Tranio** introduces Vincentio and Baptista to each other, taking the chance to plead for Bianca, *'Signior Baptista, you are happily met. Sir, this is the gentleman I told you of: I pray you stand good father to me now, give me Bianca for my patrimony.'* **Vincentio** makes it quite clear that he is in favour of the marriage, telling Baptista, *'my son Lucentio made me acquainted with a weighty cause of love between your daughter and himself: and, for the good report I hear of you and for the love he beareth to your daughter and she to him, to stay him not too long, I am content, in a good father's care, to have him match'd.'*

When **Baptista** answers with, *'pass my daughter a sufficient dower, the match is made, and all is done; your son shall have my daughter with consent,'* they decide to go to Tranio's **house**, where they cannot be overheard, to agree the details. **Lucentio**, (still disguised as the Latin teacher), is dispatched with **Biondello** to tell Bianca that she is going to be married that afternoon.

WHOOSH

Act IV scene v

On a road to Padua.

As **Petruchio**, **Kate**, and **Hortensio** journey back to Padua on horseback, **Petruchio** comments, '*Good Lord, how bright and goodly shines the moon!*' Since it is broad daylight, **Kate** initially responds with, '*The moon! the sun: it is not moonlight now.*' **Petruchio** is insistent that it must be the moon because of its brightness and **Kate** disagrees with him once more before **he** loses his temper, ordering the horses to be stopped and complaining, '*Now, by my mother's son, and that's myself, it shall be moon, or star, or what I list, or ere I journey to your father's house. Go on, and fetch our horses back again. Evermore cross'd and cross'd; nothing but cross'd!*' Tired of Petruchio's behaviour and anxious to get to Padua, **Kate** succumbs, agreeing, '*be it moon, or sun, or what you please: an if you please to call it a rush-candle, henceforth I vow it shall be so for me.*'

But **Petruchio** persists, changing his mind and deciding that it is the sun after all. Eventually, **Hortensio** persuades Petruchio that he has won the argument, '*Petruchio, go thy ways; the field is won*' and **they** re-start their journey. But **they** have not gone far before they pass an old man. **Petruchio** claims that he is, in fact, a young maid whom Kate must embrace. But when **she** complies, **Petruchio** torments her with, '*Why, how now, Kate! I hope thou art not mad: this is a man, old, wrinkled, faded, wither'd, and not a maiden, as thou say'st he is.*'

Kate continues to agree, saying that the sun was in her eyes and she was mistaken. The **old man** turns out to be Vincentio, travelling from his home in Pisa to visit Lucentio. As they travel on together, **Petruchio** tells Vincentio about his son's impending marriage to Bianca and muses on the fact that he and Vincentio will then be related.

WHOOSH

Act V scene i

In Padua, outside of Lucentio's house

Biondello is rushing Lucentio and Bianca to the **church**, where the **priest** is ready to marry them. But just as they are about to leave, **Vincentio** arrives at the **door** of the **house**. As he **knocks** loudly on the **door**, the **traveller** answers, accusing Vincentio of being an imposter and calling for him to be arrested. When **Biondello** returns from the church announcing that, '*I have seen them in the church together: God send 'em good shipping!*' **he** realises what has happened. **He** continues to keep up the pretence of the traveller being Lucentio's real father, denying every having seen Vincentio before.

Kate and **Petruchio** are bemused by what is happening and step aside to see how it will be resolved. As they watch, **Baptista** and **Tranio** join the traveller outside of the **house**. **Tranio** denounces the real Vincentio, even though Vincentio produces evidence of Tranio's identity, saying, '*His name! as if I knew not his name: I have brought him up ever since he was three years old, and his name is Tranio.*'

Just as the gathering **crowd** turns on Vincentio to arrest him and take him to jail, the newly-wed **Lucentio** and **Bianca** arrive. Realising that they are about to be exposed for their deception, **Tranio**, **Biondello** and the **traveller** disappear in the confusion. There is no option but for **Luciento** to explain what has happened, '*Love wrought these miracles. Bianca's love made me exchange my state with Tranio, while he did bear my countenance in the town; and happily I have arrived at the last unto the wished haven of my bliss.*' With the confusion cleared up, **Baptista** and **Vincentio**, although still angry with the servants, lead everyone into the **house**.

Kate and **Petruchio** have watched all of this happen. But **Petruchio**, still testing Kate, insists, '*First kiss me, Kate,*' before he will follow the wedding party. When she refuses, **Petruchio** orders the horses to be turned around for home so **Kate** agrees to kiss him and they go into the **house**.

WHOOSH

Act V scene ii

A banquet in Lucentio's house

Lucentio's **house** is crowded. The three newly married **couples** together with **Baptista** and **Vincentio**, are all sitting around the **table** chatting while they are served a banquet by the **servants**. **Tranio** and **Biondello** have been allowed to return and are helping to serve. Some good-natured teasing suddenly becomes tense when **Hortensio's wife** tells Kate that, '*Your husband, being troubled with a shrew, measures my husband's sorrow by his woe.*' Insulted, they start to argue, with **Petruchio** and **Hortensio** urging them to fight and placing bets on the likely winner. It is left to **Bianca** to calm them down, and the three wives leave to talk together in another room.

WHOOSH

Remaining at the table, the **men** continue with the conversation as they all think that Kate is a shrew. **They** tease Petruchio about it, but **he** is unmoved. **He** suggests a test of their wives to find out who is the most compliant, '*Let's each one send unto his wife; and he whose wife is most obedient to come at first when he doth send for her, shall win the wager.*'

They each agree one hundred crowns and, confident of victory, **Lucentio** sends Grumio to summon Bianca, only to be told, '*Sir, my mistress sends you word that she is busy and she cannot come.*' **Hortensio's wife** makes the same response when she is sent for. But **Kate** not only comes when asked, but also returns to the adjoining room to persuade Bianca and the widow to return to their husbands.

Baptista, amazed, congratulates Petruchio, '*The wager thou hast won; and I will add unto their losses twenty thousand crowns; another dowry to another daughter, for she is changed, as she had never been.*' Just to prove his point, **Petruchio** says to Kate, '*Katherine, that cap of yours becomes you not: off with that bauble, throw it under-foot,*' which **she** dutifully does. The other **wives** are horrified at her compliance.

She horrifies them further with a speech in which she reminds them that, '*Thy husband is thy lord, thy life, thy keeper, thy head, thy sovereign; one that cares for thee, and for thy maintenance commits his body to painful labour both by sea and land.*' **She** reminds them of her previous behaviour, saying of a wife, '*And when she is froward, peevish, sullen, sour, and not obedient to his honest will, what is she but a foul contending rebel and graceless traitor to her loving lord?*' Having shocked the other wives with her suggested subservience, **Petruchio** and **Kate** retire triumphantly to bed, leaving **Hortensio** and **Lucentio** musing on how Petruchio '*hast tamed a curst shrew.*'

WHOOSH

Follow-up activities

- For each act, ask pupils to choose one of the characters (include both main characters and those from the subplots) and rewrite the scene in prose from the viewpoint of their chosen character.
- Ask pupils to share their completed writing and discuss how it demonstrates understanding of character and knowledge of the plot lines.

7 J.B. Priestley: *An Inspector Calls*

An Inspector Calls was first performed in 1945. It is set in 1912 and all the action takes place in one evening in the home of the Birling family. They are visited by Inspector Goole, regarding the suicide of a young woman called Eva Smith. In the course of the play, it becomes clear that the family has been involved in the events of Eva's life that lead to her eventual suicide. Priestley's play is seen as a social commentary on the values of Edwardian society.

This Whoosh is a little different to some of the others in this book. The dialogue of the play is presented as narrative for all but a few key sentences. Students themselves construct the characters for this scene based on their prior understanding of the play, before then performing the Whoosh as a group. This also provides an opportunity for the teacher to assess students 'understanding through observing their discussions during the preparation and their presentation during the performance of the Whoosh. The follow-up activities encompass speaking, listening, group discussion, working in role and persuasive writing.

Choose a pupil to play Arthur. The rest of the class must help him become that character, perhaps suggesting a particular accent or sculpting his posture into one reflecting Arthur's status in the family and the household. Repeat this for the other characters in Act 3, including the inspector. Then perform the Whoosh, demonstrating through posture, gesture and improvised speech an understanding of the plot, its effect on the characters and their interaction.

Because the action is set in one room in the period of a few hours, the setting rarely changes for this play. Students should decide whether to change or replace furniture and other objects, or whether they are just arranged differently after each section of the Whoosh. This could lead to some interesting discussions about staging in future lessons.

Objective

- to demonstrate, through drama and persuasive writing, an understanding of plot and characters.

Characters	Objects	Sounds
Inspector Goole Arthur Birling Sybil Birling Sheila Birling Eric Birling Gerald Croft Edna, the maid	dining table fireplace telephone	door slamming doorbell telephone

'But just remember this. One Eva Smith has gone – but there are millions and millions and millions of Eva Smiths and John Smiths left with us, with their lives, their hopes and fears, their suffering, and chance of happiness, all intertwined with our lives, with what we think and say and do. We don't live alone. We are members of one body. We are responsible for each other. And I tell you that the time will soon come when, if men will not learn that lesson, then they will be taught it in fire and blood and anguish. Good night.' The **Inspector** leaves the room, leaving the **Birlings** sitting in stunned silence, wondering what is going to become of them all. **Sheila** is crying quietly at the **table** as **Mrs Birling** has collapsed into a chair. **Eric** is staring into space as **Birling** paces the floor. As the **front door** slams behind the Inspector, **Arthur** is shocked out of his stupor to look at the other three. **He** pours himself a drink and downs it in one.

Arthur and **Eric** begin arguing, with **Eric** laughing at **Arthur** for worrying about his nomination for a knighthood. **Sybil** is drawn in to the row, bouncing up out of her chair to repeat Arthur's warnings to Eric about drinking and picking up women in town. When **Eric** turns on him, **Arthur** tries to explain himself to the others. *'There's every excuse for what both your mother and I did – it turned out unfortunately, that's all …'* which, in turn, brings **Sheila** into the row.

WHOOSH

Their worries about a public scandal, however, are pushed to one side as **they** begin to realise how odd the inspector had been. **Mrs Birling** asks Sheila what she is talking about. *'It's queer – very queer –'*says Sheila slowly, looking at them all. *'I know what you're going to say. Because I've been wondering myself,'* said **Mrs Birling**, interrupting her excitedly. Suddenly, they are all talking over each other until **Sheila** loses her temper, pointing out what information has actually come out during the evening. Mrs Birling had put Eva out of one job and she herself had put her out of another. There was Gerald, who kept her and Eric who – she paused, because everyone knew what Eric had done. And to finish the poor girl off, Mother had turned against her. *'That's what's important,'* concludes Sheila, *'and not whether a man is a police inspector or not.'* At this point Birling also joins in, protesting loudly at the way that he was spoken to.

Eric tries to pacify everyone, agreeing with **Sheila** that it does not make much difference either way, but **Arthur** turns on him, pointing out that **Eric** has admitted to a crime. The other three may end up looking silly in public, but Eric could be in real trouble. Panic ensues as **they** all realise just how much information the Inspector has elicited from them, until **Mrs Birling** quells them with the order, '*Now just be quiet so that your father can decide what we ought to do*.' **Everyone** looks expectantly at Arthur, waiting for his advice.

The moment is interrupted by the **doorbell**. **They** look at each other in alarm. **Edna** appears, and announces Gerald's return. **Gerald** appears behind her and she leaves. **Gerald** is clearly bursting with some important news. **He** questions them closely about how the inspector had spoken to them and how he had treated them. When **Mrs Birling** shares her surprise at how rude the Inspector had been **Gerald** cannot contain himself any longer and reacts strongly. **Everyone** looks at him, realising that **he** knows more than he is sharing. **Birling** asks him what he knows, to which **Gerald** announces that Inspector Goole was not actually a police officer. It transpires that **Gerald** had questioned a passing policeman carefully about Inspector Goole, but the man did not know him. Enjoying the family's smug satisfaction that they were right, **Mr Birling** moves towards the **phone**, asking the operator for a number before turning to the others to explain that he had intended to phone the chief constable all along. '*Roberts – Birling here. Sorry to ring you up so late, but can you tell me if an Inspector Goole has joined your staff lately?*' After a few minutes conversation with Colonel Roberts, **Arthur** hangs up and turns back to the others, announcing that there was no such person on the police force. '*As Gerald says*,' he ends, '*we've been had*.'

WHOOSH

Their anger grows and **the**y all become more vociferous, arguing over the top of each other about the Inspector. The release of tension causes **them** to turn on each other until **Eric** loses his temper, accusing them of talking about how to behave as if everything is normal. '*This girl is still dead, isn't she? Nobody's brought her to life, have they?*' The argument between **Eric** and **Birling** escalates until they are screaming in each other's faces.

'*We all helped to kill her – and that's what matters*,' shouted **Eric**.

'*Either stop shouting or get out*,' **Birling** glares at Eric, adding that plenty of fathers would have thrown their sons out before now. **Eric** is now quietly bitter and does not care whether he stays or not.

The **argument** threatens to escalate until **Gerald** takes control of the situation again getting **people** thinking about how the inspector may have stitched them up. '*We've no proof it was the same photograph and therefore no proof that it was the same girl.*' **He** goes on to explain that he was tricked into responding when the inspector used the name Daisy Renton as he did actually know someone called Daisy Renton. There was no evidence that Daisy Renton and Eva Smith were the same person. The inspector was the only one who had mentioned it, and they now knew that he was an imposter. If he lied about this, how did they know if anything else was true? Then **everyone** joins in, expressing their doubts about the inspector.

WHOOSH

They decide to confirm that the whole thing was a hoax by phoning the infirmary. **Birling** goes back to the **phone** as the rest of them watch him anxiously, '*Have you had a girl brought in this afternoon who committed suicide by drinking disinfectant?*' **They** all wait nervously, fidgeting. The answer eventually comes back that there has been no suicide brought in today, or any point in the last three months. **Birling** is triumphant, revelling in the apparently confirmed fact that, '*the whole story's just a lot of moonshine. Nothing but an elaborate sell!*' **Birling** pours everyone a drink and the glasses are passed around.

Sheila is unsettled by the celebrations, still upset by the news that has come out about each member of her family and her fiancé that evening. **She** tries to leave, explaining that she could never feel the same again after hearing what the inspector said and the way he made her feel. '*And it frightens me the way you talk and I can't listen to any more of it*,' she adds. **Their** discussion is interrupted by the **telephone** ringing. **They** fall silent as **Birling** goes to answer it. After a brief conversation, **he** puts the receiver down and turns back to the **others** who are watching him closely. **He** informs them that the police are on their way to the house to talk to them because a girl has just died on the way to the infirmary. She had swallowed disinfectant. **They** stare at each other in silence, dumbfounded.

WHOOSH

Follow-up activities

- Working in groups, ask pupils to choose one of the characters in the play (including the bogus inspector) to stand trial on a charge of the murder of Eva Smith. Using evidence from the Whoosh and the wider play they should then prepare the case for both the defence and the prosecution ready for a trial.
- Working in role, each group should conduct their trial, observed by another group working in role as the jury. At the trial's conclusion, the jury, through group discussion, must reach a verdict using evidence to support their decision.
- As an extension activity when all groups have conducted their trials, challenge pupils to select one character and use evidence to write a report persuading the reader of the character's guilt or innocence.

8   George Bernard Shaw: *Pygmalion*

This five act play, written by the Irish playwright, George Bernard Shaw in 1912, was staged at a time of social upheaval. Led by Emmeline Pankhurst, a group of politically active ladies had put women's suffrage at the top of the agenda and the Women's Social and Political Union was becoming increasingly radical. The Victorian era had seen the rise of a middle class and old values were being overturned.

Pronunciation was seen as a clear indicator of class and the reason that many working class people remained in the class of their birth. The play explores the idea of self-transformation through speech – an issue which, as late as 1972, was still seen as a better indication of class than money (Wells, 1982).

Pygmalion was a character in ancient Greek mythology who brought a sculpture to life – the analogy with Professor Higgins is clear, but Shaw, with his customary wit, also uses the play to mock Edwardian social pretensions. It remains the most popular of his plays and has inspired many adaptations, including the Lerner and Loewe stage musical *My Fair Lady*.

Objective

- to consider the development of a central character.

Act I

Characters	Objects	Sounds
people/crowd lady daughter (Clara) man with notebook Freddy flower girl military gentleman cab driver	St Paul's Church market two pillars cab	cab whistles heavy rain striking clock

It is 11.15pm. Heavy **rain** is falling on Covent Garden. Cab **whistles** are sounding everywhere and **people** are running into the **market** and under the entrance to **St. Paul's Church** to get out of the rain. A **crowd** starts to gather, among them an older **lady** and her **daughter**, dressed in evening clothes. Everyone is watching the rain, apart from one **man** who seems to be absorbed in writing in his notebook.

The **daughter**, standing between **two pillars**, is starting to get fed up. *'I'm getting chilled to the bone. What can Freddy be doing all this time? He's been gone twenty minutes.'* Her mood is not improved by being told that there will not be any cabs for another fifteen minutes. *'If Freddy had a bit of gumption, he would have got one at the theatre door,'* she moans. The **mother** tries to defend **Freddy**, who suddenly appears next to them, carrying an umbrella. He has tried everywhere for a cab, without success. Eventually even his mother despairs saying, *'You really are very helpless, Freddy. Go again, and don't come back until you have found a cab.'*

WHOOSH

He is in such a rush that he bumps into **a flower girl**, knocking her basket over and damaging some of the flowers. As he picks them up he looks at her – she is quite dirty with lank hair, she has bad teeth and she's badly dressed in a black coat and sooty black straw hat. '*Nah then, Freddy: look wh' y' gowin, deah,*' she says, as he takes sixpence from his sister to pay for the damaged flowers. She is most unimpressed with this, but she has no choice as her mother tells her to hand over the money.

Even though the flowers are only a penny a bunch, **Freddy** gallantly refuses to take any change and he leaves just as a military **gentleman** arrives to escape the rain, closing his umbrella. Although the **flower seller** pesters him to buy some flowers, he refuses, giving her three half-pennies. A **bystander** warns her that she had better give him a flower, because the **man** with his back to them is writing down every word she says. Mistaking him for a policeman, she starts to get hysterical, crying, '*He's a copper's nark. I ain't done nothin' wrong. I'm a respectable girl. Garn.*'

She pushes through the **crowd** to the notetaker, pleading, '*Oh, sir, don't let him charge me. You dunno what it means to me. They'll take away my character and drive me on the streets for speaking to gentlemen. They ...*'

The **note taker** finally joins in with the conversation. '*Shut up,*' he says good humouredly. '*Do I look like a policeman?*' **He** tries to show her his notebook, but the gathering **crowd** start to jostle him so that they can see for themselves. He reads aloud, '*Cheer ap, Keptin; n' baw ya flahr orf a pore gel.*'

This is met with more hysterical crying from the **flower girl**, before the crowd finally calm her down and she goes to sit on the plinth of one of the **columns**, staring moodily into her basket. As she listens, the **note taker** starts to tell **people** where they come from. When challenged, he is even able to tell the military **gentleman** who has been watching the proceedings that he comes from Cheltenham, Harrow, Cambridge and India.

As the rain goes off and the **crowd** starts to disperse, they come to the conclusion that he is some sort of fortune teller. The **mother** and **daughter** decide to catch a bus as Freddy has still not returned.

WHOOSH

Throughout all of this activity, the **flower girl** remains on the plinth, interspersing the actions of the crowd with occasional sullen comments, '*He's no right to take away my character. My character is the same to me as any lady's ... Ought to be ashamed of himself, unmanly coward ... Hard enough to live without being worrited and chivvied ...*'

Eventually only the **note taker** and the military **gentleman** are left. They introduce themselves as Professor Henry Higgins, a specialist in the science of speech and author of *Higgin's Universal Alphabet*, and Colonel Pickering, a retired army officer and author of *Spoken Sanskrit*. Just as they start to become engrossed in a conversation about speech, the flower girl tries one last comment, '*Let him mind his own business and leave a poor girl—*'

Finally exasperated, Professor Higgins explodes, '*Woman, cease this detestable boohooing instantly. A woman who utters such depressing and disgusting sounds has no right to be anywhere – no right to live. Remember that you are a human being with a soul and the divine gift of articulate speech: that your native language is the language of Shakespeare and Milton and the Bible; and don't sit there crooning like a bilious pigeon.*'

'*Ah-ah-ah-ow-ow-ow-oo!*' is her only response, which is immediately copied by the **Professor**. '*You see this creature with her kerbstone English: the English that will keep her in the gutter to the end of her days. In three months,*' he said, '*I could pass that girl off as a duchess at an ambassador's garden party. I could even get her a place as a shop assistant, which requires better English.*'

Ignoring the **flower girl**, the two **gentlemen** decide to go for supper. She makes one last attempt to sell them some flowers pleading, '*Buy a flower, kind gentleman. I'm short for my lodging.*' But when the **Professor** points out that earlier she had said she could change half a crown, she throws the whole basket of flowers at him screaming, '*You ought to be stuffed with nails, you ought. Take the whole blooming basket for sixpence.*'

Ignoring the flowers but deciding he should be charitable, he throws his loose change into the basket. **He** leaves with **Colonel Pickering** to an accompaniment of, '*Ah-ow-ooh! Aaah-ow-ooh!*

Aaaaaah-ow-ooh! Aaaaaaaaaaaaah-ow-oo!' as the **flower girl** picks up the coins, which include a half sovereign.

Just then, **Freddy** returns in a **cab**, looking for his mother and sister. The flower girl grandly informs him that they have caught a bus before climbing into the **cab** herself, showing the handful of money to the **driver** and saying, '*Eightpence aint no object to me, Charlie. Angel Court, Drury Lane, round the corner of Micklejohn's oil shop. Let's see how fast you can make her hop it.*'

'*Well, I'm dashed*,' says Freddy, left standing outside of St Paul's Church completely alone.

WHOOSH

Act 2

Characters	Objects	Sounds
Professor Higgins Colonel Pickering Mrs Pearce Eliza Alfred Doolittle	double doors filing cabinets writing table fireplace chair clock newspaper stand piano and stool	tuning fork various voice sounds

The following morning, **Professor Higgins** is working. A window in the room looks out onto the street. There are **double doors** into the room and **two tall filing cabinets** against the walls. A **writing table** is full of equipment including several tuning-forks and a model of half of a human head. There is a leather **chair** next to the **fireplace**, above which a **clock** shows 11 o'clock. A **newspaper stand** has been placed nearby. On the other side of the room are a grand **piano**, and a **stool**. On the piano is a dish filled with fruit and sweets.

Colonel Pickering is sitting at the **table** while **Higgins** stands nearby. They have been listening to **voice sounds**. The door opens and **Mrs Pearce**, the housekeeper comes in. '*A young woman wants to see you, sir. She's quite a common girl, sir. I should have sent her away, only I thought perhaps you wanted her to talk into your machines.*'

Higgins asks for her to be shown into the room, planning to show **Pickering** how he makes recordings. The door opens again and the **flower girl** is shown in. She enters grandly, wearing a hat with three ostrich feathers. Her apron is nearly clean and her coat has been tidied. Higgins, making no attempt to hide his disappointment, points out rather peevishly that this is the girl from the previous evening. '*Why, this is the girl I jotted down last night. She's no use: I've got all the records I want of the Lisson Grove lingo; and I'm not going to waste another cylinder on it. Be off with you; I don't want you.*'

'*Don't you be so saucy. You ain't 'eard what I come for yet,*' she says. '*I want to be a lady in a flower shop. But they won't take me unless I can talk more genteel. You said you could teach me. Well, here I am ready to pay and you treats me as if I was dirt. And if you was a gentleman, you might ask me to sit down, I think.*'

'*Pickering*,' wonders **Higgins**, '*Shall we ask this baggage to sit down or shall we throw her out of the window?*'

Behaving in a much more gentlemanly way than Higgins is prepared to, **Colonel Pickering** politely invites the **flower girl**, who tells them that her name is Eliza Doolittle, to sit down. '*Don't mind if I do,*' she answers coyly. **Higgins**, meanwhile, is thinking about the offer which she has made, to pay one shilling for each lesson, which amounts to about 40 per cent of her daily income. Noticing that she is starting to cry, **he** impatiently offers her his silk handkerchief saying, '*Wipe your eyes. Wipe any part of your face that feels moist. Remember: that's your handkerchief; and that's your sleeve. Don't mistake the one for the other if you wish to become a lady in a shop.*'

Pickering, taken with the idea of passing her off as a lady, offers **Higgins** a bet. If he can do it in time for the ambassador's garden party, **Pickering** will pay all the costs himself. **Higgins** cannot resist the challenge saying, '*It's almost irresistible. She's so deliciously low – so horribly dirty –*' Ignoring **Eliza**'s loud protest of, '*Ah-ah-ah-ah-ow-ow-oo-oo!!! I aint dirty: I washed my face and hands afore I come, I did,*' they continue to discuss the plan as if she was not there, in spite of the **housekeeper**'s caution not to do anything foolish. When **Professor Higgins**, having been rude about her appearance, her family (or lack of it) and the likelihood of her drinking, decides to go ahead with the experiment, **Mrs Pearce** raises the question of what will happen to **Eliza** after the garden party.

'*When I've done with her, we can throw her back into the gutter; and then it will be her own business again; so that's all right*,' **he** answers.

At this point, **Eliza**, who has not fully understood the conversation but who suspects that **Higgins** means her harm, has had enough. **She** starts to walk towards the door but is stopped in her tracks when **Higgins** offers her a chocolate from the dish on the **piano**. As she opens her mouth to protest that it might be drugged, he puts the chocolate into her open mouth. He tries to tempt her further with promises of marriage to a Guards officer with a beautiful moustache. '*Eliza,*' he continues, '*you are to live here for the next six months, learning how to speak beautifully, like a lady in a florist's shop. If you're good and do whatever you're told, you shall sleep in a proper bedroom, and have lots to eat, and money to buy chocolates and take rides in taxis. If you're naughty and idle you will sleep in the back kitchen among the black beetles, and be walloped by Mrs. Pearce with a broomstick. At the end of six months you shall go to Buckingham Palace in a carriage, beautifully dressed. If the King finds out you're not a lady, you will be taken by the police to the Tower of London, where your head will be cut off as a warning to other presumptuous flower girls. If you are not found out, you shall have a present of seven-and-sixpence to start life with as a lady in a shop.*'

She eventually agrees to stay, but is still protesting as **Mrs Pearce** takes her away to get clean. '*You're a great bully, you are. I won't stay here if I don't like. I won't let nobody wallop me. I won't go near the king, not if I'm going to have my head cut off. If I'd known what I was letting myself in for, I wouldn't have come here. I always been a good girl.*' **Mrs Pearce** returns briefly to remind **Higgins** that he should be more careful of his manners if Eliza is to live with them. He should stop swearing, using the tablecloth as a napkin and eating breakfast in his dressing gown.

WHOOSH

Just as everything seems to have been agreed, **Alfred Doolittle**, a dustman who says he is Eliza's father, arrives at the house and demands to see **Professor Higgins**. Intrigued, Higgins agrees to see him and **Doolittle** is shown into the room by **Mrs Pearce**, sitting down rather grandly.

'*I come about a very serious matter, Governor,*' he announces.' *I want my daughter: that's what I want. See?*'

'*Of course you do. You're her father, aren't you? You don't suppose anyone else wants her, do you? I'm glad to see you have some spark of family feeling left. She's upstairs. Take her away at once. Do you suppose I'm going to keep your daughter for you?*' responds **Higgins**, surmising that he is about to be blackmailed and questioning how Dolittle knew where his daughter was.

Sensing in his turn that he is about to lose an opportunity, Dolittle responds, '*I'll tell you, Governor, if you'll only let me get a word in. I'm willing to tell you. I'm wanting to tell you. I'm waiting to tell you.*' Impressed by the natural rhetoric of Dolittle's speech, Higgins embarks on a lengthy discussion with him about middle-class morality and money. **Higgins** offers **Doolittle** £5 for Eliza, then increases it to £10 because **Doolittle** is so irresistible. **Doolittle** refuses the extra money, stating that his wife would not be happy to fritter away £10 the way she would £5. They settle on £5 now and perhaps the other £5 another time. As **Doolittle** leaves, he bumps into a Japanese lady in a kimono. She is **Eliza**, although he does not immediately recognise her because she is clean. After a brief argument, in which **Eliza** asserts that he only followed her there to get some drinking money, **he** leaves and **Eliza** rushes off to try on her new clothes, leaving **Pickering** and **Higgins** to wonder what they have taken on.

WHOOSH

Follow-up activities

- List each of the interactions in the first two acts in which Eliza is involved. On each occasion, discuss what the reader can infer about her, using evidence from the text. Include consideration of social context, how Eliza expects to be treated by people of a higher class than herself and how she is actually treated. For example, Freddy and his sister treat her very differently from each other, as do Professor Higgins and Colonel Pickering, even though they are all middle or upper class.
- Divide pupils into groups. Give each group one of the interactions from the list to create a freeze frame which shows something of her personality. At a given signal, each group should bring their freeze frame to life to show the interaction of Eliza (including appropriate accents) with at least one other character. After 10 seconds, re-freeze the frame. Then perform all the freeze frame/action/freeze frames sequentially. Remind pupils to consider posture, gesture, height and facial expression to convey meaning, including the hierarchy of each relationship.
- Through shared discussion, define what has been learnt about Eliza by the end of Act 2. Consider social context and her relationship with Higgins, Pickering and her father.
- How has Shaw developed the character of Eliza through her interaction with the other characters?
- Using this knowledge, ask pupils to predict the possible outcomes of the experiment upon which Eliza embarks.

4   Classic novels

1   Kenneth Grahame: *The Wind in the Willows*

The Wind in the Willows, published in 1908, was the outcome of Kenneth Grahame writing down the stories which he had told his son; products of his own upbringing near the River Thames and time spent, like Ratty, 'messing about in boats'. The novel is anthropomorphic, and it is the aspect of animals taking on human personalities and behaviours which is part of the book's attraction. Mole is hesitant and unassuming, the impetuous Ratty drives ideas forward, Badger is taciturn but leads with wisdom and pomposity, Toad bounces through the narrative with infectious enthusiasm for each of his latest crazes, while Weasel provides the baddie element.

Friendship and adventure are two strands running throughout the book and this Whoosh reproduces one of Toad's crazier adventures which results in his arrest and imprisonment. As a follow up activity, pupils are encouraged to discuss the circumstances which led to Toad's 20-year sentence, reflecting on why he behaved as he did.

An abridged audio version of the book, read by Bernard Cribbins, is available at http://www.bbc.co.uk/learning/schoolradio/subjects/english/wind_in_the_willows

Objective

- to use drama activities to understand how actions can be interpreted from different viewpoints.

Characters	Objects	Sounds
Mole Rat Badger Toad car delivery driver Inn keeper other guests at the inn driver of the car magistrate clerk to the court guards crowd children jailer	sun plants smashed cars hospital Toad Hall car bedroom furniture made into a car driveway to Toad Hall archway castle	knock on the door car engine key turning in a lock car horn shriek creaking key crashing door

It was a bright summer morning – one of those days when the **sun** seemed to be pulling new **plants** out of the earth as if they were on strings. **Mole** and **Rat** were finishing breakfast and talking excitedly about their sailing plans for the day, when there was a **knock** on the door. **Mole** went to answer and flung open the door to find **Badger**. '*The hour has come*,' announced **Badger**, entering the house. '*I'm going to take Toad in hand today!*'

Mole and **Rat** thought back to that day during the winter when **Badger** had told them about **Toad**'s latest craze – driving cars. The trouble was, **he** was a terrible driver and **he** had already smashed up six cars, been in **hospital** three times and **paid** countless fines for driving around the countryside too fast. At the moment, the remains of the six **cars** were piled high in **Toad**'s coach house. Just the evening before, **Badge**r had heard that **Toad** was expecting delivery of a brand new car that very day. The time had definitely come for his friends to take him in hand.

So off **they** went, only to find, when arriving at **Toad Hall**, that there was indeed a large, shiny, bright red **car** waiting outside of the **house**. And as **they** arrived, the door was thrown open and **Toad** came out, wearing goggles, a cap, the most enormous overcoat and a pair of huge leather gloves. '*Hello!*', he cried cheerfully, '*You're just in time to come with me for a ...*' but **his** voice tailed off as his noticed his **friends**' stern faces.

'*Take him inside*,' ordered **Badger** and to **Toad**'s distress, **Rat** and **Mole** marched him back into the house while **Badger** sent the **car** and its delivery **driver** away.

'*What's the meaning of this?*' spluttered **Toad**, as his **friends** laid him out on the floor. **Rat** had to sit on him before **Mole** could take his driving clothes off, but eventually they managed and pulled him to his feet. '*You've disregarded all our warnings*,' explained **Badger**, '*about your furious driving and your smashes and your rows with the police*,' he continued. **He** took **Toad** into a nearby room and shut the door. For a while, **Rat** and **Mole** could hear **Badger**'s raised voice and eventually **Toad**'s sobs. Then the door opened and **Badger** triumphantly announced, '*Toad has at last seen the error of his ways. He has undertaken to give up motor cars entirely and for ever.*'

WHOOSH

Rat was not so sure – **he** was watching **Toad** and he could definitely see a twinkle in his eye. **Badger** was just asking Toad to repeat the promise he had made when **Toad** burst out, '*I'm NOT sorry. I'd have said anything in there, dear Badger, because you put all your points so well.*'

'*Then you don't promise*,' asked an astonished **Badger**, '*never to touch a motor car again?*'

'*On the contrary*,' laughed **Toad**, '*I faithfully promise that the very first motor car I see, off I go in it!*'

That left his **friends** with no option – **Toad** was locked in his **bedroom** until he came to his senses. **He** shouted through the keyhole for a while, then **he** re-arranged the **furniture** to make a car and pretended to drive around at great speed making engine noises until all the chairs were broken and he lay in the ruins looking happy. Every day, one or other of the **trio** would keep watch on him as he gradually became quieter and quieter.

One morning, when **Rat** was left alone, **Toad** lay silently in bed. **His** voice was feeble as he begged **Rat** to go into the village and ask the doctor to call. **Rat** was alarmed at his friend's weakness and without Mole and Badger to consult, **he** decided that he must get the doctor straight away, before it was too late. When **Toad** asked for a lawyer to help him write his will, **Rat** headed rapidly for the door, remembering to lock it before he left the house.

No sooner had the key turned in the lock than **Toad** was out of bed. **He** got dressed quickly, pulled the sheets from his bed, tied them together and used them to climb out of the window. As **Rat** reached the end of the **drive** on one side of the house, **Toad**, with his hands in his pockets, was walking away from the opposite side of **Toad Hall**, whistling happily to himself as **he** went.

WHOOSH

Toad walked fast and soon arrived at a nearby town. He was feeling rather hungry so he found the local **Inn**, ordered the best meal that could be provided from the **inn keeper** and sat down at an empty table. '*Brains against force*,' **he** chuckled to himself, thinking about his **friends** and imagining their faces when they discovered the empty room. '*And brains came out on top.*' **He** was about half way through his meal when he heard a sound that made **him** start to tremble – a **car horn**. As the **car** turned into the Inn yard, **Toad** hurriedly finished his lunch and left. '*There cannot be any harm*,' **he** thought to himself as he walked around the **car**, '*in my only just looking at it.*' And then, when **he** noticed that there was nobody else around, '*I wonder if this sort of car starts easily?*' And before he knew how it had happened, **Toad** was turning the starting handle.

When he heard the familiar sound of a firing engine, **Toad** could not help himself. **His** passion for cars completely took over. As if in a dream, **he** found himself in the driver's seat. As if in a dream, **he** drove out through the **archway** onto the road. As if in a dream, **he** seemed to have forgotten about right and wrong, or the consequences of what he was doing. **He** drove faster and faster, eating up the miles as **he** sped on, reckless about the consequences of what he was doing. **He** was Toad at his best, Toad the terror, Toad the king of the open road.

WHOOSH

'*To my mind*,' observed the **magistrate**, '*the only difficulty is how we can make it hot enough for the rogue and ruffian we see in front of us*.' **Toad** listened as he was found guilty of stealing a car and (not for the first time) reckless driving and rudeness to the police. The **magistrate** looked at the **clerk** of the court, who scratched his nose with a pen while he thought about the sentence.

'*Stealing the car?*' asked the **magistrate**.

'*Twelve months*,' answered the **clerk**.

'*Reckless driving?*' **he** asked again.

'*Three years*,' grinned the **clerk**.

'*And for abusing the police, which should carry the harshest sentence?*'

'*Fifteen years*,' concluded the **clerk**.

'*I make that nineteen years*,' said the **magistrate**, turning to Toad.

'*Prisoner*,' ordered the guard. '*Stand up straight!*'

Toad, weighed down with chains, **shrieked** as the **magistrate** decided to round up the sentence to twenty years and **he** was dragged away. The **crowd** outside threw rotten food at him and **children** jeered as he was taken across the drawbridge, past the **guards** and into the castle prison. **He** was only allowed to stop when he was in front of the **jailer**. The rusty key **creaked** in the lock and the great door **crashed** shut behind him as **Toad** was imprisoned in the deepest dungeon that the old **castle** possessed.

WHOOSH

Follow-up activities

- Explore the reasons, through hot seating, for Toad's decisions about tricking his friends and stealing the car. Before starting, spend some time defining a good question, i.e. one which is open and structured in a way which encourages the character in the hot seat to offer their thinking beyond the content of the narrative. A closed question, for example, 'Do you know that stealing is wrong?' should only be asked for a specific purpose (in this case to establish that the character knew right from wrong) before questioning further to find out why Toad did something which he knew to be wrong.

- If pupils are familiar with hot seating, this activity could be conducted in pairs. Seat the class in two facing rows, one row acting as questioners and the facing row sitting in the hot seat, with all questioning conducted simultaneously. A list of questions can be agreed first, so that the same questions are asked and the varied answers can be compared. Very experienced or able hot seaters should formulate their own questions.

- Through group or shared class discussion, create a list of the evidence against Toad which could have been presented at his trial. Using information derived from the hot seating activity, discuss how Toad might have defended himself against the charges.

- As an extension challenge, pupils could write a report in role as either the arresting officer or as Toad, explaining the circumstances of his behaviour. This requires pupils to view the issue from both sides of the argument. Able pupils could write both reports, demonstrating an ability to understand a single issue from more than one perspective. Resources 15 and 16 provides sample report sheets.

Resource 15 **Police incident form**

Name:
Address:
Reasons for arrest: • • •
Evidence for incident 1:
Evidence for incident 2:
Evidence for incident 3:
Signed: Date:

Resource 16 **Statement of the defendant**

Name:
Address:
Charges: • • •
Defence for incident 1:
Defence for incident 2:
Defence for incident 3:
Signed: Date:

2   E Nesbit: *Five Children and It*

Five Children and It was initially published in 1900 as a series of short stories, later being produced as a book. It was followed by two further books to form a trilogy: *The Phoenix and the Carpet* and *The Story of the Amulet*. It has remained in print continuously for over 100 years. It was produced in 1991 as a BBC TV series and in 2004 as a film. The plot line was also revisited in 1992 by Helen Cresswell who wrote *The Return of the Psammead*, in which a different family move into the house of the original story and discover the Psammead for themselves.

Five Children and It tells the story of five children, Robert, Anthea, Cyril, Jane and their baby brother who find a grumpy Psammead buried in a gravel pit near their home. He is the last remaining type of a sand-fairy or goblin who longs for the age of the dinosaurs when Psammeads were common. He is able to grant wishes to the children although his great age and desire to be left alone mean that he will only grant them one wish each day. At sunset, the magic ceases to work.

The wishes all go wrong, with comic consequences. One day, they wish for the gravel pit to be filled with gold, but the sovereigns are so outdated that the children not only cannot spend them, but find themselves arrested when they try. On another occasion, irritated by their baby brother, they wish he would just grow up, which he does before their eyes. They then have to spend the rest of the day keeping a large baby out of trouble.

Parents are removed from the story at the beginning and after the first day, the servants are none the wiser about the children's antics after they wish for the servants to see nothing. The Whoosh retells their wish from the first day.

Objective

* to explore the fantasy novel genre.

Characters	Objects	Sounds
Robert Anthea Cyril Jane the baby the Psammead other Psammeads children Martha	The White House hole dinosaurs dinosaurs turned to stone window hedge sun	scream door banging bell ringing

The White House, their new home, seemed quiet and empty to the **children** after their parents left. **They** wandered from one room to another, wishing that they could think of something to do. To fill the gap, the **children** decided to go and explore the gravel pit near their **house**. Because their father had said that it had been the seaside thousands of years ago, **they** took their spades so that they could pretend that **they** were digging on the beach.

On the way to the pit, **they** had to take it in turns to carry the **baby** and **he** would keep trying to eat the sand when they got there, but eventually **he** curled up and fell asleep. That was when **they** had the idea of digging to Australia. For a while **they** dug as though they really did mean to dig right through the earth, but then **they** got tired and one by one, **they** climbed out of the **hole** and sat on the edge. Only **Anthea** carried on and even **she** was about to give up when her **scream** from inside the hole made the others jump. '*Come here. Come quick – it's alive! It'll get away. Quick!*' Of course, by the time they got back into the hole, It, whatever It was, had got away.

They were still discussing whether it was a rat or a snake and **Anthea** was still pulling at the sand with her hands when a voice said, '*You let me alone.*' And there it was – a **creature** with eyes like a snail on long stalks that moved in and out like telescopes, ears like a bat and a fur-covered body that looked a bit like a spider. Its arms and legs were furry, but it had hands and feet like a monkey.

'*What on earth is it?*' wondered **Jane**. '*Shall we take it home?*'

The **creature** turned to look at her, stared at her hat and said, '*Does it always talk nonsense, or is it only the rubbish on her head that makes her silly?*'

'*She doesn't mean to be silly*,' soothed Anthea. '*Don't be frightened. We won't hurt you. Who are you?*'

'*Well, I knew the world had changed*,' he said, sounding astonished and a bit angry at the same time, '*but do you mean to tell me you don't know a Psammead when you see one?*'

WHOOSH

While **they** sat on the sand, the **creature** explained to them that **Psammeads** had been around for several thousand years, although most of **them** had caught colds and **died** when they got soaked by the sea. **They** used to give daily wishes to **children**, he explained, in particular whatever **dinosaur** they wanted for their dinner. At the end of the day, any dinosaur meat left over **turned** to stone. But then **he** moved on to the really interesting bit – the fact that **he** could still give one wish each day.

For a while the **children** sat there and **thought** about what they could wish for, but nothing came to mind. It was only when the **Psammead** started to burrow impatiently back into the sand that **Anthea** said in a hurry, '*I wish we were all as beautiful as the day.*' The **Psammead** held his breath until he swelled up before suddenly letting go of his breath and going back to his normal size. '*Good day*,' he said suddenly, before scratching at the sand with his hands and feet and disappearing.

For a few seconds the **children** stood completely still, wondering who the other strange children around them were and where their brothers and sisters had gone. It was only when **Jane** said, '*Excuse me, but have you seen my brothers and sister anywhere?*' that **they** recognised her voice and the hole in her dress. '*You look like Christmas cards – silly Christmas cards*,' said **Robert** angrily to the girls. But there was nothing they could do to change themselves – the Psammead had already explained that the magic would keep working until sunset. **They** were starting to feel hungry, too, so **they** decided to wake the **baby** up and go home for lunch. But their troubles were only just beginning.

WHOOSH

The **baby** looked exactly the same as always, but when **Anthea** tried to pick him up, **he** just cried and tried to scratch her. **He** refused to let anyone touch him and it was a while before the awful truth dawned on **them** – **he** did not recognise them. It took over an hour before **he** calmed down and got to know these strangers well enough to let **them** carry him **home**. By then, **he** was crying with hunger and thirst so they were glad when they finally got **home**, very late, for their lunch.

'*Thank goodness he's safe back*,' said Martha, their nursemaid, as she snatched the baby from them. '*Who are all of you?*'

'*We're us, of course*,' said **Robert**, but **Martha** told them to clear off to their own homes and then she **banged** the door. **Cyril** rang the **bell** until **Martha**'s head appeared through a bedroom window and she shouted, '*If you don't take yourselves off I'll go and fetch the police.*'

'*They can't put us in prison for being as beautiful as the day, can they?*' wobbled **Jane**. But **none** of them knew and **they** were too hungry and worried to talk about it. **They** tried three more times to get someone inside the house to listen to their story and eventually **they** got so hungry that **Robert** even tried to climb in through a **window**. When **Martha** soaked him with a jug of cold water, **they** decided there was nothing for it but to sit under a **hedge** and wait for sunset.

There was one moment of real panic when **they** remembered that at sunset they might turn to stone and **Cyril** thought that it was already beginning to happen to him. But then **he** realised that his foot had just gone to sleep. At last, hungry, frightened and tired, **they** all fell asleep.

WHOOSH

Anthea was the first to wake up. The **sun** had set and it was starting to get dark. **She** pinched herself to make sure that she had not turned to stone. Then **she** pinched all the others, too, waking them up as she did so. '*Cyril*,' **she** said almost in tears with relief, '*how nice and ugly you look.*'

When **they** got **home**, they found that **Martha** was very angry. **She** had just started telling them about the strange children who had been so rude when **she** thought to ask, '*And where on earth have you been all this time?*'

'*In the lane*,' answered **Anthea**. '*We couldn't come home because of them. They kept us there until after sunset.*'

Then **Martha** turned her anger on the child strangers and said that if she ever saw them again, she would spoil their beauty for them. **She** was so sorry for the children that she gave them a huge supper.

'**Let's ask the Psammead to make it so that the servants don't notice anything different, no matter what wishes we have**,' suggested Jane, before **they** all went gratefully off to bed.

WHOOSH

Follow-up activities

A fantasy novel allows the reader to move into an imaginary world – what other examples of the genre can children think of, for example J. R. R. Tolkien's *The Hobbit* and *The Lord of the Rings*; C. S. Lewis's *The Chronicles of Narnia*; J.K. Rowling's *Harry Potter* series; Philip Pullman's *His Dark Materials* trilogy; Eoin Colfer's *Artemis Fowl* and Garth Nix's *Keys to the Kingdom*.

In *Five Children and It*, the characters live in a realistic world and the fantasy element rests with a single sand fairy who has survived for several thousand years before he is found. He is able to grant a wish and his magic works until sunset.

- With this structure in mind, invite pupils to divide into groups of four or five to discuss what wishes they would make if they were in the position of the children in the novel.
- Ask them to choose one wish and improvise a short story around the granting of their wish. What are the consequences – funny, sad, frightening or helpful? Ask groups to share their ideas with each other.
- Challenge each group to produce their story either in written form or as a short film. When complete, pupils will have written a class book based on *Five Children and It*.
- As an additional challenge, pupils could create their own fantasy creature with its own good or evil powers.

3 Robert Louis Stevenson: *Treasure Island*

Treasure Island was first published in serial form between 1881 and 1882, before being published as a book the following year. It is classified as a *bildungsroman*, or a story in which the protagonist, Jim Hawkins, grows to maturity in the course of the novel. Narrated in the first person, it tells the story of a boy who unwittingly gets caught up in an argument between pirates during which a treasure map falls into his hands. He joins the adventure to find the treasure, spies on the double-dealing Long John Silver thus preventing a full mutiny and, through a series of other events, saves their ship, the *Hispaniola*.

The book is divided into six parts, the opening of which suggests a back story surrounding the pirate Billy Bones. As the narrative progresses, the back story is gradually revealed until the treasure is found and the roles of all the characters become clear. It is set in the south-west of England at some point in the middle of the eighteenth century. Although the book was written 140 years ago in a setting over 250 years old, the themes of greed, honour, treachery and heroism are still relevant today and pirate stories remain enduring favourites with pupils of all ages.

The influence of Stevenson's creation on popular perception is huge, including the concept of a treasure map in which X marks the spot of the buried treasure and talking parrots squawking, 'Pieces of eight!' on the shoulders of one-legged pirates. The Black Spot was entirely Stevenson's creation and it was used in the book as a form of communication between pirates when a character had been found guilty of something. One side of a circular piece of paper was black and the other side carried a message. The literary device has found its way into other novels, including Arthur Ransome's *Swallows and Amazons* when the children decided that their uncle should be deposed, and *The Pirates of the Caribbean: Dead Man's Chest* in which Jack Sparrow is given a Black Spot by Davy Jones. The novel has also inspired many film versions, including *Muppet Treasure Island*.

This Whoosh concentrates on the opening of the novel, using the first four chapters as a means of hooking pupils into the story. As an introduction, fill a wooden box or chest with various items suggested by the text, for example, a skull and crossbones flag, a bottle of rum, a sword and some gold treasure. Discuss the items in the chest, deciding to whom they might belong and what the story behind the items might be. Then move into the Whoosh, which contains plenty of opportunity to improvise any dialogue which has not been provided.

Objective

- to introduce the characters, setting and plot of an adventure story.

Characters	Objects	Sounds
Jim Hawkins father mother captain man pushing the barrow people walking past the inn strangers guests one-legged sailor doctor Black Dog Blind Pew neighbours	Admiral Benbow inn Black Hill Cove and beach door tables neighbours' houses sea chest	whistling rapping on the door snort wind shaking the house waves breaking against the cliffs pirate songs shouting chairs and tables being overturned fighting cry of pain tapping stick ticking clock logs falling in the fire knocking on doors clock striking six door handle turning bolts rattling

I will never forget the day that **he** walked into the **Admiral Benbow**, the inn that my **mother** and **father** kept. **He** plodded to the door, an old, brown seaman with his sea chest pushed behind him by a **man** with a barrow. **He** was tall, his ponytail falling over the shoulder of a dirty blue coat which had been patched so many times that it seemed to be almost all patches. His hands were scarred and his nails black and broken. Across one side of his face, a thick red scar was evidence of a sword cut.

He whistled as he looked around outside – the old song, *Fifteen men on a dead man's chest, Yo, ho, ho and a bottle of rum!* was a favourite of his. Then **he** rapped on the door with his stick, calling for a glass of rum when my **father** answered his insistent knocking. Eventually, after looking around at the cliffs **he** said, '*This is a handy cove. Much company, mate?*' When my **father** replied that apart from local folk we were very quiet at the **Admiral Benbow**, the old **man** threw a few gold coins in the doorway and informed my father that he intended to stay with us. '*I'm a plain man; rum and bacon and eggs is what I want. You can call me captain.*'

And that is how **he** came to live with us. **He** was usually silent and spent the day walking along the cliffs peering through a brass telescope. In the evenings **he** would sit by the **fire** and drink rum and apart from the occasion **snort** which sounded like a fog horn, **he** kept himself to himself. Occasionally **he** would ask if any of the **people** passing by on the road outside were sailors and when **strangers** entered the **inn, he** would hide, as quiet as a mouse, behind the **door. I** had already become part of this fear, because **he** had promised me a silver coin every month if **I** would look out for a seafaring man with one leg and let him know the moment one appeared.

WHOOSH

How that one-legged **sailor** haunted my dreams. On stormy nights, when the **wind** shook the four corners of the house and the **sea** waves roared up the cliffs, **I** would see him in my nightmares. But **I** was not as frightened of the captain as others were. Some evenings **he** would force our **guests** to join him in his pirate songs, **telling** dreadful stories about walking the plank, storms at sea and wild deeds on the Spanish Main. **He** would eventually get so drunk that **he** would stagger off to bed. Although my **father** was afraid that we would lose business, most **guests** seemed to enjoy being scared out of their wits and it certainly added some excitement to our quiet, country life.

I only ever saw him cross once and that was after my **father** was taken ill. The **doctor** called one afternoon and took it upon himself to warn the **captain** that drink would be the death of him and that he should consume less rum. The **captain** leapt to his feet, opening a knife and threatening to pin the **doctor** to the wall. The **doctor** did not flinch. He merely mentioned that he was not only a doctor but the local magistrate and if the **captain** carried out his threat, **he** would find himself in court. The **captain** soon sat down, muttering to himself. For many evenings after that, **he** was very quiet.

WHOOSH

Soon afterwards, the first of several strange events occurred. One cold January morning, the **captain** left for the **beach** earlier than usual. I was laying the **tables** for breakfast (my father still being ill) when a pale **man**, with two fingers missing on his left hand, walked in and ordered a glass of rum. '**Come here, sonny, come nearer here**,' he demanded when I served the rum. '**Is this here table for my mate, Bill?**' he asked. Although I knew no one by that name, I soon recognised the captain in his description. When I mentioned that Bill had gone down to the beach, **he** finished his rum and said, '**You and me'll just get behind the door and we'll give Bill a little surprise – bless his 'art.**' Somehow, I did not feel that he was going to be as friendly towards Bill as his words suggested.

He pushed me towards the **door**, hid himself and me behind it, then pulled out his sword. When the **captain** returned for his breakfast, the **visitor** called to him. The **captain** swung round and suddenly went white, as if he had seen a ghost. '**Black Dog**,' he gasped.

'**Black Dog as ever was**,' he laughed, '**come for to see his old shipmate Billy.**' The **visitor** seemed to have taken a liking to me and asked me to get him some more rum. I managed to serve it even though my hands were shaking, then I left them together, seated at a **table**. For some time I just heard low voices, but then suddenly there was **shouting**, the **sound** of chairs and tables being overturned in a fight and a **cry** of pain. Then I saw **Black Dog** running away.

The **captain** was lying on the floor with closed eyes. My **mother**, hearing the noise, had come downstairs, appearing just as the **doctor** arrived to visit my father. Apparently the **captain** had suffered a stroke brought on, the **doctor** said, by too much rum. **We** carried him to his room where the **doctor** gave him one more warning. '**The name of rum, for you, is death**,' **he** said, before going to see my **father**.

WHOOSH

Although the **captain** was weak and needed care, **my** attention was taken from him by the death of my **father**. The day after the funeral, I was standing sadly at the door of **inn** when I heard a stick **tapping**. A dreadful **man** appeared and I realised that the tapping was his stick on the ground. **He** was hideous; most of his face was covered with a green shade and **he** was hunched into a huge cloak with the hood pulled up. '**Will any kind friend inform a poor blind man in what part of the country he may now be?**' **he** called, sensing my presence.

'**You are at the Admiral Benbow at Black Hill Cove**,' I answered.

'**Will you give me your hand, my kind young friend, and lead me in?**' **he** asked. When I gave him my hand, **he** pulled me close to him, hurting my arm. As soon as **we** entered the **inn**, **he** demanded to be taken to the **captain**, wrenching my arm to make sure that I did as I was told. The **captain**, meanwhile, had passed beyond fear and looked as though he was near to death. The blind **man** pressed something into the captain's hand, then skipped out of the inn and along the road with a great deal of energy. '**Ten o'clock**,' the captain whispered. '**We've got six hours**,' he continued, before falling dead on the floor.

WHOOSH

I lost no time in telling my **mother** everything. Every sound terrified us, even the clock **ticking** and the logs **falling** in the fire. We knew that we had to get out of the **inn**, because Blind Pew would be coming back. **We** wasted precious time **knocking** on our **neighbours**' doors and asking for help, but our appeal was useless – the cowards all shook their heads and were too scared to leave their own **homes**.

Returning to the inn, **we** decided to search the captain's **chest**, take any money which he owed us, and leave the place for good. I searched his pockets for a key, finally finding one around his neck. The message on the Black Spot read, '**You have till ten tonight**,' and as the clock **struck** six, I realised that **we** would need to work quickly.

The **chest** smelt of tobacco and contained a neatly folded suit of clothes, two pistols, some silver trinkets, and some shells. Right at the bottom, hidden by an old cloak, was a canvas bag full of gold and a packet of papers wrapped in an oilskin. It was while my **mother** was counting the money that I heard the tapping of **Blind Pew's** stick on the path again. **We** held our breath while the tapping got nearer and the stick was used to hammer on the door. **He** turned the handle and **rattled** the door bolts, but then we heard the sound of the **tapping** stick fade into the distance as he left again.

But I knew that he would soon be back with reinforcements. I urged my **mother** to collect the gold as quickly as she could while I got ready to leave. At the last moment, I picked up the wrapped papers. What was in there? Why were they important enough to be locked in the chest? Was this why Blind Pew had given the captain the Black Spot?

WHOOSH

Follow-up activities

- Create a packet of papers tied up in waterproof paper and show it to the class. Discuss what the papers might contain and why they were so important to the captain. How might the papers be connected with the Black Spot?
- Working in groups, ask pupils to list their predictions about the papers.
- Create a black spot, a circle of paper which is black on one side and has the message 'You have till ten tonight' on the reverse. Discuss what this message might mean. What did Blind Pew and his friends expect the captain to do in the six hours that they gave him? List predictions.
- The story is narrated by Jim Hawkins. How might he figure in the rest of the story? Predict possible scenarios, bearing in mind that the book is called *Treasure Island*. The original title read *Treasure Island or the Mutiny of the Hispaniola*. Provide this information to support discussion.
- Continue to read the story of *Treasure Island* – the book is summarised in 10 short video sections designed for 9-11 year olds at http://www.bbc.co.uk/learning/schoolradio/subjects/english/treasure_island
- When the story is completed, compare predictions with what actually happened.

4   Charles Dickens: *A Christmas Carol*

Charles Dickens wrote *A Christmas Carol* in 1843. It is structured in five stanzas, or verses, to mirror the structure of an actual Christmas carol. The novel reflects a Victorian love of ghost stories and it is also seen as a significant contribution to the Victorian creation of the modern Christmas.

Throughout his adult life, Dickens used books, lectures, magazines and newspapers to bring the plight of the poor and destitute to the attention of the wealthy and the emerging middle class. In this novel, Scrooge is the mouthpiece for Thomas Malthus who said that starvation and death were a natural way to control a population. Dickens himself supported reform, including a Poor Law which allowed for provision proportional to the number of children in a family. Opponents to welfare reform felt that this just encouraged poor people to have large numbers of children without having to take responsibility for their care.

As a result of visits from the ghosts of his former partner Jacob Marley, Christmas Present, Christmas Past and Christmas Yet to Come, the miserly Scrooge is reformed and becomes a benefactor, celebrating Christmas with his family and generously sharing his great wealth with people less fortunate than himself.

The following two Whooshes consider Dickens' characterisation, contrasting the mean and grasping Scrooge at the outset of the story with the genial and benevolent Scrooge at its conclusion.

Meet Mr Scrooge

Objective

- to consider how an author creates the character of the protagonist in a novel.

Characters	Objects	Sounds
Jacob Marley Ebenezer Scrooge people Bob Cratchit Scrooge's nephew two local businessmen people with torches workmen cooks child singing carols boys sliding in the road Marley's face	sign clock houses desk office fire candle door streets torches carriages fog church tower shop windows tavern house road front door room	striking clock stamping feet creaking door clapping muffled kitchen sounds carol singing laughter

Jacob Marley was dead. There was no doubt about it – **he** was definitely dead. Only his name lived on, painted on the **sign** 'Scrooge and Marley' above the door. **Ebenezer Scrooge** refused to pay to have the sign changed, so there Marley's name stayed for many years. **Scrooge** was a tight-fisted, grasping old man. In summer and winter alike he was as cold as ice; **his** shrivelled face, red eyes and blue lips frozen from inside of his own body.

    Nobody ever greeted him as they passed by. He wanted nothing more when walking along streets crowded with **people** than to be left alone. **Nobody** spoke to him. **Nobody** smiled at him. That was just the way **he** liked it.

    This story starts one Christmas Eve. It was already dark even though the city **clock** struck only three o'clock. It was cold – so cold, that **people** stamped their feet on the pavement to try and keep warm. Freezing fog poured through every open door and turned the shapes of **houses** into ghosts. **Scrooge** was sitting at his **desk** in his **office**, occasionally looking up from his work to glare frostily at his clerk, **Bob Cratchit**, sitting at another **desk** in the tiny **office** next door. Even though it was freezing outside, Scrooge's **fire** was small; his clerk's **fire** even smaller. Earlier that afternoon, when **Cratchit** had tried to put some more coal on his tiny **fire**, **Scrooge** had made it quite obvious that if he did it again, he would lose his job. So **Cratchit** just wrapped his white scarf round his neck and occasionally tried to thaw his freezing fingers around the **candle**.

WHOOSH

'***Merry Christmas, Uncle***,' called a **voice**, as the **door creaked** opened.

    '***Bah! Humbug!***' growled **Scrooge** as his **nephew**, warm and glowing from his fast walk through the icy **streets**, appeared.

    '***Humbug?***' repeated his **nephew**. '***You don't mean that.***'

    '***Why are you merry? You're poor enough***,' grumbled **Scrooge**.

    '***Why aren't you merry?***' his **nephew** smiled. '***You're rich enough.***'

    '***Humbug***,' snarled **Scrooge** again, lost for a suitable answer. '***Any idiot who thinks that Christmas is merry should be buried with a stake of holly through his heart.***'

    '***Christmas is a good time, a time to be kind***,' answered his **nephew**, refusing to be silenced. At that comment, **Bob Cratchit**, sitting in his office, **clapped** loudly but after a hard stare from **Scrooge**, **he** suddenly pretended that he was actually poking the **fire**, which was enough to put the tiny **fire** out completely.

'*Good afternoon*,' snarled **Scrooge** to his nephew, turning back to his work.

'*Merry Christmas, Uncle*,' smiled his **nephew** in return as **Bob Cratchit** got up and walked across the **office** to open the **door**. When the **nephew** wished him '*Merry Christmas*,' **Cratchit** shook him warmly by the hand and returned the greeting.

WHOOSH

In opening the **door** to let the **young man** out, **Bob Cratchit** had also let in **two** other **people** carrying books and papers. **One** of them handed **Scrooge** a piece of paper introducing himself.

'*Mr Marley?*' **one** of them enquired as they removed their hats.

'*He's dead*,' growled **Scrooge**. '*What do you want?*'

Not to be put off, the second **gentleman** explained that they were collecting for the poor at Christmas and they were wondering how much Mr Scrooge might like to give.

'*Nothing*,' said **Scrooge**. '*Send them to the workhouse.*'

'*Sir*,' explained the **gentleman** patiently, '*many people would rather die.*'

'*Then let them*,' barked **Scrooge**. Realising that there was no point in discussing the situation any further with a man whom everyone knew to be mean, **they** replaced their hats and turned to leave. **Scrooge** returned to his work looking more pleased with himself than he had for a long time.

WHOOSH

Outside, the temperature fell with the darkness. **People** ran about with flaming **torches**, offering to walk ahead of **carriages** to help them see through the thickening **fog**. The clock on the **church tower** that normally looked down on Scrooge became invisible. **Men** on the corner of the street mending gas pipes had lit a **fire** around which **people** gathered to warm their hands. Bright **shop windows** reflected cold faces as **people** hurried by. Fifty **cooks** worked continuously in the Lord Mayor's kitchens, the sounds of their **pots** and **pans** muffled by the fog. One brave **child** even pressed his nose up against Scrooge's window and started to sing, 'God rest you, merry gentleman,' until **Scrooge** terrified him by advancing towards him with a ruler in his hand. **Everyone** was getting ready for Christmas.

Everyone, that is, except Scrooge. Eventually and grudgingly, **he** agreed to let **Bob Cratchit** have the following day off on condition that he was at work earlier than ever the morning after. Happy to have been given Christmas Day off, **Bob Cratchit** slid down the road, **laughing** with a group of **boys** as he went on his way to his family in Camden Town.

WHOOSH

Scrooge, meanwhile, went on his lonely way. **He** sat alone at a **tavern** table to eat his dinner. **He** read the newspapers alone. **He** passed the evening by checking his bank book then **he** stood up to make his way to his empty home. He lived in rooms in the **house** which used to belong to Jacob Marley. The **road** was so dark that **Scrooge** had to feel his way to the **front door** even though he knew the **house** so well. There was nothing unusual about the **door**, except that the brass door knocker was rather large. Scrooge knew the **door** as well as he knew anything, so why, he puzzled, did the knocker suddenly turn into **Marley's face** as he put his key in the lock?

The **face** glowed vaguely in the surrounding darkness, which made it look quite ghostly. **It** looked at him in just the way that Jacob Marley used to look at him when he was alive. The eyes were wide open and the hair looked as though it had been blown by the breeze. Then just as suddenly as it had appeared, the **face** vanished and the door returned to normal. **Scrooge** stared at the **door** for a moment, then opened **it**, walked through **it** and locked **it** firmly behind him.

Lighting just one **candle** because darkness is cheaper than light, he made his way up the gloomy stairs to his **room**. Then, sitting close to the dying **fire**, he picked up his bowl of thin gruel. '*Humbug*,' he muttered several times, as he started to eat.

WHOOSH

Follow-up activities

- Use Role on the Wall to explore pupils' understanding of Dickens' characterisation. Draw a large outline of a person on paper and attach it to the wall. Provide each pupil with one or two sticky notes on which they should write a fact about Scrooge which they have learnt from the Whoosh. Ask pupils to share their fact then stick their note on the outline. This will build a picture of Scrooge and his character.
- Challenge older students to decide if the comments are about external appearance (in which case stick them around the outside of the outline) or internal character (in which case stick the comments inside the outline). Alternatively, ask students to make one comment about external appearance and one comment about internal character.
- An extension challenge would be to ask students to write two comments, one reflecting how Scrooge sees himself (stuck on the inside) and one reflecting how he is seen by others (stuck on the outside).
- Through shared discussion, define the character called Scrooge which Dickens has created.

Mr Scrooge becomes a new man

Objective

- to reflect on the changes in the character of a protagonist at the conclusion of a novel.

Characters	Objects	Sounds
Scrooge	bed room	laughter
boy	clothes	church bells
delivery boy	sitting room	'Merry Christmas'
cab driver	door	party sounds
Bob Cratchit	window	clock striking nine o'clock
Mrs Cratchit	shop	
Tiny Tim	turkey	
five other Cratchit children	front door	
people in the street	cab	
two local businessmen	Bob Cratchit's house	
children	Scrooge's house	
beggars	street	
maid	church	
nephew and niece	nephew's house	
nephew's friends	dining room	
	table full of food	
	desk	
	office	
	fires	

Scrooge woke up the next morning, his face wet with tears. **He** checked that he was in his own bed – he was. He checked that the **room** was his own – it was. **He** jumped excitedly out of bed, putting his **clothes** on inside out and taking them off, only to drop them or put them on again upside down. And all the time **he** jumped and danced around singing, '*Merry Christmas everybody. I feel as light as a feather. Merry Christmas!*'

He half ran and half fell into his **sitting room**, trying to put his socks on as he went. Finally **he** stopped, out of breath from his rushing around. **He** checked around the room, lifting the saucepan in which he had heated his gruel the night before. **He** opened and closed the **door** through which Jacob Marley had entered. **He** walked into the corner where the Ghost of Christmas Present had been sitting. **He** looked out of the **window** through which he had watched the wandering spirits. And then **he** started to laugh.

For someone who had not laughed for many years, it was a splendid **laugh**; loud, long and happy. **He** only stopped laughing when he realised that he could hear church **bells**. It seemed that every church **bell** in London was **chiming**, **ringing** and **clanging**. **He** realised that he had no idea what day it was, so throwing open the **window** to let in the clear, frosty air, he called to a **boy** in the street below, '*What day is it?*' Looking up at the **window** in surprise the **boy** laughed, '*Today? It's Christmas Day*.' And no sooner had **he** answered than **Scrooge** asked him to go around the corner to the **shop** and buy the biggest **turkey** that he could.

WHOOSH

While the boy was away, **Scrooge** made his way downstairs and opened the **door**. He looked at the door knocker, patting it as though he was seeing it for the first time. **He** started laughing again and **he** was still laughing when a **turkey** twice the size of Tiny Tim was delivered and **he** ordered a **cab** to send it off to Bob Cratchit's **house**. **He** laughed while he paid the cab driver. **He** laughed while he paid the **boy** for his efforts. **He** laughed while he imagined **Bob Crachit**'s face when the **turkey** was delivered without a note telling him who had sent it. He imagined the Cratchit **family**, Bob, his wife, Tiny Tim and their other five children sitting down to enjoy a huge turkey dinner. **Then** he sat in a chair and laughed until he cried.

Shaving was quite hard because his hands were shaking so much, but even if **he** had cut off the end of his nose, **he** would still have laughed. By the time **he** had dressed and was ready to leave the **house**, the **street** was filling with **people**. As **he** strolled along with his hands behind him, **he** smiled at everyone, wishing several people, '*Merry Christmas*'. When people wished him '*Merry Christmas*', in return, **he** thought it was the nicest sound he had ever heard.

He had not been walking for long when **he** saw the two business**men** who had visited his office the day before. Remembering with embarrassment how rude he had been, **he** went up to them. '*Merry Christmas*,' he called, before quietly **telling** the men how much money he would like to give to their collection for the poor. **They** were so astonished by his generosity that **they** were scarcely able to wish him a merry Christmas in return.

Then he went to **church**, walked the **streets**, watched **people**, patted **children** on the head, talked to **beggars**, looked through **windows** to see people busy in their kitchens and **he** found that everything was making him happy. **He** had no idea that people could give so much pleasure.

WHOOSH

Then as the afternoon wore on, **Scrooge** turned his steps towards his nephew's **home**. He walked up and down past the **door** at least a dozen times before **he** finally managed to find the courage to knock on the **door**. The **maid** let him in but **Scrooge** insisted that he would go to the **dining room** alone. Instead of the **maid** announcing him, **Scrooge** quietly turned the door handle and crept unseen into the **room**. His **nephew** was standing with his **wife**, checking a great spread of food on a **table**. '*Fred*,' called **Scrooge**, making them both jump.

He was made more welcome than **he** could have imagined. **Fred** and his **wife** both shook **Scrooge** by the hand until his arm was in danger of falling off. Then later, when their **friends** arrived, there was **eating**, **dancing**, **games** and **laughter**. Everything about the **party** was wonderful.

WHOOSH

The next morning though, **Scrooge** was sitting at his **desk** earlier than normal. **He** watched as the **clock struck** nine. **He** watched as another 18 minutes passed before **Bob Cratchit** arrived for work. **Bob** took off his hat and scarf and settled to work so fast that it looked as though he was trying to catch up with the clock. But it was no good – **Scrooge** summoned **Bob** into his office in his sternest voice. '*I'm sorry I'm late, sir*,' he pleaded, '*but it's only once a year*.'

'*I'm not putting up with any more of this*,' shouted Scrooge. '*So I'm going to … I'm going to … raise your salary*.' And before the astonished **clerk** could respond, **Scrooge** went on, '*Merry Christmas. Before you do anything else, put a lot of coal on those fires to keep us warm*.'

Scrooge was as good as his word. **He** raised Bob's salary. **He** helped **Tiny Tim**, who did not die. **He** became as good an employer, friend and master as anyone had ever known.

Sometimes **people** laughed at the change in him, but **he** took no notice because **he** was laughing in his own heart. The ghosts never visited him again and **he** celebrated many more merry Christmases with generosity and cheerfulness.

WHOOSH

Follow-up activities

- Using the Role on the Wall activity described in the previous Whoosh, repeat the activity in the same way for this Whoosh.
- Through shared discussion, define the character of Scrooge at the end of the novel. Compare and contrast it with the opening of the narrative. In what ways has he changed?
- What are Dickens viewpoint and intention in creating the character of Scrooge in the way that he did?

5   Charles Dickens: *Oliver Twist*

Oliver Twist was Dickens' second novel which was published in serial form between 1837 and 1839. He wrote it to draw attention to the 1834 Poor Law and the conditions in which many of London's children lived and worked as a result of the establishment of workhouses. For part of his childhood, Dickens lived near a workhouse and he would have witnessed the reality of the scenes which he describes in the book.

The novel is a perceptive analysis of Victorian society and its attitude to poverty and starvation. The two following Whooshes each examine a scene in Oliver's life which typifies the lives of many poor Victorian children. Families were split up when they entered the workhouse, so children all lived and worked together. Other children, either orphaned or homeless, lived on the streets and many became members of pickpocket gangs which were managed by gangmasters such as Fagin.

Life in the workhouse

Objective

- to consider the historical and social context of a novel.

Characters	Objects	Sounds
Oliver Twist	workhouse	sneeze
Oliver's mother	cellar	crying baby
workhouse nurse	gate	gate being bolted
Board gentlemen	large room	crying child
Mrs Mann	ropes	
Mr Bumble, the Beadle	hall	
young children	copper	
servant		
workhouse boys		
workhouse master		
serving ladies		

Among its public buildings, almost every town has a **workhouse** – a dark, grim place built to care for people who could no longer work and care for themselves. It is in one of these workhouses that **Oliver Twist** was born. Being born in a **workhouse** is not the best start in life and **he** lay gasping on a tiny mattress, ignored by everyone. It took **Olive**r some time to decide whether he was going to breath or not but eventually a tiny **sneeze** announced that he had decided to live and so yet another orphan child would be relying on the parish to be fed and clothed.

His **mother** had been found ill and exhausted the day before, her shoes worn out as if she had walked a long way. **She** wore no wedding ring and lived just long enough to give a gold locket for her son into the care of a **nurse** who was more interested in the beer in her green bottle than in caring for her patient. **Oliver**, crying loudly by now, was dressed in a yellowing cotton gown, wrapped in a blanket and given a number. A **Board** meeting of important gentlemen decided that he should be sent to the farm where babies were cared for until they were old enough to return to the main workhouse.

The old nurse, **Mrs Mann**, was given enough money by the **Beadle** every week to feed all the young workhouse **children**, but since most of the money mysteriously disappeared into her own pocket, **they** were always hungry. Occasionally, the important gentlemen of the **Board** would visit the farm, but because **Mr Bumble** the Beadle always called the day before to announce the visit to **Mrs Mann**, the **children** were scrubbed clean and fed before they arrived. As a result, the **Board** always saw neat, clean **children** who appeared to be well cared for and they had no idea that anything was amiss.

WHOOSH

So **Oliver**'s life progressed until the day of his ninth birthday. **He** was a short child; underfed and very thin. But what he lacked in height he made up for in courage; **he** was celebrating his birthday locked in the **cellar** with two other **boys** for daring to complain that they were hungry. **He** had just been locked up when **Mrs Mann** spotted **Mr Bumble** trying to open the **gate**. Quickly sending the **servant** to fetch the **boys** from the cellar and give them a good wash, **she** went to let **Mr Bumble** in. By the time **she** reached the gate, **Mr Bumble**, who was an impatient man, was **kicking** it to try and get it open.

While the **boys** were scrubbed, **Mrs Mann** led the **Beadle** into her parlour, providing him with a glass of gin (kept only, of course, as medicine for the children when they were ill) to calm his mood. **He** was visiting, he announced, to remove Oliver Twist who was now old enough to return to the main **workhouse** and be trained for work. A reward of twenty pounds had failed to produce any information about his mother's identity so it was assumed that he had no family to claim him.

So **Oliver** was brought to the parlour and told that he would be leaving Mrs Mann. **He** was quick enough to pretend that this news made him sad and because **he** cried, **Mrs Mann** gave him what he really wanted, which was an extra piece of bread and butter. Then off **he** set, wearing the brown cloth cap that announced to the world that he was a workhouse boy. But although **he** was glad to be leaving **Mrs Mann**, who was very fond of smacking the **children** in her care, **he** realised as heard the **gate** being bolted behind him that **he** was also leaving behind the only friends he had ever known. Suddenly, **he** felt very lonely.

WHOOSH

As **he** trotted along, holding firmly to the Beadle's gold laced sleeve, **Oliver** asked every few minutes if they were nearly there yet. **Mr Bumble** answered very snappily and **he** was glad, when they arrived at the **workhouse**, to hand Oliver over to another **nurse**. **He** had hardly finished demolishing another slice of bread and butter when **he** was told by the nurse that he had to appear before the Board.

Having no idea that the **Board** was a collection of the gentlemen who had visited his old home, **Oliver** was not sure what to expect and he started to **cry**. A poke in the back from **Mr Bumble**'s cane only made matters worse as the important **gentlemen** told Oliver that he would start work picking oakum at six o'clock the very next morning. **He** had no idea what this involved and **he** had no time to ask before he was taken to a large **room** where a great many **boys** all slept on hard beds with rough covers. **Oliver** cried himself to sleep.

WHOOSH

The morning after his ninth birthday, **Oliver** started work. Picking oakum was a horrible job that involved unwinding the thick, heavy **ropes** that had been used on ships until they became single strands of thread. Often the **ropes** were sticky with tar; the **children** worked long hours and ended the day with sore, tired fingers.

Oliver happened to have arrived at the **workhouse** just after a new way of feeding the inmates had been found. Having been given a free supply of water, the **Board** had decided to mix a little oatmeal with the water three times a day to make gruel. Twice a week an onion was added and on Sundays each resident was given half a bread roll. **Everyone** had become very thin and hungry, but the gentlemen of the **Board** were delighted because they were saving so much more money.

Things went on this way for six months. The **boys** ate their meals in a large, stone **hall** with a **copper** at one end in which the gruel was cooked by the **master**, who always wore a large apron. The **boys** would then line up to be given one small bowl of gruel, spooned out by one or two **women** who helped to serve the food. On some occasions the **boys** celebrated when they were given a small piece of bread to go with the gruel.

The **boys** would sit on benches at long tables to eat, licking their bowls and spoons clean and looking longingly at the **copper**. **Oliver** and the other **boys** eventually became so hungry that **one** of the larger boys started to suggest that if he did not get another bowl of gruel, he would have to eat one of the other children instead. A meeting was held, the **boys** decided that they must ask for more food, and it fell to **Oliver** to do the asking.

WHOOSH

So that evening, with the **master** in his apron and the serving **women** standing next to him, **Oliver** was pushed forward by his **friends**. Although **he** was scared, **he** was so desperate with hunger that **he** found the courage to hold up his bowl and say, '***Please, sir, I want some more.***' The **master** aimed a blow at Oliver's head with the ladle that he used to stir the gruel, then pinned his arms behind him until **Mr Bumble** arrived.

The gentlemen of the **Board** were involved in a very serious discussion when the **Beadle** burst through the door in great excitement informing them, '***Oliver Twist has asked for more!***' There was pandemonium; **Oliver** was locked up alone and a poster was stuck to the **gate** of the **workhouse** the very next morning offering a reward of five pounds to anyone who would take the boy as an apprentice.

WHOOSH

Follow-up activities

* Through shared discussion, review the facts of Oliver's life which have been learnt from the Whoosh. List them.
* Governed by the Poor Law, workhouses were a compulsory provision which each parish had to make for its homeless, unemployed and orphans. In 1833, with growing concern about workhouse conditions, a Poor Law Commission was set up to investigate the issue nationwide. Many workhouse inhabitants, including children, were interviewed as part of this.

    Pair pupils, with one pupil working in role as an interviewer and the other working in role as Oliver. Using the list of facts generated as a result of the Whoosh, role play an interview with the intention of obtaining accurate facts about Oliver's life. Although feelings will enter into the interviews, particularly about hunger, pupils need to be aware that expectations were very different at the time when Dickens was writing. Many thousands of children were orphaned and hungry and even more children started work when they were very young so children like Oliver would not have expected anything better.
* Conclude with a class discussion about the historical and social context of *Oliver Twist* with regard to life in the workhouse for orphaned children.
* As an additional challenge, older pupils could write in role as a journalist seeking to expose the treatment of workhouse inhabitants.

Fagin's Den

Objective

* to consider the historical and social context of a novel.

Characters	Objects	Sounds
Oliver	streets	sausages sizzling
Mr Jack Dawkins aka the Artful Dodger	shops	box lid slamming
homeless children	building where Fagin lived	laughter
Fagin	room	splashing water
four or five dirty children	table	street noise
Charley Bates	fire	'Stop thief! Stop thief!'
boys in the street	candle	
market stall sellers	trap door	
old gentleman	small box	
police officer	shop windows	
crowd	market stalls	
	court	

After walking for several days, **Oliver** finally arrived in London, immediately falling into company with a **Mr Jack Dawkins**, who kindly offered to show him somewhere to stay. As **Oliver** was led through the **streets** of London, he looked around. The **streets** were narrow and very muddy, with horrible smells everywhere. There were a lot of small **shops** and Oliver wondered whether he had ever seen quite so many **children** as there were trying to sleep in the doorways.

Eventually, they arrived at a dark **building**. **Oliver** climbed the dirty and broken stairs, trying to feel the wall with one hand while **Jack Dawkins** pulled him by his other hand. The **room** which he was taken into was black with dirt. There was a **table** in front of a **fire** and one **candle**, stuck in a beer bottle, giving light. A shrivelled old **man** was standing in front of the **fire** toasting bread while a frying pan full of sausages **sizzled**. Four or five dirty **boys** were sitting around the **table**.

Along the walls of the room were several beds made of nothing but sacks. The only colour in the room came from a great many silk handkerchiefs which were hanging over a clothes horse to dry.

WHOOSH

Oliver was introduced to the old man as **Fagin**, who bowed low, took Oliver's hand and said he hoped that he would get to know Oliver much better. Laughing, the other **boys** then shook both his hands very hard – one **boy** took his cap to hang up, **one** checked Oliver's pockets in case he was too tired to empty them himself and **they** all wanted to help him put down the tiny bundle which he was carrying.

Their helpfulness was brought to a halt by **Fagin** hitting the **boys** over their heads with the toasting fork. **Oliver** was given some toast, some sausages and a drink of gin and water. It was not long before **he** fell asleep in front of the **fire** and he was gently lifted onto one of the sack beds.

WHOOSH

When **Oliver** slowly started to wake up the next morning, the **room** was empty apart from the **old man**, who was making himself some coffee. Then, checking that Oliver was still asleep, the **old man** lifted a **trap door** in the floor and brought out a small **box**. While **Oliver** watched through half closed eyes, **Fagin** took out a gold watch, followed by rings, bracelets and other pieces of gold jewellery. **He** turned them over in his hands, admiring them and smoothing them.

As **his** eyes wandered around the room, **he** suddenly noticed that **Oliver** was watching him. As quick as a flash, **Fagin** slammed down the lid of the **box**, grabbed the bread knife from the table and started to shout at Oliver. '*I am very sorry if I disturbed you, sir*,' whispered the terrified **child**, at which **Fagin** seemed to calm down. Putting the knife down, **he** showed **Oliver** where to wash his face and hands, then how to throw the water out of the window when he had finished.

Hardly had **he** eaten breakfast than **Jack Dawkins**, who was apparently better known as the Artful Dodger, returned with **Charley Bates**, one of the other boys whom Oliver had met the night before. For some reason which **Oliver** could not understand, the **boys** gave **Fagin** some silk handkerchiefs and a couple of wallets, which **Oliver** could only assume they had made – an assumption that reduced the **boys** to helpless laughter.

Then a game followed, in which **Fagin** walked up and down the **room** with a pocket handkerchief hanging out of his pocket while the **Artful Dodger** and his **friend** tried to steal it without Fagin knowing. It was **Oliver**'s turn to be reduced to laughter as **Fagin** pretended to peer into **shop windows**, walking around the room with a stick like an old man and constantly tapping his pockets to make sure that he had not been robbed.

After the game had been played a great many times, the **boys** went out again, apparently, Oliver was told, to go back to work. Then it was **Oliver**'s turn to play the game and **he** removed the handkerchief so quickly and carefully that **Fagin** did not even realise it was gone. '*You're a clever boy, my dear*,' said **Fagin**, patting Oliver on the head, '*If you go on like this, you will be the greatest man of the time*.' **Oliver** was not sure how the handkerchief game could ever make him great, but he thought it best not to ask.

WHOOSH

For several days, **Oliver** stayed in one **room** with **Fagin** while the other **boys** went to work. **He** was shown how to pick marks out of the great many silk handkerchiefs that the boys brought home and **he** played the game regularly both with **Fagin** and the other **boys**.

Eventually **he** started longing to be outside and **he** pleaded with **Fagin** to let him go to work with the others. This became particularly important to **Oliver** after he saw the **boys** come home one day with nothing and watched them go to bed without any food. Then one day, after there had been no handkerchiefs for two or three days, **Fagin** decided to let **Oliver** go out with the **Artful Dodger** and **Charley Bates**.

Oliver enjoyed the noise and bustle of the market **stalls**, but **he** was quite worried to see that the **Artful Dodger** had a nasty habit of pulling caps from the heads of smaller **boys** and throwing them away. **Charley** had an even nastier habit of stealing apples and onions from the roadside **stalls**. **They** were just at the end of a narrow lane when the **Artful Dodger** stopped. '*Do you see that old man over at the book stall?*' he asked. '*He'll do.*'

The old **gentleman** looked very respectable. **He** had picked up a book from the stall which he had become completely engrossed in reading. From a distance, **Oliver** watched in alarm as the **Artful Dodger** crept up behind the **gentleman**, slipped his hand into his pocket and pulled out a silk handkerchief. Then **Charley** and the **Artful Dodger** were off round the corner before the old **gentleman** could even realise that he had been robbed.

'*Stop thief! Stop thief!*' **everyone** started to shout. In his fear and confusion, **Oliver** started to run after the **Artful Dodger**, but because **he** could not run as fast and the **crowd** grew quickly, **Oliver** soon found himself lying face down in the mud. **He** was pulled roughly to his feet by a **police officer**. '*It wasn't me, sir. Indeed, it was two other boys.*' **Oliver** pleaded. '*They are here somewhere.*' But he was not believed and when the old **gentleman** agreed that this was the child who had robbed him, **Oliver**'s legs gave way beneath him.

Seizing him by the collar of his jacket, the **police officer** dragged **Oliver** along the street towards the **court** house. **They** were accompanied by the **old gentleman** who pleaded with the officer not to hurt the poor child. As they walked, other **boys** jeered at Oliver and some of the people in the **crowd** stared as he was taken away.

WHOOSH

Follow-up activities

*   This activity seeks to explore the thoughts of the characters (principally Oliver) at key points in the Whoosh. Divide pupils into six groups and give one of the following scenarios to each group.
    *   Oliver meeting Fagin and the boys
    *   Oliver seeing Fagin's treasure
    *   Oliver learning the game
    *   Oliver at the scene of the robbery
    *   The Artful Dodger at the scene of the robbery
    *   The old man at the scene of the robbery.
*   In each case, the aim is to create a thought collage. To do this, one pupil takes the role of the key character (i.e. Oliver, the Artful Dodger or the old man) and stands in silence. The other members of the group position themselves around the character and each person speaks a thought which the character might be having. For example, when Oliver is first introduced to the Fagin and the boys, he will be thinking about what he sees, the smell of the food, the oddity of his position, the unusual friendship that he is being shown and an awareness of his own weariness. Each person in the group speaks their thoughts randomly as many times as they wish, creating a collage. Sometimes just one person may be speaking and sometimes several people will be. Encourage groups to experiment with varied tones of voice from whispering to shouting, depending on context.
*   Perform the collages as a sequence.
*   Through shared discussion, define what has been learnt about the historical and social context of street gangs in Victorian times.

6   Charles Dickens: *Great Expectations*

Great Expectations, published between 1860 and 1861, is set in Kent. Pip, the protagonist, recounts his story, starting at the age of seven. Although initially happy enough with his life and future prospects as a blacksmith, this changes after encountering Estella and her adoptive mother, the wealthy Miss Havisham. The novel reflects the social divide of Victorian society and traces the fictional life of a character who becomes committed to his own social mobility at the expense of his caring family.

The Whoosh is centred around Pip's visits to Miss Havisham and the self-realisation that results from his conversations, in particular the comments that Estella makes about him. The way in which Pip sees and values himself and his family changes as a result of this. The Whoosh encourages pupils to consider how we value people and the judgements that we make about each other based on our values.

Pip meets Miss Havisham

Objective

*   to understand how a character's values influence judgement about self and others.

Characters	Objects	Sounds
Pip Uncle Pumblechook Estella Miss Havisham three lady visitors one gentleman visitor Pip's sister, Mrs Joe Joe Gargery, the blacksmith	Satis House gate locked and chained door Miss Havisham's room table stopped clock room door long table spiders mice beetles fireplace forge	door bell wind whistling knocking on the door scuttling mice

Uncle Pumblechook took **me** to **Satis House** at ten o'clock, as arranged. Who could live in such a house? It was old brick and it was very dismal. Some of the windows had been bricked up and those that remained were barred with rusty iron bars. After ringing the **bell**, we had to wait some time before a window was opened and a voice demanded, '*What name?*' A self-possessed **young lady** carrying some keys eventually came across the court yard and unlocked the huge **gate**. '*This is Pip*,' said my **Uncle** to the pretty young lady, who let me through the gate but made it clear that Uncle Pumblechook was not to follow.

Locking the **gate** behind me, the **young lady** led me across the paved courtyard. Grass grew in the cracked paving slabs and a cold wind **whistled** around the **building**. Although the **young lady** was about my age, she called me 'boy' a great deal in a tone of voice that suggested that she was grown up and a great deal better than me. The huge front **door** of the house was locked and chained, so we went into the **house** through a side door, which led into a very dark passage. '*Don't loiter, boy,*' **she** said scornfully as I followed her.

There were a great many more dark passages and stairways before we finally stopped outside of one of the doors. '*Go in,*' **she** said. Although **I** stood aside to let her enter first, **she** looked at me scornfully and turned to walk away saying, '*Don't be ridiculous, boy. I am not going in.*' I was now quite afraid, but **I knocked** on the door and heard a voice inside saying, '*Enter,*' so I opened the door and found myself in quite a large **room**. There was not a sign of any daylight, but I could see a **table** with a gold mirror in the light of the candle that lit the **room**. Resting on the **table** was the elbow of the strangest **lady** I have ever seen. **She** was sitting in an armchair and her head was leaning on her hand.

She was dressed in satin, lace and silk, all of which had once been white and there was a long yellowing veil hanging from her hair. Jewels, gloves and flowers were heaped around the mirror and several dusty old dresses half folded into trunks gave the appearance of someone packing to go away. The old **lady** may have been dressed as a bride, but to me, she looked more like the skeleton that I had once seen dug out of a church vault. The only difference was that her **eyes** followed me round. I noticed, as I looked around a little more, that both her watch and a **clock** had stopped at twenty minutes to nine.

'*Who is it?*' asked the **lady**.

'*Pip, ma'am,*' I answered, '*Mr Pumblechook's boy.*'

She asked me if I was frightened and I'm not ashamed to say that I lied. I would gladly have run away, but did not want to get into trouble with my sister. I watched as she touched her heart, uttering just one word, '*Broken!*' before slowly moving her hand back into her lap as though it was very heavy. '*Call Estella,*' she ordered next, '*Call Estella. At the door.*'

WHOOSH

I felt very uncomfortable standing in a dark corridor shouting Estella's name at the top of my voice. For a while, nothing happened, but then I saw her candle moving towards me. When **she** entered the room, **Miss Havisham** beckoned to her and told her to play cards with me. '*With this common labouring boy?*' sneered **Estella**. As **she** dealt the cards, I had a chance to look around again. **Miss Havisham** was wearing just one shoe, with the other abandoned on the dressing table. The shoe was yellowing with age, but it had clearly never been worn.

'*What coarse hands he has,*' said **Estella** during the first game. '*And what thick boots!*' I had never looked at my hands before, but I did now. I had never thought of being ashamed of them, but now they seemed to me very inferior. **Estella** won the game and seemed to be waiting for me to do something wrong; when I misdealt the cards, she sneered, '*Stupid, clumsy boy.*'

Miss Havisham, observing that Estella had said plenty about me, asked me what I thought of her. '*I think she is very proud,*' I whispered, '*and very pretty.*' I noticed her looking at me with disgust, '*I think she is very insulting and I should like to go home,*' I ended. When we finished the next game, **Miss Havisham** told me to return in six days, then told **Estella** to take me downstairs and give me something to eat.

We went into the courtyard. '*Wait here, you boy,*' ordered **Estella**, before disappearing into the house. I took the opportunity to look again at my hands and my boots. They had never troubled me before, but now they seemed to me very vulgar. Then **Estella** returned with a plate of food which she put down on the ground as if I were a dog. I was so hurt that tears sprang to my eyes, which **Estella** noticed with great pleasure. **She** left me alone for a while to eat, then returned with the keys. **She** looked triumphant as she unlocked the **gate** and pushed me through it with a contemptuous laugh.

As I trudged the four miles home, I had plenty of time to reflect on how common I was and how coarse my hands and how thick my boots were. I realised how ignorant I really was.

WHOOSH

The next time I visited, **Estella** took me to a different **room**, opening the **door** and saying very rudely, '*You are to go and stand there, boy, till you are wanted.*' There were other people in the room – **three ladies** and a **gentleman**. **Their** conversation stopped when I entered and I felt very awkward as they all looked me up and down. Eventually, **Estella** returned and told me to follow her. **She** stopped suddenly in the corridor, turned to me and asked, '*Am I insulting?*'

'*Not so much as you were last time,*' I answered. In reply, **she** slapped my face hard saying, '*You coarse little monster.*' As I continued along the corridor behind her, I was determined not to let her see how badly she had hurt me.

On this visit, **Miss Havisham** took me into a different **room**. Everything was covered in dust and mould. A feast was laid out on a **long table** but it had long ago gone mouldy with age. A black, mouldy centrepiece, which **Miss Havisham** later told me had once been her wedding cake, was now full of **spiders**. I could hear **mice** scuttling around and black **beetles** crawled around the **fireplace**.

My job today, it appeared, was to walk her around the room. I was grateful that Estella was not there, but my relief was short lived when I was told to call her and **she** not only entered the room, but brought the other **visitors** with her. '*Walk me, walk me,*' commanded Miss Havisham and so we continued walking while her **visitors** tried to engage her in conversation.

Eventually **Estella** picked up a candle and **led** them away and only then did **Miss Havisham** stop walking. Stabbing at the cobwebs which hung around the wedding cake with her walking stick, **she** said with a ghastly look, '*It and I have worn away together.*' After that, **Estella** and I played several games of cards, all of which **she** won. This time as **she** unlocked the **gate**, **she** said that I may kiss her, but as I kissed her on the cheek I felt that she had allowed the coarse, common boy a kiss in exactly the same way as she would have given me money – it meant nothing.

WHOOSH

I continued to visit **Miss Havisham** when she required me to attend and **Estella** was always around. **She** would let me in and out through the locked **gate** and her moods were many; sometimes **she** was cold and superior, sometimes **she** was familiar and often **she** told me energetically that she hated me.

As time went by, I became more and more influenced by these surroundings. At home, **my sister** and **Mr Pumblechook** held endless conferences about my prospects and what Miss Havisham might be expected to do for me. **Joe** took no part in these conversations, although as **he** sat by the fire in the evenings **he** was usually told at length about my **sister**'s expectations for me. This went on for a long time until one day **Miss Havisham** said quite suddenly, '*You are growing tall, Pip. You had better be apprenticed. Would Gargery come here with you and bring your indentures?*'

This was not what I wanted at all, I pondered as I walked back to the little forge which, after all this, was going to be my only home. When I told Joe what Miss Havisham had said, my **sister** went on a rampage such as we had never seen before. I was to be nothing – nothing but a blacksmith after all. When **she** had finished screaming at Joe and me about being nothing but a doormat beneath our feet, **she** burst into tears and threw a candlestick at Joe. Then, still sobbing, **she** put on her apron, turned **Joe** and **me** out into the yard and set to cleaning every inch of the house. It was ten o'clock at night before **we** dared to venture back inside.

WHOOSH

Follow-up activities

Apart from his sister's occasional tempers, Pip had been very happy up to this point in the novel. He enjoyed helping Joe Gargery in the forge and his expectation was that he would become Joe's apprentice. But when Pip is introduced to a new social experience, he suddenly starts to assess himself against the values of Miss Havisham and Estella.

- Review Estella's comments about Pip and discuss his reaction at various points in the Whoosh. How does his view of himself change as he visits Satis House? What happens to his expectations of the future as a result? He tells Miss Havisham that he thinks Estella is proud and he knows that she is also cruel. Why does her opinion matter to him so much?
- After discussing these issues, ask pupils to construct a soliloquy – this is a literary device in which a character talks to himself and reveals thoughts and feelings which are not explicated elsewhere. Perform the soliloquys.
- Using this information and knowledge about Pip, ask pupils to write in role, creating a letter which Pip writes to his future self. To do this, write about what Pip is feeling and thinking at this point (including his perceptions about Estella and his impressions of Miss Havisham), how his expectations for his future are changing as a result and what he expects to value in himself in the future.
- Retain the letters and revisit them when the story is fully known.
- Then compare the values which Joe had implicitly taught him with the values of Estella and Miss Havisham. Which person's values should Pip have adopted and why?

7 Charlotte Brontë: *Jane Eyre*

Charlotte Brontë's best-known novel *Jane Eyre* was published in 1847 under the pen name Currer Bell. Written in the *bildungsroman* genre, it tells a story through the eyes of the orphaned Jane Eyre, tracing her life from a cruel childhood to maturity. Some aspects of the novel reflect Brontë's own experience – Lowood School, for example, is based on Brontë's first school, the conditions at which may have contributed to the death of two of her sisters from tuberculosis. Like Jane, she worked throughout her adult life as a governess and teacher.

The settings of *Jane Eyre* are very rich in detail, from the terrifying red room of Jane's childhood to the burnt out remains of Thornfield Hall to which she eventually returns. Each of the settings reflects Jane's feelings in some way as she grows to maturity. The terror of being locked in the red room stays with her for many years; the deprivations and harshness of Lowood School shape her as a woman and a teacher; Thornfield Hall has many faces, each one reflecting a key development in Jane's life.

It is the various facets and changing nature of Thornfield Hall that form the basis of this Whoosh. The four sections each describe a different aspect of the Hall, which together build a picture of the people who live there and the events that surround them. The writing is very atmospheric and there is ample opportunity for adding more sounds than just those suggested, as the bustle of the house party preparations and the eerie atmosphere of the ruined Hall are recreated.

When the Whoosh is complete, pupils are invited to consider how the author uses these contrasts of setting to reflect Jane's life and the changes in her mood and feelings as the narrative unfolds – on the morning after her arrival at Thornfield, Jane observed that, 'Externals have a great effect on the young,' and it is this which the Whoosh examines.

Objective

- to examine contrasts within a single setting, considering how setting is used to reflect mood changes in a character.

Characters	Objects		Sounds
Jane	horse	drawing room	gates clashing
driver	gates	arch	ticking clock
maid	drive	couches	cawing rooks
Mrs Fairfax	house	mirrors	busy kitchens
servants/cleaners	window	carvings	noisy servants' hall
Adele	doors	hangings	doors opening and
cook	hall	trap door	closing
Mr Rochester	Mrs Fairfax's room	fields	rain
house guests	fire	wood	
haymakers	gallery	church	
	sun	grounds	
	Jane's room	rain	
	portraits	coaching inn	
	clock	hedges	
	meadow	road	
	thorn trees	orchard wall	
	hills	stone pillars	
	Thornfield	ruins of Thornfield	
	dining room		

My arrival at Thornfield Hall (Chapter XI)

The **horse** walked very slowly and it took nearly two hours to cover the six miles between the coaching inn and Thornfield Hall. Eventually a **voice** called, '***You're noan so far fro' Thornfield now***,' so I dropped the window to look out as the **driver** got down and opened a pair of heavy **gates**. As they **clashed** shut behind us and we began to ascend the **drive**, all I could see was the long front of a **house** in darkness, except for a candle gleaming in one **window**.

But although all was darkness from the outside, once I passed through the high **doors** into the square **hall**, I was warmly welcomed into a small, snug **room**. It was occupied by a little elderly **lady** whom I took to be Mrs Fairfax. She sat in an arm chair by a cheerful **fire** and was occupied with some knitting. **She** was genuinely pleased to see me, but **I** was too tired to talk much, so after eating a sandwich, I was shown to my **room**.

I followed Mrs Fairfax as she took her candle, checked that the hall **door** was locked and led the way up an oak staircase. A high **window** and a long **gallery** from which the bedroom **doors** opened gave it the appearance of a church. The space seemed cheerless and cold – I was glad to be shown to my room.

The **sun** shone brightly through the blue **curtains** on the following morning, showing a **room** with papered walls and carpet on the floor – it was so unlike anything at Lowood that I began to expect that my future held something pleasant. As I left my room, I noticed two **portraits** in the long **gallery**, one of a severe man in armour and one of a lady with a powdered wig. A great oak **clock** was black with age and a bronze lamp hung from the high ceiling.

It was all very grand and imposing, so I was glad to step through the hall **door** to look at the outside of the three storey **building**. It was grey, with battlements around the top and surrounded by a great **meadow** full of old, strong **thorn trees** inhabited by rooks. Farther off were **hills** that seemed to surround and seclude Thornfield. It seemed a great place to live.

Seeing that I was already up and about, **Mrs Fairfax** offered to show me the inside of the house. The **dining room** was imposing, a room with purple **chairs** and **curtains**, wood panelled walls and one vast **window**. A huge **arch** separated it from the drawing room, a carpeted room with moulded grapes and vine leaves at the ceiling, crimson **couches**, and large **mirrors** between the windows. The rest of the house was equally grand, especially the front bedrooms. Some of the third floor rooms were dark and gloomy, but everywhere I went, it was decorated with oak **carvings** and rich tapestry **hangings**.

And finally, there was the view from the battlements, which was reward enough for the climb up the narrow attic stairs and the ladder to the **trap door**. I could see the land around me like a map – the **fields**, the **wood**, the **church** and the peaceful **hills**, all lit by the autumn sun. But then, on my return from the roof, the darkness and gloom of the passage suddenly struck me and it felt like a corridor in some Bluebeard's castle.

WHOOSH

The Thornfield Hall house party (Chapters XVII–XVIII)

A while after Mr Rochester's return, **Mrs Fairfax** announced that there was to be a house party. I thought the rooms at Thornfield were beautifully clean and well arranged, but **women** were brought in to scrub, wash, beat carpets, dust and polish. **Fires** were lit in all the rooms and feather beds aired and shaken.

Mr Rochester's ward, **Adele** ran quite wild around the house, jumping on the beds and lying on the mattresses and pillows which she piled up in front of the roaring **fires**. I spent all day in the storeroom helping **cook** to produce custards and pastries and tie the game birds ready for roasting.

We were all busy and happy – the work was completed the evening before the guests were due to arrive. Carpets were laid down, bed hangings draped, **tables** arranged, **furniture** dusted, flowers piled high in vases and the rooms looked as fresh and bright as we could make them. The hall and **clock** were polished to the brightness of glass, the **sideboard** in the dining room groaned under the weight of the silver and flowers bloomed on all sides.

It was a mild spring day, with summer just around the corner. It was still warm as the day drew to an end and **I** sat at work in the school room with the window open, waiting for **Mr Rochester** and his **guests** to arrive.

Life at Thornfield Hall was very different now from my first three months of solitude and monotony. All sadness and gloominess had been driven from the house and there was **life** and **movement** all day long. The **gallery** had once been hushed and empty, but now you could not enter it without meeting someone's **maid** or **valet**.

The kitchen, the pantry, the servants' and entrance halls – they were all **alive** with **people** and the **main rooms** were only empty when the blue sky and spring weather called the **guests** out into the **grounds** of the **Hall**. The enjoyment was not dampened even when continuous **rain** set in. Then the **guests** would settle to a game of charades that lasted all afternoon.

But my pleasure was short lived, as **I** was summoned to Gateshead by news of the impending death of my Aunt Reed, who, it appeared, particularly wanted to see me before she died.

WHOOSH

My return to Thornfield Hall (Chapter XXII)

It was a month before **I** was able to return to **Thornfield**, by which time the house party had dispersed. I had not told Mrs Fairfax the exact day of my return and so **I** was able to walk from the **coaching inn** to the **Hall**. It was about six o'clock in the evening when I set out along the old road to Thornfield. The road mostly lay across **fields** and **haymakers** were hard at work under a blue sky which promised well for the future. **I** stopped once or twice to enjoy the feeling that I got from knowing that I was returning.

With just another couple of **fields** to cross, I could see the **gates** of the Hall in the distance. The **hedges** were full of roses which normally I would have stopped to pick, but today I was in too much of a hurry to reach the house. And there on the stone stile by the steps sat **Mr Rochester**, writing in a book. Seeing me before I could take a different route to the house, **he** called out, '*Are you coming from Millcote and on foot? Yes, just one of your tricks, not to send for a carriage but to steal into the vicinage of your home along with twilight.*'

He had spoken of Thornfield as my home – would that it were my home! Little did I know then that in just one month's time I would look at the great closed and **locked gates** as I left the Hall. I did not know then that I would cross the **fields** again, choosing a **road** from Thornfield which I had often noticed but never travelled as I prepared to leave for ever.

WHOOSH

The end of Thornfield Hall (Chapter XXXVIII)

But it was not for ever. Summoned by **Mr Rochester**'s voice, I went back one more time. It took me thirty six hours by coach, but as we stopped to water the horses, I recognised the **hills** as part of the landscape that I loved. As Thornfield was just two miles away, I decided to walk; I could see the stile ahead of me and the **fields** through which I had run blindly on the morning that I had fled from Thornfield. And I ran now, realising that I knew nothing of Mr Rochester or the other inhabitants of the Hall.

At last I saw the **woods**, still thick with cawing **crows**. I was filled with delight as I crossed another field knowing that I would soon see the outline of my beloved **Thornfield**. I wanted to see the battlements and Mr Rochester's window, so I ran along the **wall** of the orchard, planning to turn through the **gate** from the meadow, and peep around one of the two stone **pillars** crowned with stone spheres. I moved carefully then, in case anyone inside the house should see me.

I looked nervously towards the Hall and saw nothing but a blackened **ruin**. There was no roof, no windows, no chimneys and no battlements – all had crashed in. I wandered around the shattered walls; there was nothing but the silence of death.

WHOOSH

Follow-up activities

- There are four scenes of Thornfield Hall included in this Whoosh. Group pupils, assigning one scene to each group. Ask pupils to create a coloured storyboard sequence for the setting of their scene – the number of images in the sequence will vary according to the complexity of each scene. Pupils should concentrate on setting, using evidence from Brontë's original text to shape and inform their decisions and to reflect the changing faces of Thornfield Hall.
- Images should then be annotated.
- As a further challenge, pupils could create moviemaker videos of their settings, adding music as a further enhancement.
- View storyboards and/or movies in sequence and discuss how Brontë uses contrasts of setting to reflect Jane's mood.
- Compare the storyboards with the original text, asking pupils to peer evaluate understanding.
- To complete the activity, ask pupils to write an analysis of Brontë's use of language to create settings which reflect mood.
- As an extension task, challenge pupils to repeat this activity based on the Red Room in Chapter II.

8   Sir Arthur Conan Doyle: *The Hound of the Baskervilles*

A Sherlock Holmes excerpt has been included, not only because the stories are currently *en vogue* as a result of the BBC drama series, but also because this book will have a broad appeal to teachers in all schools, both mixed and single-sex. Studying Sherlock Holmes stories not only engages students in a range of language deduction activities, but also presents a significant challenge to students' thinking and deduction skills as they attempt to solve the case before

Sherlock, or at least before Watson, does. *The Hound of the Baskervilles* is arguably one of the more famous Sherlock Holmes stories. Studying it opens up some interesting possibilities for comparisons of the various TV and film adaptations that have been made over the years.

This Whoosh is a little different to some of the others – it could be termed a 'Whoosh within a Whoosh.' It is based primarily around Dr Mortimer's visit to 221b Baker Street in Chapter 2, where he describes in detail to Holmes and Watson exactly what has been happening on the moors, both in the past and at the time of the more recent death of Sir Charles Baskerville. Each section of the Whoosh will require a Dr Mortimer, a Sherlock Holmes and a Dr Watson. Holmes and Watson are part of the first and last sections of the Whoosh, but in other sections they are merely listening to Dr Mortimer's account, so they will need to improvise reactions to what they are hearing as the Whoosh progresses. These key roles can be taken by the same students throughout, or they can be changed with each section. Others will be whooshing the various parts of Dr Mortimer's account. The narration could also be passed to the character of Dr Mortimer rather than remain with the teacher.

Objective

- to engage pupils in understanding the language of a classic text.

Characters	Objects	Sounds
Dr Mortimer Sherlock Holmes Dr Watson Hugo Baskerville neighbours the girl stable hands 13 men shepherd	Holmes' dining table sofa Baskerville Hall upstairs room Sir Hugo's dining room two stones hounds the beast	drunken carousing chaos horses' hooves a sound of hell laughter whimpering hounds

Dr Mortimer is standing in the front room of 221b Baker Street smoking, whilst **Holmes** and **Watson** are watching him, one sitting at the **dining table** and one on the **sofa**. They are clearly waiting for **Mortimer** to explain himself. **Holmes** notices that **Mortimer** is fidgeting with a piece of paper in his pocket and encourages him to take it out and tell them the purpose of his visit. **Dr Mortimer** reluctantly takes out the paper, explaining that '*This family paper was committed to my care by Sir Charles Baskerville, when he died just three months ago. I was a trusted friend as well as his doctor, you see. He was a strong-minded man, perceptive and practical with very little imagination, yet he took this document very seriously and his mind was prepared for just such an end as did eventually overtake him.*' **Dr Mortimer** tails off as **Holmes** stretches out his hand for the old manuscript and flattens it out on his knee. **Watson** looks over his shoulder, reading '*Baskerville Hall, 1742*' under his breath. **Dr Mortimer** desperately explains to them both that there is a hugely important matter regarding this document that must be settled within 24 hours, imploring them to listen to his account of the situation. **Holmes** leans back on the **sofa**, places his fingertips together and closes his eyes, indicating that **Mortimer** should continue.

WHOOSH

Sir Hugo, said **Mortimer** to his listeners, owned **Baskerville Hall**. It was a dark, brooding house, matched well to its wild and untameable owner. Such was his reputation that even his own **neighbours** whispered about him behind his back. **He** fell in love with the **daughter** of a rich merchant who held lands near the Baskerville estate, but the **girl**, scared by his bad behaviour, kept her distance and eventually would avoid **him** whenever **he** sought her company. One day in late September, when her father and brothers were working away from home, **Hugo** and **six** of his henchmen raided her home and kidnapped the **girl**. When they arrived back at **Baskerville Hall** she was locked in an **upstairs room** whilst **Hugo** and his **men** enjoyed a loud, drunken dinner. Hearing the noise from the **dining room**, the **girl** became terrified and started to look for a means of escape. **She** soon found that the wall underneath her window was covered in ivy so **she** climbed down it, quaking with fear that she would be discovered. When **she** reached the ground, **she** began to run in the direction of her father's house.

WHOOSH

A little time later, **Hugo** left his **friends** carousing in the **dining room** and took some food and drink upstairs to his prisoner. **His** anger at discovering her absence was indescribable; suffice to say it gave credence to some of the things his neighbours had said of him. **He** burst back into the **dining room** and leapt up on to the table scattering plates and cups everywhere, leaving his **guests** diving for cover. **He** bellowed '*With you all as my witnesses, I will surrender my body and soul to every Power of Evil if I can but recapture this wench.*' Despite their friendship, his **guests** were horrified at the extent to which **Hugo** was willing to go to get his own way. All, that is, except one who stumbled forward suggesting that the **hounds** of the manor should be sent out to find her. At this suggestion, **Hugo** ran to the stables, shouting for his **grooms** to saddle his horse and unleash the **hounds** from their kennel. He gave the **dogs** the scent with a handkerchief that the girl had dropped in her hurry to escape and the whole evil band galloped away over the moors.

WHOOSH

This happened so fast that Hugo's **guests** were left standing around the dining table, shocked into silence by what they had witnessed. But as the shock slowly subsided, they realised what was about to happen out on the moor. Then there was uproar as the **men** ran about, **some** shouting for the horses while **some** looked for pistols and other weapons. Eventually, all **thirteen** of them set off in pursuit of **Hugo** and the **hounds**. **They** had barely gone a mile when they came across one of the night **shepherds** with his dog and they stopped to ask him whether he had seen the dogs. He was almost speechless with fear but at last managed to stammer, '*I saw her, a girl, and then the hounds almost on her. They were followed by Hugo Baskerville on his black mare.*' The men started to move on, but the shepherd continued, '*and behind him there was such a hound of hell as God forbid should ever be at my heels.*' **They** laughed at this ridiculous claim and rode on over the moor, but when they were met by Hugo's riderless and terrified horse, they shuddered as they remembered the words. Riding a little closer to each other, they expressed relief that they were together; had they been alone there is no doubt that they would have turned back.

WHOOSH

On **they** rode, watching closely for **Hugo**, imagining that he had been thrown from his horse. Eventually they came upon the **hounds** who, despite having been chosen for their fearlessness, were clustered together and whimpering on the edge of a deep dip in the moor. **Some** were slinking around the pack and **others** growling with their hackles raised as **they** looked along the valley in front of them.

The **men** drew their horses to a stop. The **three** boldest of them rode on, seeing that the valley opened out into a broad space with two great **stones** in the middle of it. Between the **stones** was the **girl**, unconscious with fear and fatigue. It was not **her** body, nor that of **Hugo Baskerville** lying near her, which scared the men the most. It was the fact that standing over **Hugo**'s body was a great black **beast**, shaped like a hound yet larger than any hound they had ever seen. As **they** watched, frozen in terror, the **beast** ripped out **Hugo**'s throat and turned to them with blazing eyes. The three **men** shrieked in fear, turning their horses and riding for their lives. **They** were followed closely by the other ten **men** who, although having seen nothing, sensed their friends' fear.

WHOOSH

After concluding the story, **Dr Mortimer** looks up from the paper, '*It is said that one of the men died that night, and the other two were never sane again. The hound is said to have plagued the family ever since, with many of their deaths having been sudden, bloody and mysterious.*' **Mortimer** pushes his glasses up his forehead and looks expectantly at **Holmes**. **Holmes** yawns and tosses his cigarette butt into the fire.

'*Well?*' asks Mortimer. '*Do you not find it interesting?*'

'*Yes, to a collector of fairy tales,*' scoffs **Holmes**, trying not to smirk. **Dr Mortimer** seems unmoved by this reaction, merely drawing another piece of paper out of his pocket, which **Watson** leans forward to read. It is a recent newspaper article from the Devon County Chronicle.

This seems to capture **Holmes**' interest as **Mortimer** explains that it is about the death of Sir Charles Baskerville. He had only lived at Baskerville Hall for a short time before his death and he had been well loved by those around him.

Readjusting his glasses, **Mortimer** begins to read the public facts surrounding the death. The coroner had decreed that there were no suspicious circumstances, with servants and friends giving evidence that pointed toward a heart problem. **Dr Mortimer** looks up from the paper and, seeing both **Holmes** and **Watson** utterly intrigued by what he is reading, continues.

WHOOSH

Follow-up activities

- Complete the reading of the story in its original text.
- Challenge students to write their own Whoosh. This can be based either on the newspaper article describing Sir Charles' last moments or the conversation that follows it between Mortimer and Holmes, in which Mortimer describes that evening in his own words.
- Both of these scenarios are suitable to whooshing and the activity would help pupils develop their understanding both of the characters and of the language and setting of the story.

9   Mary Shelley: *Frankenstein*

The epistolary novel, *Frankenstein*, was published in 1818 and was the result of a competition between Mary Shelley, Percy Bysshe Shelley, Lord Byron and John Polidori to write the best horror story. It is credited with influencing the growth and popularity of the horror story genre.

It is written in three distinct parts – the central narrative, written by Victor Frankenstein after his rescue at the North Pole, tells the sad story of his life. This is framed on either side by letters from Captain Walton to his sister Margaret Walton Saville which provide an introduction and conclusion to the narrative. Captain Walton is exploring the North Pole when he finds and rescues Victor Frankenstein. The overarching meta-narrative lends itself to the Whoosh format, as it allows pupils to see the three sections as separate entities, with the first and third sections framing the central narrative. This Whoosh focuses on the first section, allowing the finale to be written by students as a follow-up activity.

For the purposes of this Whoosh, the teacher/narrator acts as the voice of the letters. Whether the person playing Walton is changed with each section or whether that actor stays the same throughout is one decision to be made. There is also an option for the seated, writing Walton to get up and involve himself with the action of the Whoosh; alternatively, he could merely sit and observe, with his part played by another actor. For an added level of complexity a pupil could act the part of Mrs Saville showing her responses to what Walton is writing.

Objective

- to explore the tripartite structure of a novel.

Characters	Objects	Sounds
Mrs Saville Captain Walton ship's lieutenant ship's master ship's crew a giant a stranger	a room in Walton's house ship ice fields ice-bound ship anchor dog-sledge ice sheets cabin deck stove	breeze gale-force winds breaking mast eerie silence cracking ice gnashing teeth

Part 1: Captain Walton's introduction

A **man** is sitting at a table in his **room**, writing a letter to his sister. He describes the cold, northern **breeze** in the streets of Peterborough that gives him a taste of what is to come at the North Pole. The dangers of the journey are overcome in his mind by his excitement about his forthcoming trip. After reflecting on the fact that he will not return to his homeland for months or perhaps even years, he describes how he has hired a **ship** and has started to employ courageous, dependable people to sail it. He is sad, however, that he has yet to find a real friend with whom to share his trip.

He describes various of his men, including his **lieutenant** who is exceedingly brave and desperate for glory and recognition. The **master** of the ship is a gentle, mild man who is so friendly to everyone he meets that he will not even hunt because he hates pointless killing. He is also hugely generous, but, after a failed engagement (where he not only released his fiancée to marry someone else but gave them money to start their new life) he has spent his entire life on a ship and knows little of the real world or society around him.

WHOOSH

In another letter, **he** describes how they have sailed through ice fields and gale-force winds which have moved them towards the North Pole far quicker than they were expecting. The **men** are bonding well, particularly through some difficult situations such as the **mast breaking**, but nothing significant has happened to challenge the expedition.

That was, however, until one particular day when the **ice** surrounded the **ship** and she could barely move any more. There was a thick fog in the air, which made visibility very poor and created an eerie silence. **They** lowered the **anchor** to wait for the fog to clear, but when it did, all they could see was **ice**. In every direction, as far as the eye could see, were huge, irregular plains of **ice** which seemed to have no end. Some of the **sailors** were upset by the sight, and **Walton** describes how he himself was starting to panic, when **they** were suddenly distracted by the appearance of a low carriage, fixed on a **sledge** and drawn by **dogs**, about half a mile ahead of them. There was a flurry of activity on the boat as the **men** grabbed their telescopes to see that there was a **giant** of a man sitting on the sledge holding the dogs' reins. They watched the curious sight until it disappeared into the mist and fog that was rolling back in on their **ship**.

WHOOSH

There was huge excitement amongst the **men**. They were hundreds of miles from any land that they knew of, so who was this **giant person**? Why was he there? Was there anyone else out there with him? The excitement generated such discussion amongst the **men** that two hours passed before anyone noticed that the **ship** was moving on the tide. This movement turned their attention to the **ship**, and before nightfall, the **ice** had **cracked** enough for them to drift at **anchor**. As it was already dark, **they** decided to stay put for the night – the **ice fields** were cracking into large **sheets** of **ice** that could still sink the ship if struck in the wrong way.

Walton goes on to describe how, when he emerged from his **cabin** the next morning, he saw the rest of the **crew** gathered at one side of the **ship**, leaning over the rail. When **he** joined them, he saw that they were looking at a **sledge** similar to the one which they had seen the day before, drifting towards them on a block of ice. Only one dog was still attached to the reins, but a **man** seemed to be resisting joining the men on the **ship**. As **Walton** approached, the **master** stepped back from the group, saying '***Here is our captain and he will not allow you to perish on the open sea.***'

WHOOSH

As the **man** looked up from the broken **sledge**, he spoke, '***Before I come on board your vessel, can you please tell me where you are going?***' **Walton** admits to being surprised that a man who was clearly suffering had the presence of mind to even ask rather than just accept help, but once **he** explained that they were on a voyage to the North Pole the **stranger** willingly boarded the **ship**.

He had clearly been out on the **ice** all night; his limbs were frozen, and his body was so emaciated by fatigue that **he** passed out as soon as he was carried into the **cabin**. The **crew** carried him back into the fresh air of the **deck** and dosed him with brandy to bring him round. Once **he** had regained consciousness, **they** wrapped him in blankets and moved him near the **stove** to warm up. **Walton** writes that the **man** did not speak for two days and that they were starting to worry about his mental state. **Walton** tended to him personally, describing how **his** eyes were wild and even showed occasional flashes of madness. However, as soon as someone did something for him or was kind to him, they glowed with appreciation and his whole face lit up. His general mood, though, was one of melancholy and the **man** often **gnashed** his teeth as if he were in the depths of despair about something in his life.

When the **man** had recovered a little, **Walton** found himself having to act as a barrier between him and the **crew** who were desperate to question him and get to know him further. But Walton judged that his mental state was still too fragile for such an inquisition. One day, however, the **lieutenant** had struck up a conversation with the strange guest. '**Why had you travelled so far on the ice in such a small sledge?**' he asked.

'**To seek someone who had fled from me,**' the **stranger** replied.

'**This person who ran away ... did he travel in the same way?**' asked the **lieutenant**, realisation dawning in his eyes.

'**Yes, why?**'

'**Then we have seen him, I think, in the distance the day before we found you.**' The **stranger** brightened up suddenly, asking a great many questions about what they had seen and holding the rapt attention of the **crew**.

WHOOSH

Once the **crew** had returned to their work, **Walton** was left alone with the stranger. '**I can see that you are curious,**' said the **stranger** to Walton, '**but you are too nice to question me further.**' The **men** talked, hedging around the unasked questions, but the **stranger** eventually asked the question he has clearly been pondering since he talked to the lieutenant. '**Do you think that the other sledge would have been damaged like mine was when the ice broke up?**' **Walton** writes that he answered in a very noncommittal way, hoping that the other person may have reached safety before the ice broke.

After that chat, the **stranger** seemed very keen to be up on **deck** as much as possible, watching for the sleigh, despite **Walton**'s protestations that he was still too weak. **Walton** commanded one of his **men** to keep an eye out for the sledge, which seemed to pacify the stranger. Despite the continuing, brooding silence, **Walton** writes of his growing companionship with the stranger, feeling pity for his obvious grief and worry. As time goes on, **Walton** increasingly describes how amiable his **guest** is, gentle and wise with a highly educated mind and an exceedingly eloquent vocabulary.

WHOOSH

As soon as **he** was allowed, **he** spent all of his days on deck as a lookout for the other sledge. The **men** chatted amiably as **he** watched, discussing all manner of things from Walton's history to the point of the trip.

When **Walton** brought up his desire for a real friend on the trip rather than just his colleagues in the crew, the **stranger** grew quiet before saying sadly, '**I agree with you in believing that friendship is not only a desirable but a possible acquisition. I once had a friend, the most noble of human creatures and am entitled, therefore, to judge respecting friendship. You have hope, and the world before you, and no cause for despair. But I ... I have lost everything and cannot begin life anew.**' **Walton** was so saddened by his obvious distress that he brought the conversation to an end, although he still observed from a distance how moved this stranger was by the nature around him.

The following day, the **stranger** approached Walton and asked if he might share his story ...

WHOOSH

Follow-up activities

- The concluding section of the novel acts as a frame narrative with the introductory letter. Read Captain Walton's concluding letter in which he recounts the death of Victor Frankenstein, the discovery of the monster mourning the death and his decision to allow the monster to die by his own hand rather than be killed as Frankenstein had requested.
- Challenge pupils to write their own Whooshes based on this concluding section.
- Through shared discussion, define the effectiveness of the novel's tripartite structure, and its effect on the reader.

- Working in role as Mrs Saville, ask pupils to write return letters to Captain Walton showing her reactions to his adventures. This can also be used to assess pupils' understanding of the story.

10 George Eliot: *Silas Marner: The Weaver of Raveloe*

George Eliot published this, her third novel, in 1861. It tells the story of a weaver called Silas Marner, who leaves his home town in the north of England after begin falsely accused of theft by his best friend. He settles in a Midlands village called Raveloe where he becomes a virtual recluse, spending all his time weaving fine cloth and hoarding the gold which he earns from his work.

One night his gold is stolen and he is completely desolate. But he later finds an abandoned child in his house and decides to bring her up himself, naming her Eppie after his mother and sister. He becomes part of his community again and hope is restored to him, along with his gold which is found sixteen years later. It had been stolen by Dunstan, the worthless son of Squire Cass. Events unfold quickly as the older son, Godfrey, confesses to his childless wife that Eppie is actually his daughter from an earlier marriage which he had hidden after his drug-addicted wife was found dead. He expects to be able to reclaim Eppie, but finds instead that she sees the man who brought her up as her real father, not the man who denied her existence to avoid social disgrace. She would rather be the poor daughter of a weaver who loves her than the rich daughter of a squire who has behaved so badly.

This Whoosh contrasts Squire Cass and Silas Marner as parents. In one respect, the comparison is straightforward as both men raise children alone, without the support of the children's mothers. But socially there is no similarity – the Squire is a rich landowner with status, whilst Marner becomes poor after the theft, living in a rented cottage with nothing other than his skill as a weaver to feed and clothe himself and Eppie.

Objective

- to compare and contrast the role of parents in a novel, drawing parallels with contemporary life.

Characters	Objects	Sounds
Squire Cass Dunstan Cass Godfrey Cass two other sons villagers Mr Bryce other riders at the hunt Silas Marner Silas's neighbours Dolly Winthrop Eppie Eppie's mother guests at the New Year's Eve party doctor crowd Miss Nancy Lammeter Aaron Winthrop	church Red House stables pub door Snuff, a brown spaniel cottage Wildfire hounds fence fire party weaving loom	horses' hooves hunting horn party church bells weaving loom

Squire Cass was the most important man in the village of Raveloe. He lived opposite the **church** in the **Red House**, a large building with an impressive flight of stone steps to the front door and **stables** behind the house. But although his home was big, the Squire spent more time in the **pub** than he did at home. His wife had died many years ago, his home was disorganised and he had not really cared properly for his four **sons**. As a result, **they** had all turned out rather badly. The **people** of the village were not often critical, but they did wonder why the Squire allowed all his sons to be so lazy, particularly his second son, **Dunstan**, a spiteful young man who was given to drinking and gambling. The eldest son, **Godfrey**, who would one day inherit the estate, used to be a good-natured young man, but recently **he** had become quite bitter and withdrawn. **People** were beginning to wonder if he was following in Dunstan's footsteps, in which case he would lose the chance to marry Nancy Lammeter.

One afternoon, **Godfrey** was standing in front of the fire looking particularly anxious. As the **door** opened and **Dunstan** walked in, **Godfrey**'s face seemed to change from anxiety to hatred and even **Snuff**, his brown spaniel, retreated to hide under a chair.

'*Well, what do you want with me?*' mocked **Dunstan**. '*You're my elder, you know, so I had to come when you sent for me.*'

'*What I want,*' answered **Godfrey** savagely, '*is the hundred pounds that I lent you. You know what the Squire threatened if you ever made off with his money again.*'

'*Oh,*' sneered **Dunstan** in return. '*Suppose you get the money yourself and save me the trouble.*' At this **Godfrey** clenched his fist and threatened to hit his brother but **Dunstan** turned away with a laugh saying, '*No you won't. I might tell the Squire about that nice young woman you married.*' Realising that he had won the argument, **Dunstan** began to torment **Godfrey**, suggesting that he should borrow the money or sell his favourite horse.

Eventually, tired of being blackmailed, **Godfrey** gave up. '*I may as well tell the Squire everything myself,*' he complained. '*I should get you off my back, if I got nothing else.*' Seeing that he had pushed Godfrey too far, **Dunstan** threw himself into a chair and waited. It was not long before **Godfrey** decided that selling his horse was preferable to telling the Squire the truth and then either having to work for a living or become a soldier. A deal was agreed – Dunstan would sell the horse the following day and pay the Squire the money.

As **Dunstan** slammed the door behind him, **Snuff** came out of hiding, expecting a pat from his owner. But **Godfrey** merely pushed his pet aside with his leg and went to the **pub**.

WHOOSH

As **Dunstan** set off on horseback the following morning, he passed the **cottage** of the weaver, Silas Marner. It suddenly occurred to him that the man was supposed to have a hoard of gold. Maybe Godfrey could scare the weaver into lending him some of it. But any further thoughts of gold were driven out of his head by the negotiations to sell the horse. **Wildfire** was well known and much admired in Raveloe and **Dunstan** struck a good deal with **Mr Bryce**, one of the hunters, agreeing to accept £120 when **Wildfire** was delivered to **stables** in the neighbouring village later that day.

What **Dunstan** should have done next, of course, was to ride the horse straight to its new stable. But **Wildfire** was such a fine horse that **he** decided to join the hunt for a while and enjoy the admiring looks of the other **riders**. The **horn** sounded the start and off **he** rode, following the **hounds** and the other **riders**. It was only when **he** tried to take a **fence** too fast to catch up with the **hounds** that were streaming away into the distance that tragedy struck. **Wildfire** fell onto a stake, rolled over and died.

Fortunately, nobody had seen the accident, but **Dunstan** was annoyed about having to walk home. It was only when **he** passed the weaver's **cottage** that **he** remembered the gold – the answer to all his problems. Who would know? **He** looked carefully into the cottage but Marner was nowhere to be seen. His dinner was cooking over the bright, warm **fire**, so obviously he was not far away. The **cottage** was simple and it took just a few minutes to examine the floor, see the patch of sand with handprints in it, brush away the sand and find the gold. His problems were over. **He** grabbed the bag and rushed out into the darkness.

WHOOSH

The next day, the village was alight with news of the robbery – **people** could talk about little else. Most of the **villagers** found time to visit the weaver's **cottage** near the Stone Pits if only to look pityingly at the ghostly figure of **Silas Marner**. **Godfrey** went too, just out of curiosity. Dunstan had not returned home, but **Godfrey** was not worried, assuming that he had decided to spend the night at an inn, rather than walk home in the dark.

It was not until **Mr Bryce** called out to him, '*Well that's a lucky brother of yours,*' that **Godfrey** realised there was anything wrong. Out came the whole story – how the deal was agreed, how Dunstan had decided to ride with the hunt and how **Wildfire** had been found dead much later in the day when someone noticed that Dunstan was missing.

'*He couldn't have been hurt*,' added **Mr Bryce** optimistically, '*for he must have walked off.*'

'*Hurt?*' said Godfrey bitterly. '*He'll never be hurt – he's made to hurt other people.*' There was nothing for it – **Godfrey** would have to tell the Squire everything.

As Dunstan had still not come home, **he** decided to confess during breakfast the following morning, although **he** stopped short of mentioning his unfortunate marriage. The **Squire** was first shocked, then angry. '*I've been too good a father to you all – that's what it is.*'

'*Quite the opposite,*' mused **Godfrey**, keeping the thought to himself, '*some rules and some discipline might have saved us from this.*'

WHOOSH

Christmas arrived and with it the promise of parties and dances. Dunstan had not returned. Silas's money had not been found. Life in the village had returned to normal. A few of Silas's **neighbours**, in particular **Dolly Winthrop**, had tried to befriend him but **he** grieved for his gold and worked even harder at his loom. **He** had developed a strange habit of opening his door and looking out from time to time, as if he expected to see his money somewhere. That is what **he** was doing, lost in thought for a long time, on New Year's Eve.

It was only when **he** closed his door and went to sit down by the **fire** that he realised that he was not alone. Curled up on the floor, fast asleep, was a little golden-haired **child**. It only took a few minutes to find her **mother** but what he found sent **Silas** rushing to the **Red House**, even though a **party** was in full swing.

'*How's this? What's this? What do you do coming in here this way?*' demanded the **Squire** angrily.

'*I'm come for the doctor. I need the doctor. It's a woman. She's dead, I think – dead in the snow at the Sand Pits – not far from my door.*'

The **doctor** rushed off, closely followed by **Godfrey**. **He** had recognised the **child** in Silas's arms as his daughter. Was his wife really dead? Could he be so fortunate?

WHOOSH

Several of the **ladies** tried to take the **child**, but **Silas** hugged her close saying, '*It's come to me. I've a right to keep it. It's a lone thing – and I'm a lone thing.*' Nobody argued further. The child's **mother** was, indeed, lying dead in the snow. And she was Godfrey's wife. **He** managed to remove her wedding ring without being noticed by the gathering **crowd**.

Dunstan was missing. His wife was dead. What should **he** do about the **child**? Would her life be happy if her father did not own her? '*I'll see that she is cared for,*' he thought to himself. '*I will do my duty but my life will certainly be happier if I do not own her as my daughter.*'

So, once again, life in Raveloe returned to normal. Dunstan never came home. The church bells rang when **Godfrey** married **Miss Nancy Lammeter** and **he** eventually became the Squire. The only sadness in his life now was the death of their only child. **Silas** named his daughter **Eppie** after his mother and his sister and **he** loved her dearly. **She** made many demands of Silas's time and energy as she grew, but where his gold had made him weave harder and harder, **Eppie** called him away from his loom. **They** were often seen picking flowers near the Sand Pits or sitting on the bank and listening to birds.

He began to think of the other **villagers** as his neighbours and **Dolly Winthrop**, in particular, became a great help. When she was about three years old, **Eppie** started to discover ways of causing mischief. **Silas** decided that while **he** was working, **he** would tie her to his **loom** with a long piece of linen so that **she** could play near him without getting into trouble. **Silas** started work and **Eppie**'s chatter was drowned in the noise of the **loom**. Unseen by her father, **Eppie** reached out for the scissors, cut the tie and toddled out of the door into the sunshine. How **he** panicked when he noticed her missing. How frantically **he** searched all places that they went together, all the time fearing that she had fallen into the Stone Pits and drowned. And where was **Eppie**? Sitting in a hole using one of her boots to pour out water and make mud. **Silas** tried hard to punish her after this, but **she** even thought being shut in the coal house was some sort of game. So eventually, **Silas** brought her up without punishment.

WHOOSH

For sixteen years, life passed happily for **Silas** and **Eppie** as she grew into a fine and beautiful young woman. **Aaron Winthrop** built Eppie a garden and **Silas** took to sitting in it in the evenings to smoke a pipe. Nothing, it seemed, could disturb their happiness. Until, that is, the skeleton of Dunstan Cass was found deep in the Sand Pits, along with Silas's gold.

Distraught at the memories that Dunstan's crime recalled, **Godfrey** confessed to his wife that **Eppie** was his child. **Nancy** cried for a while, but felt that her husband should do his duty. '*So we can take Eppie now*,' he smiled, '*I won't mind the world knowing at last.*' They set off to visit Silas Marner straight away. Finding **Silas** and **Eppie** alone, **Godfrey** wasted little time in telling them why he was visiting. '*We should like*,' **he** announced, '*to have somebody in the place of a daughter to us – we should like to have Eppie.*' **Silas** started to shake violently, but before he could speak, **Eppie** had already answered, '*Thank you, sir, but I can't leave my father, nor own anybody nearer than him.*'

'*I've a claim on you, Eppie*,' **Godfrey** responded angrily. '*It's my duty, Marner, to own Eppie as my child. I've a natural claim on her that must stand before any other.*'

'*Your coming now and saying, "I'm her father" doesn't alter the feelings inside us. It's me she's been calling father ever since she could say the word*,' answered **Silas**.

The argument continued for a while. **Silas** became more animated as he pointed out the fact that Godfrey had abandoned his daughter. **Godfrey** became more angry as he accused Silas of being unreasonable and denying Eppie the chance to become a wealthy lady. **Eppie** listened, looking pale and anxious, but she would not change her mind. '*I should have no delight in life any more,*' she cried, '*if I was forced to go away from my father. He's took care of me and loved me from the first and nobody shall ever come between him and me.*'

WHOOSH

Follow-up activities

- Using the discussion cards provided as Resource 17, divide students into groups to discuss the issues raised by the parenting choices of Squire Cass and Silas Marner.
- Ask each group to select the two points from their discussion which they think are the most clearly articulated and share them with the rest of the class.
- In the centre of a large piece of paper write, 'A good parent is …' Provide each student with a sticky note on which to write one definition. Stick the notes around the central sentence. Evaluate Squire Cass and Silas Marner against the criteria for good parenting that has been created.

Discussion card 1

The argument between Dunstan and Godfrey centred around money and a secret which Dunstan threatened to tell their father. Who was to blame for their situation and their anger?

In what ways is their relationship similar to that of brothers and sisters today?

Discussion card 2

Contrast the affection which Silas showed Eppie with the Squire's emotional relationship with his sons. In what ways were they different? How did this affect their children?

How does affection, or lack of it, affect children as they grow up today?

Discussion card 3

Neither the Squire nor Silas punished their children, so how did Eppie learn to be kind and thoughtful when the Cass boys did not?

Is punishment always effective? In what other ways can parents raise caring, respectful and independent children?

Discussion card 4

Both Squire Cass and Silas were single parents from very different social backgrounds. What made Squire Cass a bad father and Silas a good father?

How can we define good and bad parents in modern life? Are social status and money important? How do our parents' values influence us?

Discussion card 5

How did accepting help allow Silas to become part of his village community? Why did the Squire never ask for help in the years after his wife died?

In what ways are we influenced by belonging to a community? How would we define community in today's world?

Discussion card 6

Godfrey denied his daughter's existence for selfish reasons, then expected to adopt her when it suited him. Was this a reasonable view? Was Eppie's final decision the best one?

Define a parent. What do we most want from our parents?

5   Modern novels

1   Andrew Norriss: *The Touchstone*

Andrew Norriss won the Whitbread Children's Book of the Year award in 1997 with his novel *Aquila*. A common feature of his books for children is the ability to make the reader think, 'What would *I* do if … ?' They are also laced with subtle comedic touches, evidence of the author's experience as a TV sitcom writer. *The Touchstone* was published in 2004 and tells the story of Kai, an alien fugitive who needs to save her planet. She engages the help of Douglas, an ordinary boy with an extraordinary ability to remain calm in every kind of crisis.

This Whoosh uses the first chapter of the book to introduce pupils to the narrative and to create time to explore the ingredients of a strong story opening. There are opportunities in this Whoosh to improvise the dialogue. In paragraph three of the second section of the Whoosh, for example, the reader could pause after each phrase to allow the pupils acting the parts of Douglas and Kai to add the dialogue. The extent to which speech is added is dependent on the age and confidence of the participants. Video this Whoosh to assist with the follow-up activities.

Objective

* to explore a story opening.

Characters	Objects	Sounds
Mrs Paterson Douglas Kai Guardians of the Federation people of Kai's planet Gedrus	supermarket house front door trees bushes wall necklace grey metal box planet stairs three stones bed library shelves of books desk	closing door 'Douglas' rustling leaves crash crunching

Mrs Paterson worked on the checkout in the local **supermarket**, so she always left the **house** before **Douglas**. But one morning, just as he shut the **front door**, he thought he heard someone saying his name. The voice was very quiet. It was quieter than a whisper, but he definitely heard a voice say, '*Douglas*'. As he was thinking that maybe it was just the breeze **rustling** the leaves on the **trees**, he heard it again. This time it was a definite whisper. '*Douglas!*' the voice said. Some **bushes** lined the front **wall** of the garden, but the strange thing was that although the voice appeared to be coming from the **bushes**, the garden seemed deserted when **Douglas** looked around.

WHOOSH

When he heard his name, '*Douglas!*' for the third time, **he** decided to find out if there was actually anyone there. So, walking across the grass, **he** pulled the **bushes** apart, somewhere in the area where he had heard the sound. And there was someone there – a young **woman**. She was sitting down, leaning against the **wall** and holding her shoulder as if she was hurt.

Douglas noticed a lot of things about her very quickly – the boots, combats and khaki vest that made her look like a soldier, an unusual green **necklace** hanging on a silver chain around her neck, and her **lunchbox**. Well, it looked like a child's lunchbox anyway, except that it was grey and made of metal, which actually made it quite different from any lunchbox that **Douglas** had ever used.

He was just wondering who she was, how she knew his name when he had never seen her before and whether he should call an ambulance when she spoke again. **She** definitely disapproved of the ambulance idea – she seemed to think that 'they' might find her.

She, apparently, was **Kai**. They, it turned out, were the **Guardians of the Federation**, who wanted to stop her getting the **lunchbox** to her home **planet** to save her **people**. And **Douglas**, definitely, was the only *coda* who could help her. Gedrus had said so. '*Will you help me?*' pleaded **Kai**.

Now **Douglas** never panicked. **He** was always calm in a crisis. But on this occasion, even **he** felt the strain. **His** first reaction was a sort of trance. **His** second reaction, as **Kai** tugged at his arm saying, '*Please? Will you help?*' was to look back at his **house** and decide on a course of action.

WHOOSH

He unlocked the front **door** and started to help **Kai** up the **stairs**. Pretty soon, **Douglas**'s calmness was put to the test again because half way up, **Kai's** left arm fell off at her shoulder. He pushed it back in, but it dropped off again fairly quickly, so in the end **Douglas** just carried it.

After **he** finally managed to get **Kai**, pale and weak, into his bedroom, he went to find some sticking plaster. When he returned, something blue was oozing from the hole in her shoulder. **Kai** was lying with her eyes partly closed, holding her necklace and talking to herself almost, **Douglas** thought, as if she was praying. As **he** set about taping her arm back on, **Kai** seemed to rally her strength enough to tell him what was about to happen. Apparently, **Douglas** was to keep her existence a secret while **he** hid her for 48 hours, in which time **he** was to ignore her and **she** would heal herself.

But there was no time for **Douglas** to decide where to hide her, because **she** was opening the **metal box** to reveal three more green **stones**, similar to her necklace. So this is what the Guardians wanted. This is what Kai was risking her life for. Taking **Douglas**'s **hand**, she pushed it into the box and told him to pick up a stone. But it wasn't a stone. It wasn't even glass. It moved and formed itself like a liquid in his hand. '*It's a Touchstone*,' said Kai, showing him how to wrap his fingers around it.

WHOOSH

No sooner had **he** done so than his whole body felt a shock of energy which reached even to the ends of his fingers and his toes. **Douglas** dropped the **Touchstone** with a cry. And as if things weren't bad enough, **Kai** was fading away, telling **Douglas** that he should use the Touchstone to contact Gedrus, who could answer any questions that he wanted to ask.

And then **she** was gone. **She** fell heavily to the floor with a loud **crash**. All but her head had landed on his rug. There was no pulse. Well, there may have been, but **Douglas** was trying to find it in the arm that had fallen off. Anyway, Kai was no longer breathing. He would have to somehow slide the rug under his **bed** where nobody could find her.

While **he** walked around her body, thinking about how he could find the strength to mover her, he picked up the **stone** where it had fallen. That was when he got another surprise. A bright, clear picture appeared in front of his face. The picture was of a **library** with **shelves of books** as far as he could see in any direction. But that wasn't all. There was a young **man** with his feet propped on a **desk**, reading a book and crunching an apple.

'*Hi. I'm Gedrus*,' he said. '*What can I do for you?*'

So it was true. This was Gedrus, the person who could tell him anything. Absolutely anything he wanted. All he had to do was grasp the **Touchstone** and ask.

WHOOSH

Follow-up activities

- Watch the video of the Whoosh. As they watch, ask pupils to note questions which occur to them. Then brainstorm a list of the questions that Douglas might want to ask Gedrus in their first conversation, for example:
  - Who are you?
  - What is going to happen to the body under the bed?
  - Why does Kai need to be left alone?
  - Where is Kai from?
  - Who are the Guardians of the Federation? Are they good or bad people?
  - How did Kai know his name?
  - Kai referred to him as a *coda*. What did she mean?
- Then attempt to answer the questions. Challenge pupils to demonstrate the difference between an evidence-based answer and a prediction. Be clear about how the answers have been derived.
- Through shared discussion and using the outcome of the previous activity, define how the author has set up the plot in this first chapter of the narrative.
- Working in groups, ask pupils what they would ask for if they had a Touchstone. Consider the advantages and disadvantages of each idea. For example, they could ask Gedrus for answers to all of their school work, but what would the consequences be? They could ask him about their future lives, but are they sure they would want to know? How could a Touchstone be used to help everyone, not just the owner? List the ideas and vote to choose the best three.
- Consider the setting. Why might the author have chosen a very ordinary setting for the story?
- Douglas is the protagonist, or central character, in the novel. Although he is very calm, he must have experienced a range of emotions during these events. Watch the video of the Whoosh and list everything that is learnt about Douglas in this opening chapter, both about his personality and his emotional reactions. Provide evidence for each inference. Resource 18 provides a grid to complete, with one suggestion to start the discussion.
- What makes this book engaging? Why do you want to read on? How has the author built that motivation into the story opening?

2   Frank Cottrell Boyce: *Cosmic*

Cosmic, published in 2008, is Frank Cottrell Boyce's third novel, following on from *Millions* and *Framed*. It explores the question of what it means to be a dad and it exploits the intrinsic humour of a child who is so tall that he is mistaken for an adult. At the point of this Whoosh, the central character, Liam, has already been mistaken for a new teacher on his first day at secondary school, a father wanting to test drive a Porsche and a responsible adult who can accompany scared children on Cosmic, a famous theme park ride. In each case, he allows the mistake to go uncorrected with hilarious consequences until he is rescued by his Dad at the last minute. Use the Whoosh when you reach 'The Vomit Comet' chapter in the book.

Liam is now undergoing training in China with his surrogate daughter Florida and three father/son teams. The children have started voting for the dad whom they wish to take into space. On the first vote, all the children voted for Eddie Xanadu who had taken ice cream on the desert trip, even though Liam had saved their lives and solved the team puzzle. After the second training exercise every dad got one vote, even though Liam had accidentally got drunk and did not expect to get any votes. The rationale for the children's voting eludes him as they enter the third day of training.

Video this Whoosh to facilitate the follow-up activity.

Resource 18 All about Douglas

Information	Evidence
Douglas was curious.	He looked around to find out who was calling his name.

Objective

• to explore relationships between characters.

Characters	Objects	Sounds
Liam Digby	diggers	alarm
Florida Kirby	lakes and gardens	plane engine
Samson Two Toure	rocket-shaped rides	wailing
Samson One Toure	Infinity Park entrance	pleading
Hasan Xanadu	desert	voice
Eddie Xanadu	trees	scream
Max Martinet	caterpillar minibus	yells of excitement
Monsieur Martinet	meadow	
Dr Drax	rocket orchard	
Shenjian	long bench	
doctor	soft cushions	
	trail of vomit	
	sick bag	
	gravity	
	Earth	
	moon	

Liam still felt like someone was drilling a hole in his head when the **alarm** went off. **Florida** patiently explained that he was suffering from a hangover. '*They happen*,' she told him, '*when people drink too much alcohol. A big fried breakfast and a cup of coffee are the best treatments. Oh, and adults joke about hangovers when they meet up.*' Unfortunately, food was forbidden before the training that day and the last thing **Liam** felt like doing was meeting up with anyone and going on a ride at Infinity Park.

When they **all** arrived at Infinity Park, though, they could see why it was going to be the best theme park in the world. There were still **diggers** everywhere, but there were **lakes, gardens** and a lot of **rocket-shaped rides** which were half built. Even the **entrance** to the park had two rockets crossed to create an arch. **Liam** looked at the contrast. Outside, nothing but **desert** and sand mountains. Inside, **lakes, trees** and bright colours.

Dr Drax gave them **all** a guided tour in one of the park's **caterpillar minibuses**. The tour ended in a **meadow**, populated with **rockets** rather than trees. '*A sort of rocket orchard*,' mused Liam. One plane was of particular interest, because it was the one they were going to fly on. It was a bit odd though – there were no windows and **Dr Drax** was saying something about going on a parabola.

WHOOSH

Samson Two, of course, got it straight away. '*Zero gravity,*' he announced. '*He's a genius*,' said his **dad**. **Dr Drax** ignored them both and explained that they were about to experience weightlessness. They were definitely **all** excited about that. They finally understood the no-food rule when **Dr Drax** informed them that although the plane was actually named the Draxcom Zero Star, it was informally known by its testers as The Vomit Comet, '*because most people who ride on it,*' she said, '*throw up.*'

Inside was one **long bench** for them to sit on. The rest of the plane was a huge open space lined with **soft cushions**. It looked like a children's play area. As they fastened their lap belts, **Dr Drax** wished them good luck. '*Sick bags,*' she informed them as she left, '*are under the seat.*'

Listening to all of this, **Florida** had got very excited about the idea of suddenly losing weight. **Liam** tried to explain about gravity but as the plane climbed relentlessly upward, the **noise** was so deafening that it was hard to hear. **They** had to hold tightly to the **bench** and **Liam** thought his head was going to blow up.

Samson Two, as usual, demonstrated his detailed knowledge about the process until **Max** started to **wail**. All this earned him was a lecture from **Monsieur Martinet** about dealing with fear. **Hasan** just kept begging someone, anyone, to let him off the plane. Although he knew a good deal when he saw one, **he** didn't stop begging even when **Eddie** pointed out that NASA charged a couple of thousand pounds for an experience which he was being given free.

WHOOSH

Florida, meanwhile, was clinging to **Liam** as they **all** sat and waited. **His** ears were really hurting and the more the plane climbed the more they hurt. But **he** also remembered feeling like it before. Suddenly it came to **him** – the log flume. It was just like climbing to the top of a log flume. After that, the sensation didn't seem so bad, **Florida** relaxed a bit and by the time a **voice** told them that **they** should unfasten their seat belts, **they** were **all** feeling too excited to think about anything else.

Florida was quick to let go of **Liam**. **She screamed** just as though she was on a log flume. But **Liam** couldn't follow her. **Monsieur Martinet** was hanging onto his other arm and instead of joining in with **all** the others, **he** showed every intention of just gripping tighter and tighter. **His** eyes were closed as **he** breathed deeply. **Liam** opened **Monsieur Martinet**'s fingers and tried to walk away. But **his** steps were odd – much longer than he expected them to be. And after his third long step, **he** was flying. **His** feet, though, kept on going upwards so **he** ended up turning a perfect double somersault.

With **yells** of excitement, **he** found himself facing **Florida**. Without really thinking, **she** pushed him and shouted, '*Tig!*'. As **he** spun back the other way, **Liam** passed **Samson Two**. But as **Liam** tigged him, **Samson Two** just looked puzzled. **He** didn't look as though he had ever played tig before.

Then, just as suddenly as it started, it was over. **They** were **all** standing normally, with the exception of **Monsieur Martinet** who hadn't even undone his seatbelt.' *No one was sick*', whined Florida, in a tone of voice which suggested that Liam ought to do something about it.

WHOOSH

But there was no time. '*Please prepare for the second parabola*,' intoned a **voice** and **they** were **all** off again, floating and somersaulting along the plane. **Samson Two** tigged **Liam** (**he** had obviously got the idea of the game) and **Hasan** was still whinging about wanting to get off. **Monsieur Martinet** seemed to be having some sort of crisis, shouting, '*Stop!*' at the top of his voice and yelling that the pilot had lost control. But as **he** was shouting, a trail of **vomit** slid out of his mouth and started to float along the plane.

Florida was fascinated by it and while **everybody** else watched, **she** opened her **sick bag** and caught the vomit trail. '*Look. I caught it*,' **she** said when the plane landed. **She** sounded rather proud of herself and even though **Liam** tried in a fatherly way to dissuade **Florida**, she showed it to **Dr Drax**. When **Dr Drax** said that she had shown good agility and that she had the makings of a good taikonaut, **Florida** beamed with pride, checking that **everybody** had heard. Except nobody was looking.

Instead, **everyone** was watching a **small girl** leaving the plane and **everyone** was thinking the same thing – where had she come from? She wasn't on the plane when they were floating, was she? Well, according to **Dr Drax**, she was. The girl was her thirteen year old daughter **Shenjian** and she had been piloting the plane. '*Thirteen?*' screamed **Monsieur Martinet** as **Dr Drax** went on to explain that she herself had learnt to fly at the age of nine and that Infinity Park was all about giving children opportunities. **She** was enjoying their reaction.

Samson One seemed to understand. After all, **he** pointed out proudly, **Samson Two** could already do plenty of things that adults couldn't do. **Florida** wanted to know if she could have a flying suit the same as Shenjian's because she was rather taken with the design detail of the pockets.

WHOOSH

Then the **adults** had to go and have medical tests. The **doctor** told Liam that he had the metabolism of a twelve-year-old and, according to **Monsieur Martinet**, he had the brain of a twelve-year-old, too. **He** took a poor view of Liam playing games while the pilot was losing control of the plane. Afterwards, **Florida** wanted to know how they had suddenly become weightless. **Liam** started to explain about **gravity**. **He** was fine about explaining how it pulls you towards the **Earth** and that there is less of it the further you move away from the **Earth**. But when **he** got to the effect of the **moon** on tides, **he** started to realise how much he didn't know.

It didn't matter though; **Liam** was just looking forward to getting all the votes that evening. He was the only adult who had actually enjoyed the experience and after all, he had played with the children.

Each dad got just one vote. And **Florida** didn't even vote for her own dad. '*Why?*' asked **Liam**, puzzled. '*I voted for Mr Martinet*,' Florida giggled. '*He was scared. He threw up. Wasn't that great?*'

WHOOSH

Follow-up activities

- Stand nine pupils in a circle. Each pupil should represent one of the following characters: Liam, Florida, Samson One, Samson Two, Hasan, Eddie, Max, Monsieur Martinet or Dr Drax.
- Next, provide each character with several pieces of string, each one long enough to reach across the circle. In turn, each character should hold one end of a piece of their string and give the other end to a character with whom they interacted in this Whoosh. Consider how to represent comments which were not for any particular person (e.g. Max's wailing, Hasan's pleas to be let off the plane or Monsieur Martinet's outburst about the loss of control).
- Discuss the web which has been created. How many of the interactions are personal and how many are comments aimed for a general audience? Which character communicated with the most people? What does this say about the characters? What does it tell the reader about their ability to listen?
- Reproduce the web as a diagram, marking the direction of the communication using arrows – an example is provided in Resource 19 together with a blank template for pupils to complete as Resource 20. How much of the communication was two-way? Was there any difference in the adult–child communication than the child–child interactions? If so, what were the differences?
- Compare Liam's interaction with that of the other fathers. What are the differences? Are there any similarities?
- Based on this evidence, decide why Liam expected to receive all the votes that day. Discuss why this did not happen and suggest some possible reasons.
- Although Liam is tall and easily mistaken for an adult, in what ways do his interactions with the other children demonstrate that he is not an adult? How would Liam have acted differently if he was an adult?

3 Nina Bawden: *Carrie's War*

Carrie's War tells the story of three children who are evacuated to a Welsh mining village during World War II. The novel gives a detailed insight not only into evacuation, but also the social and cultural life of the village. Carrie and her brother Nick are billeted with Mr Evans (the local grocer, a councillor and a deeply religious man) and his anxious, timid sister. There is much to learn about wartime homes, lives and families through the perceptive eyes of the twelve-year-old Carrie.

The purpose of this Whoosh is to introduce the novel and consider the historical setting before commencing a closer study of the text. The language of the narrative in the opening chapter is rich; full of imagery and powerful description. The narrative technique of flashback is used, providing opportunity to consider the contrast between the lives and expectations of war-time and modern children. Flashbacks are also used in the Whoosh, as a series of memories or pictures in Carrie's mind. This allows for the dramatisation of her memories as a series of mini-scenes within the Whoosh itself.

Resource 19 Character interactions on the Vomit Comet: example

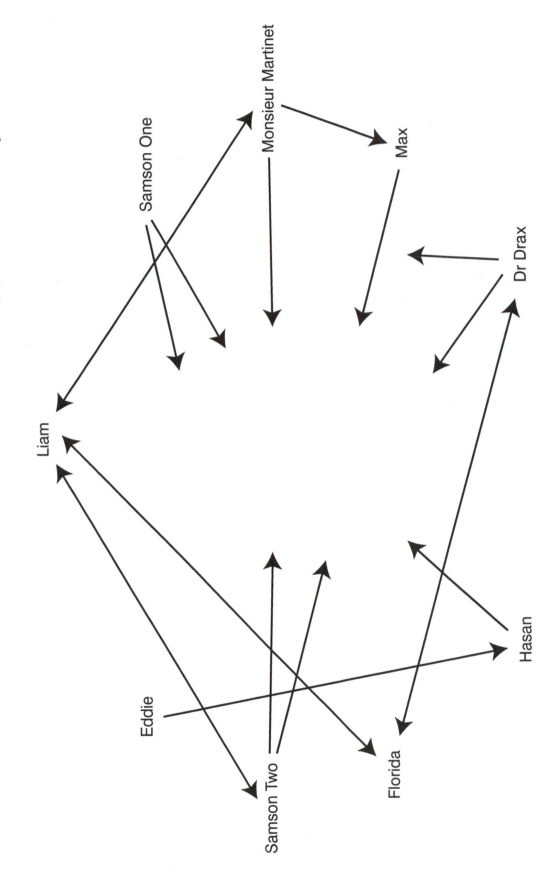

Resource 20 Character interactions on the Vomit Comet: template

Liam

Samson One

Monsieur Martinet

Eddie

Max

Samson Two

Florida

Hasan

Dr Drax

Objective

• To consider the historical, social and cultural context of a novel.

Characters	Objects	Sounds
Carrie (adult) oldest boy little children Carrie (child) Uncle Nick (child) mothers school children Miss Fazackerly engine drivers train passengers Johnny Gotobed Hepzibah Green Albert Sandwich old people coal miners families	yew trees house railway line school bend in the railway line trains sheep Druid's Grove Druid's Bottom library chickens sun tunnel entrance skull path boarded-up shops narrow streets coal mines slag heap Ebenezer Chapel village school	giggling hissing chickens train whistle

In her dreams of Druid's Grove and the railway, **Carrie** had always gone back. She was just twelve, still wearing socks and sandals, the **yew trees** pulling at her hair and her skirt as **she** ran. **She** was always running in the same direction; even though it was uphill, she was always running away from the **house** and towards the **railway line**.

Then one day **she** did go back, taking her own **children** to show them. A lot had changed though. The **railway** wasn't used any more. The track had been taken up and instead it was a mass of overgrown and tangled brambles. Her **children** laughed as they pulled the brambles off of their jeans. A picture came into **Carrie's** mind …

She was eleven years old and she was going to **school**, like she did every morning. But this morning was different. **Mothers** were trying not to cry as they waved off **children** equipped with gas masks and packed cases. **Miss Fazackerly** was being really kind as they hung their labels around their necks and got on the train. **She** had had to look after **Nick**. He was only a year younger than her, but you would never know it. As **they** waved goodbye, they had no idea where they were going. **They** had no idea when they would be coming home…

Carrie's attention returned to her own children. '***We were sent here away from the bombs. Uncle Nick and I.*** '*Without your Mummy?*' one of her children asked. The **children** started to **giggle** at the thought of their Uncle Nick ever being a child. But they listened entranced as **Carrie** told them that in those days there weren't many trains and because the line wasn't electrified, they could walk alongside it quite safely. She pointed out the **bend** in the line where the lumbering, **hissing** steam **trains** had to slow down.

She smiled, half to herself, as she imagined the **engine drivers** climbing down from their cabs to drive **sheep** off of the track. Sometimes, she remembered, **passengers** would even get off the train and walk around, picking blackberries and stretching their legs before they continued their journey.

WHOOSH

Carrie explained that sometimes she and Uncle Nick would pick blackberries on their way to visit Johnny Gotobed and Hepzibah Green. Then the children really did giggle. '*They sound like people in a story,*' laughed the oldest boy. But **Carrie** assured the children that they were real alright. She showed them **Druid's Grove**, the valley where they used to live.

Even after thirty years, she could still imagine the big, old **house** with its tall **chimneys** – **Druid's Bottom**, everyone called it. She could still picture **Albert Sandwich**, the boy who had been sent to live there, poring over some old books in the **library**. She could still see **Johnny** calming the noisy **chickens** as he shut them up for the night and **Hepzibah** the housekeeper, smiling as she pulled a freshly made cake from the oven.

The **children**'s silence suddenly called her back to the present. **They** seemed worried at the change in her mood. So **they** chattered as they wandered on and soon found the **sun** disappearing as they moved closer to the **tunnel entrance**. The **yew trees** of Carrie's dreams grew thickly here, twisting and turning on the edges of the steep slope. **Carrie** smiled again, remembering how frightened **Nick** used to be. '*He was even scared of the old skull,*' mused **Carrie** aloud, explaining to the children about the old **skull** at **Druid's Bottom** which could never be taken out of the house.

WHOOSH

The **oldest boy** was glad when the ruins of the **house** came into sight. As **Carrie** pointed it out in the valley below, her **daughter** noticed a **path**. But for some reason, **Carrie**'s mood changed again. She seemed frightened, somehow, and the **children** were frightened with her. **She** refused to go down the **path** and when she put on her dark glasses so that the **children** couldn't see her eyes, the **oldest boy** decided it was time to leave.

Sending the **younger children** ahead, they turned around and started to retrace their steps. '*Not much of it, this town, is it?*' asked the **oldest boy**. They paused on the hillside to look down on the **boarded-up shops**. It was an ugly town now, with its **narrow streets** and slate roofs and only the **old people** left. **Carrie** told him that it used to be different. When the **mines** were open, the town was bustling and busy with **miners** and **families** coming and going. Then the **mines** were closed because the country didn't need such expensive coal any more. The **miners** had no jobs so they moved away to find other work and soon after the railway would have gone, too. **Carrie** pointed to the **slag heap**, a huge pile of useless coal waste that they used to slide down on tin trays. She showed him **Ebenezer Chapel**, where she had to go to school because the **village school** wasn't big enough for all the London children. And just before they started down the hill to go back to the **village**, she stopped and showed him where they used to stand and listen to the **train whistle**. It used to echo around the valley and the first time they heard it, **Uncle Nick** had been sick. And that was really where the story started…

WHOOSH

Follow-up activities

The novel goes on to tell the story of Carrie and Nick as evacuees in a Welsh mining town. The wealth of historical and social detail throughout the book makes it an ideal text to develop children's understanding of life on the Home Front during World War II.

- Resource 21 is a chart which lists some of the areas of information which can lead to discussion about life then and now. Some of these contrasts are already made in the text. For example, the twelve-year-old Carrie wears a skirt; her children are wearing jeans. Carrie herself contrasts the speed and frequency of trains and the fact that they could walk alongside the railway line while electrified lines on modern railways have to be fenced off.
- Enter any information already gained. As the novel progresses, further information can be added. When the story is complete, this resource can lead to non-fiction writing (an information text) or creative writing (a diary entry for Carrie or letters to their mother from either Nick or Carrie).
- When making entries to the chart remind pupils that they need to note evidence from the text.
- The language of Chapter 1 is rich in imagery. Once the Whoosh has familiarised pupils with the characterisation, plot and setting, they could focus on selected examples of the language in order to develop understanding of an author uses language effectively in storytelling.

Resource 21 **Life on the Home Front**

	Information	Evidence
Clothes		
Homes		
Transport		
Jobs		
Food		
Leisure		

4   Louis Sachar: *Holes*

Holes was first published in 1998. The twists and turns in the plot, the descriptions, lively characterisation and ironic humour combine in a narrative which appeals to a wide range of readers.

The central character, Stanley Yelnats, finds himself falsely convicted of theft. Camp Green Lake Juvenile Correctional Facility in Texas falls short of his expectations, but it leads him on a detective trail that ends in the uncovering of some surprising truths.

Reading the early chapters of the book always prompts the question, 'Why are they digging the holes?' This Whoosh gives pupils a chance to reflect on the characters and setting revealed at the opening of the novel. These reflections can then be used to discuss and predict possible plot lines and outcomes for Stanley, including why he has to dig holes every day.

Objective

* to develop skills of prediction and open-minded thinking.

Characters	Objects	Sounds
campers Stanley Yelnats (IV) judge Derrick Dunne teachers Sweet Feet Livingston Dad police Mum Stanley Yelnats I Kissin' Kate Barlow driver guard Mr Sir Mr Pendanski boys in tent D Zero Armpit	rattlesnakes scorpions holes yellow-spotted lizards lake trainers stagecoach bus tents buildings space bed crate	rattlesnakes bus engine splashing squad car siren creaking snoring

Camp Green Lake is in Texas. There used to be a lake there, but there isn't any more. There used to be a town called Green Lake, too, but there isn't any more. Apart from the **campers**, there's nothing but earth baked hard by the fierce heat and the **rattlesnakes** and **scorpions** that hide in the shelter of the **holes**. Oh, and the **yellow-spotted lizards**. Avoid those – if one of them bites you, you'll die.

The court had decided that **Stanley Yelnats** was a bad boy. The **judge** let him choose between jail and Camp Green Lake, but he had to choose quickly because spaces at Camp Green Lake went fast. **Stanley** was poor and he'd never been to camp before. He liked the sound of Green Lake. So there **he** was, sitting on a **bus**, handcuffed to the seat. **He** was looking forward to splashing around and swimming in the **lake**. He was looking forward to making new friends. Nobody told him that the bad boys at Camp Green Lake just dug holes.

Stanley was innocent. The **trainers** had fallen on his head, but the court didn't believe his story. He shouldn't even have been there. If **Derrick Dunne** hadn't stolen his notebook and thrown it down the toilet, then **he** wouldn't have missed his bus, he wouldn't have had to walk home and it wouldn't have been his head that the **trainers** fell on. **Derrick Dunne** was always teasing him, but because **Derrick** was small and **Stanley** was big, nobody ever believed him. Even the **teachers** laughed at him when he said anything. And how was **Stanley** to know that the **trainers** belonged to **Sweet Feet Livingston**? How often did **trainers** belonging to such a famous baseball player fall on someone's head?

Actually, for a while **Stanley** thought that the **trainers** were a sign. His **dad** had been trying unsuccessfully for ages to find a way of recycling trainers, so when a particularly smelly pair fell on him, **Stanley** naturally took it to mean something. But instead, he found himself followed by a **squad car**, arrested by the **police** and charged with theft. The Yelnats family had always been unlucky. It must be something to do with the curse.

WHOOSH

Mum liked to point out that not everyone in the family was cursed. The first **Stanley Yelnats** was really rich so he must have been lucky. She didn't usually add that he had then lost the lot when he was robbed by **Kissin' Kate Barlow** when she held up his **stagecoach** at gunpoint.

After eight weary hours, the **bus** was finally stopping. There was no lake. There was nothing green. There was nothing but a few **tents,** a few **buildings** and a lot of **space**. '*Welcome to Camp Green Lake*,' said the **driver** as the **guard** unlocked Stanley's handcuffs and took him into the camp.

Mr Sir was the first person that **Stanley** met. **He** chewed sunflower seeds and seemed fond of reminding **Stanley** that he wasn't in the Girl Scouts any more. **He** checked that **Stanley** wasn't carrying any weapons, either on himself or in his backpack, then gave him two sets of orange clothes. Apparently, all Stanley had to do was dig a hole every day which was five feet wide and five feet deep. Then he could please himself for the rest of every day. There was just one rule – don't upset the Warden. There was a **hammock** swinging in the only shade in the Camp. They belonged to the Warden – the hammock and the shade. Getting up at 4.30 every morning for breakfast didn't sound so good, either.

Then **Mr Sir** did something odd. Taking **Stanley** outside, he asked him if he would like to run away. There were no guards or fences. Mind you, there was no water for a hundred miles either, so anyone who ran away would die pretty quickly. There was nothing but desolate, empty space. **Stanley** didn't think running away was a good idea.

WHOOSH

The **boys** were just coming back to camp after finishing their holes for the day. **Mr Pendanski** seemed kinder than **Mr Sir** (who apparently had got quite grumpy since he'd given up smoking and taken up chewing sunflower seeds) and he introduced **Stanley** to the boys in tent D. **Squid** and **X Ray** were still covered in dirt and dust, but **Magnet, Armpit** and **Zigzag** had already showered. And there was **Zero,** so called because, according to **Mr Pendanski**, there was nothing in his head. **Mr Pendanski** encouraged them all to shake hands, then they showed **Stanley** his bed and the **crate** he would use for his locker.

Stanley remembered he was thirsty. He had been thirsty for hours. He thought he might be thirsty a lot more in the next eighteen months. He asked one of the **boys** where he could get a drink, only to find himself grabbed by the collar and thrown to the floor for using the boy's real name instead of calling him **Armpit**. Maybe making friends was going to be hard here, too.

Showers were cold and lasted for just four minutes. The food was supposed to be stewed meat and vegetables but it could have been anything. His **bed** creaked and threatened to collapse under his weight, it smelt of sour milk and **Armpit** snored. And none of the boys had believed him when he told them that he was there for stealing Clyde Livingston's trainers.

On his first morning at Camp Green Lake, after breakfast at 4.30, **Stanley** started to dig the first of many holes.

WHOOSH

Follow-up activities

This Whoosh covers the first six chapters of the book, in which most of the characters are introduced. After reading these chapters and acting out the Whoosh, use the following questions to prompt thinking about possible outcomes in the unread narrative. This can be done as a class discussion or in groups which then feed back to the whole class. Remind students that predictions must be based on available evidence so far.

- List the characters who have been introduced. What has the reader already learnt about them?
- How might Stanley's relationships with Mr Sir and Mr Pendanski develop?
- Stanley was hoping to make some new friends. Which boy appears to be in charge of tent D? How should Stanley interact with this person?

- Zero apparently has nothing in his head. Why might Stanley identify with Zero? What hidden depths might Zero have?
- All the boys have a nickname. What might be an appropriate nickname for Stanley?
- Stanley was bullied at school. What hints are there that this might continue at Camp Green Lake? How could Stanley change this and earn respect from the other boys?
- Digging holes was supposed to turn bad boys into good boys. What other reasons might there be for digging holes in a wasteland?
- Poisonous animals used the holes for shelter. What might the insertion of this information foreshadow? Are there other examples of information which might be foreshadowing events later in the story?
- Suggest some ways in which the plot might unfold. For example, how might Stanley prove his innocence?

5   Michelle Magorian: *Goodnight Mister Tom*

Goodnight Mister Tom was published in 1981 and it quickly became a very popular children's book. Set against the backdrop of World War II, it tells the story of eight-year-old William Beech, a deprived and abused child who is evacuated to the country. Whilst living with Tom Oakley, the taciturn man with whom he is billeted, he discovers values and a view of life which contrast sharply with the only life he has known in London.

Some preparation is needed before embarking on this Whoosh. Draw two large outlines of a child to represent William. One should be smaller and thinner than the other – label this one 'William in London'. Label the other one 'Little Weirwold – six months later'. Use these for a Role on the Wall to compare and contrast Tom's two lives. Providing pupils with sticky notes, ask them to write on each note anything they know about William so far. This can be about his appearance, the people he knows or his behaviour and personality. Then invite pupils to stick their notes onto the correct outline, depending on whether their information relates to William at the beginning of the story or after six months in Little Weirwold. Comments about external appearance should be stuck around the outside of the outlines. Comments about his personality or about William as a person should be stuck inside. To support their thinking, pupils could question each other to discover what they know about:

- William's external appearance, what he looked like, the clothes he wore and the food he ate
- his two schools and his teachers
- his skills and gifts
- the two environments and how he interacted with them
- friendships
- how his mother and Mister Tom cared for him
- how he developed as a person.

Then, through shared discussion, compare and contrast William's life with his mother in London and with Mister Tom in the country. For example, he learnt to read, write, draw and paint. He grew physically because he was well fed. And most importantly, he was happy because he was respected, cared for and encouraged.

The Whoosh takes place as William's happiness is about to shatter. He has worked hard at school and moved into Mrs Hartridge's class. He has the lead role in the school production of Dickens' *A Christmas Carol* and he is responsible for the artwork in the gazette which he and his friends are producing. Fear and physical punishment are things of the past and Tom is flourishing in his new life. Suddenly, at the height of his happiness, a letter arrives from his mother asking for him to return to London as she has been unwell. His two worlds are about to collide.

Where dialogue is suggested but not provided, encourage pupils to improvise. This Whoosh also includes some thought tracking. This is a useful strategy in helping pupils to consider what William might be thinking when his actions do not reveal his thoughts. Stop the Whoosh at the points indicated and ask for suggestions about what William might be thinking. Start the Whoosh with a thought track about William's feelings as he prepares to leave Mister Tom and all his friends. Is he sad? Is he excited about seeing his mother again? What might he want to share with her about his new life?

Objective

• to explore how a character matures in the course of a novel.

Characters	Objects	Sounds
Tom Oakley William Beech Mrs Beech billeting officer soldiers sailors young soldier vicar ticket inspector warden baby	Dobbs, the horse the village of Little Weirwold blacksmith's forge station Sammy train carriage door cafe Mrs Beech's home	clopping hooves train whistle crying baby

Thought track: What are William's thoughts about his return to London?

As **Dobbs** clopped steadily on, pulling the cart past the fields of **Little Weirwold**, **William** and **Tom** had nothing to say. As they came to the edge of the **village**, **Tom** thought about how he had tried to persuade **Mrs Beech** to visit them and how he had pleaded with the **billeting officer** to find a way for **William** to stay. But there was nothing anyone could do – **Mrs Beech** was his mother and **she** wanted him back. It was only until **she** felt better, she said, but **Tom** was filled with dread anyway.

Leaving **Dobbs** at the **blacksmith's forge, they** sat on a bench at the **station,** still with little to say to each other. William's rucksack was crammed full of all his new possessions; his clothes, his books and the presents his friends had given him when he left. His paints, though, he had left behind. He held **Sammy**'s lead, perhaps for the last time.

'**Don't forgit to write**,' reminded Mister **Tom**.

'**I will come back. I will, won't I?**' pleaded **William**, thinking of the paints which he had left at the place he now thought of as home. There was just time for Mister **Tom** to remind William that it might take time to get to know his mother again, when a cloud of smoke rising through the nearby trees announced the arrival of the train. The **sound** got louder and louder as Mister **Tom** picked up **Sammy**. **William** sniffed but **he** could not get rid of the lump in his throat as tears rolled down his face.

The train was crowded with **soldiers** and **sailors** looking out of the open windows; so many of them that there was standing room only. **Tom** opened one of the **doors** and a young **soldier**, seeing **Tom**'s worried face, pulled **William** up into the carriage and found him a seat by the window. The **whistle** blew as **Tom** and **William**, both choking back the tears, said goodbye for the last time.

Thought track: Is William thinking about London at this point? What is likely to be his uppermost thought?

WHOOSH

The **soldier** was very kind. For a while, seeing **William**'s face, the **soldier** left him alone to stare out of the window. After a while, **he** tried to start a conversation, by way of cheering William up. At one point, **he** asked about William's mother which made **him** stop and think. His mother was just a dim memory now. '**She's got dark hair**,' he said, '**and she's medium size**,' before he ran out of information about her. It was only when **he** asked about the contents of the rucksack that **William** came to life, showing the soldier his sketchpad. '**Your mother must be terribly proud of ye,**' **he** mused as he looked through the drawings.

Would she be proud of him, **William** wondered. For a while **he** imagined what it would be like when she met him at the station. He imagined how **they** would laugh and smile with the pleasure of seeing each other again. **He** imagined how **they** would hug when he got off of the train. But then **he** remembered that she was ill and might not be there to meet him at all. Perhaps **she** was dying and the **vicar** would meet **him** from the train and take **him** to his **mother**. **He** imagined how **she** would tell him weakly how much she loved him. **His** imagination became his dreams as **he** fell asleep.

When the **soldier** shook him awake, **William** expected to see the light around the blackouts in his own room. **He** felt quite wobbly as he realised that he was in London. It was cold on the platform, so **he** buttoned up his coat and put on his gloves and balaclava.

'*Another one, eh?*' sighed the **ticket inspector**. '*Don't you know it's safer in the country?*' **he** asked, as **William** showed him his ticket. Then the **inspector** seemed more concerned about whether anyone was there to meet the child. He was just about to call the **warden**, when **William** spotted his **mother** standing next to a pile of sandbags.

'**Mum!**' **he** called, running over to her, '**Mum!**' **She** stared past him and was just about to tell him to go away when **she** realised that this upright, warmly-clothed child was actually her son.

'*I'm awfully pleased to see you, Mum. I've such a lot to tell you*,' **William** said.

'*I'm sorry. I'm not very well. You've changed*,' **she** answered.

William looked at the thin, pale woman standing in front of him. She had changed, not him. There was a bag leaning against her leg, which **William** stepped forward to pick up. '*I'll carry that, Mum*,' he said gently. **She** slapped his hand back down. The meeting which William had imagined on the train evaporated.

Thought track: *William shows little reaction to his mother's harsh welcome. How might he feel, though? What comparisons might he be making with the adults who cared for him in Little Weirwold?*

WHOOSH

Mrs Beech had to be in charge; she had to assert her authority. **She** decided that she would go easy on him for one evening before reminding him who was in charge.

'*Everything will be fine*,' thought **William**, remembering that Mister **Tom** had warned him that it would take time. Before going home, **Mrs Beech** decided that they should go for a cup of tea in a nearby **cafe**. **She** was horrified to see **him** smile at the suggestion. **She** was horrified that he was so well fed and as **they** sat and drank their tea, things went from bad to worse. The presents in his rucksack which had been so kindly offered were nothing but charity and **Mrs Beech** would not take charity. **William** dared to disagree with her so **she** decided that **he** was still as bad a child as ever. And there was the matter of his letters. '*Your letters*,' she said, '*I thought you'd grown out of lyin'. That writing was not yours.*'

William felt that he was slipping into a bad dream. **He** was two people. There was the Little Weirwold William, or Will, and there was Willie, the name his mother used.

Thought track: *Speak aloud William's conflicting thoughts about his double identity. What does he hope that his mother will do? What, based on his knowledge of her, does he expect her to do?*

They took the bus to their **home** in Deptford. The journey was littered with reprimands and when **they** arrived at the **house**, his **mother**'s behaviour was very odd. It seemed that **she** didn't want anyone to know that he was **home**, so **she** told **him** to run in quickly when **she** opened the door. She did hint that inside the **house** there was a surprise that she wanted him to see. **She** was obviously frightened of something as **she** unlocked the door and hurried inside. The house smelt awful.

Thought track: *William had been looking forward to sharing the presents and telling her his news. What are his thoughts about her accusations and complaints? What is he thinking about the surprise his mother has promised?*

WHOOSH

He was told off for asking questions about the tape on the windows. **He** was told off for answering back. But then **he** noticed the box in the corner. There was the surprise. A **baby**, with tape over its mouth to stop it crying or making a noise. '*A present*,' his Mum explained, '*from Jesus.*' Then **he** was told off again for wanting to pick the **baby** up when **she** cried.

But that was nothing compared with the nightmare that followed. **He** got her presents and his own possessions out of his bag. '*You begged them*,' she said. Had he carried on reading his Bible, **she** asked, before telling him to recite some verses. **He** showed her his pictures. '*You stole them*,' she accused. '*You play with girls*,' **she** criticised when **he** told her about his friends. And things spiralled completely out of control when **he** mentioned that Zach could not go to church because there was no synagogue in the village. '*You've been poisoned by the devil*,' **she** screamed. Something hit him on the head and **he** fell to the ground. Although everything had gone dark, **he** could still hear **her** screaming and feel **her** hitting him.

When **he** came round **he** was in complete darkness and **he** ached badly. **He** was wearing nothing but his underclothes and **he** was very cold. **He** knew where he was though. **She** had locked him under the stairs. **He** thought of his own little room at Mister Tom's. **He** thought of his warm clothes, the paper Mister Tom had given him to write letters, the money Mister Tom had sewn into his coat. **She** will have sold it all, apart from Zach's poem. **She** would have burnt that, because Zach was a Jew.

As **he** lay there in pain, **he** knew that he was no longer two people. He was just Will. '*Mister Tom*,' he cried. '*I want you, Mister Tom*.'

Thought track: *Why does William no longer have two identities? Why has he decided this? What other thoughts does he have as he lies locked under the stairs?*

WHOOSH

Follow-up activities

- Review what pupils have learnt from the thought tracking.
- Before he left, Mister Tom asked William to write. Using information from the Whoosh and the thought tracking, ask pupils to work in pairs or groups to write a letter to Mister Tom in role as William. How much of his letter would be factual, about the journey and about his mother, her health, etc? How much of his distress would he reveal to the person whom he trusts most in the world? Would he tell Mister Tom about the baby? Would he ask for help?
- Share the letters.

6   Michael Morpurgo: *Kensuke's Kingdom*

Kensuke's Kingdom has proved to be one of Michael Morpurgo's most enduring favourites since its first publication in 1999. Possibly one of the most frequently asked questions about the book is whether it is a true story, the idea being initiated in the reader's mind by the Postscript. As with many Morpurgo novels, it was inspired by a true story; that of a Japanese soldier left behind on an island after World War II. He remained there for 40 years. The hunting of orang-utans and the journey of turtles to the sea are also factual occurrences, so the novel weaves its narrative around real events.

The Whoosh explores how setting is developed – in this case, water and the sea. In the novel the sea is many things, from the location for a hobby, an adventure and the cause of a catastrophe to a source of food, enjoyment and eventual rescue. The author depicts the many moods and functions of the sea, which this Whoosh attempts to capture. It would best be used when exploring aspects of the text once the whole story is known.

Objective

- to explore how setting is created.

Characters	Objects		Sounds
Michael (narrator)	dingy	Doldrums	wind
Dad	reservoir	Australia	storms
Mum	waves	life jacket and	cheering
Stella Artois	yacht	harness	crashing waves
Gran	icebergs	sharks	drumming rain
Barnacle Bill	storms	wooded island	shrieking wind
friends	super tankers	shells	thundering waves
Eddie Dodds	sea	poisonous jellyfish	singing
Kensuke	rain	orang utans	lapping waves
hunters	sun	outrigger	shouting
	sea animals	bottle	splashing
	sails	baby turtles	thunder
		beacon	thumping waves
			gunshot

On Sundays **we** used to go **dinghy** sailing. OK, it was on the local **reservoir** not the sea, but **Dad** loved the clean air and the chance to fix things, **Mum** loved working the tiller and skippering the **boat** and **Stella Artois** and **I** just loved sailing. It was especially good when there was enough wind to make **waves** that were so big that nobody else ventured on the water. **We** even enjoyed it when there was no wind at all, because then **we** used to fish.

That all changed, of course, when Mum and Dad both lost their jobs. **Dad** went mad, or so everyone thought, sold everything and bought a 42 foot Bowman **yacht**. I didn't think he was mad at all – I thought it was a brilliant idea. No school for two years while we sailed around the world. **Gran** frightened me for a while, with her scary warnings about the hazards of the sea (**icebergs**, **storms**, **supertankers**, sudden **waves** the size of houses, things like that) but nothing really dampened our enthusiasm. **Barnacle Bill** taught **Mum** to skipper a **boat** at **sea**, **Dad** was the first mate and **I** was the ship's boy. There were times when **I** was terrified. The **waves** on the **reservoir** were nothing compared with the 20-foot **waves** at sea, but if **Mum** was scared, she never showed it.

WHOOSH

And so the day came, our **boat** loaded with stores, when we set sail. **Gran** came to cheer us off, together with **Barnacle Bill** and lots of **friends**. My best friend, **Eddie Dodds**, was there too, with a football for me. Water covers two thirds of the earth, apparently. I could believe it; if it wasn't the **sea** crashing onto the side of the **boat** it was the **rain** relentlessly **drumming** on the deck. We were constantly wet; even the sleeping bags were damp. But when the **sun** shone and the **sea** was still, we watched **porpoises** and **dolphins** diving and splashing in the waves. There were **whales**, **sharks** and **turtles**. And when I was terrified in the Bay of Biscay as the force-10 winds **shrieked** through the **sails** and the **thundering waves** threatened to engulf the *Peggy Sue*, I would curl up on my bunk, taking comfort from hugging **Stella Artois** until the storm passed.

Of course, it wasn't all storms. There were the **Doldrums** off the west coast of Africa – areas of the **sea** where there's no wind at all. **Boats** just get stuck there for weeks. Sometimes the **sea** was so huge and so empty that we were alone on the ocean for days. There was that terrifying day when **Stella Artois** fell overboard and even though **we** had practised the drill, it took three attempts of coming alongside and a lucky wave before **Dad** managed to grab **her** out of the sea just as **her** energy was gone.

WHOOSH

We felt like real explorers the day we spotted **Australia** – I wonder if that was how those first explorers felt? Our elation didn't last, though. We were hit by **storm** after terrifying **storm** as we sailed up the east coast of **Australia** and into the Pacific Ocean. **Mum** was ill and the **boat** was damaged, so **I** had to take my turn on watch at night. And that was when it happened.

I knew it was **stormy** and the **boat** was pitching and lurching. I knew I didn't have my **life jacket** or **harness** on, even though **Mum** and **Dad** were both asleep. I knew I should have just let the football go. But I didn't. And instead of steering the *Peggy Sue* across the waves, I found myself washed overboard and sinking in the waves, as the *Peggy Sue* disappeared from view, taking my sleeping **parents** with her.

The **waves** were too strong for me to swim. It was too dark to see anything. My football washed into me, which meant that **I** had some buoyancy, but all **I** could do was tread water in the darkness, trying not to be frightened, trying not to think about **sharks** homing on in me as I got colder and colder, and **singing** *Ten Green Bottles* at the top of my voice to keep myself awake. I knew that **I** was going to die at sea and somehow, **I** found that I didn't really mind.

WHOOSH

I didn't die. The **sea** washed me ashore. I have a vague memory of being pulled from the waves and when **I** woke up, **Stella Artois** was there and everything seemed better. The **sea** was calm as the tiny **waves lapped** against the white sand, but it was very, very empty. An empty **sea**, all the way to the horizon. **I shouted** for my parents until I couldn't shout any more, then **I** had to accept that the sea had taken them away. Oddly, though, when I finished exploring and found that I was on a small, wooded **island** completely surrounded by **blue, jewel-like sea**, I felt quite excited.

For several days, someone left food for **me**, so I was obviously not alone. And the **sea** took on a new meaning. It was a place for **me** to **splash** and play while the salt water healed my bites. It was a gentle force which washed up beautiful **shells**. And **I** soon realised that the sea was my means of rescue. **I** just needed to wait my chance.

It wasn't all peaceful on the **island**. Once, a huge storm lasted for four days, with crashing **thunder** overhead and mountainous **waves thumping** on to the beach. And **I** learnt the hard way that the sea could carry other dangers. **Kensuke**, the little old man who had rescued me, ran down to the beach one day while I was floating in the **sea**, shouting to me to get out of the water. But **I** didn't. **I** deliberately jumped around and swam about, making the water leap around me. Only after **he** nursed me back to health did **I** realise that the **sea** was full of **poisonous jellyfish** and my defiance of his warning had nearly cost me my life.

WHOOSH

The **sea** brought another danger, too; evil **men** hunting the orang-utans. **Gunshot** rang around our **island**, but **Kensuke** knew what to do. And as **we** got to know each other better and **he** started to trust me, he showed me where he kept an **outrigger** that he had made. **We** regularly went fishing together out on the open **sea**. Sometimes **he** would let **me** row back to shore, standing up in the stern of the boat like he did.

One day, **I** found a Coke **bottle** bobbing near the shore. Another idea came to me. **I** wrote a note, put it in the bottle and threw it far out to **sea**. Somebody would find my message. Somebody would rescue me.

Kensuke was very hurt when **Stella** appeared one day with the **bottle** in her mouth. The **sea** has just washed it straight back to shore. Even the night that **we** watched over the hatching of the turtle eggs, making sure that the gulls couldn't devour the tiny **creatures** before they made it back to the safety of the **sea**, didn't really restore his trust.

But **he** did realise how much **I** wanted to go home. And the day that we saw a **yacht** on the horizon, he finally let me light my **beacon**. Turning towards us, the **yacht** glided across the **sea**. As the *Peggy Sue* came into full view, **I** knew that the **sea** was finally going to take me home.

WHOOSH

Follow-up activities

- The sea shows many faces in this Whoosh, demonstrating how the strong contrasts of a single setting can enhance plot tension, narrative pace and emotional intensity. Through paired talk which is then shared across the whole class, brainstorm the different roles and functions of the sea as a setting. This could include:
  - storms with mountainous and thundering waves
  - the Doldrums
  - a calm, peaceful swell
  - a vast, empty space
  - a source of adventure
  - a source of food
  - a source of salt water healing
  - somewhere to play
  - a home for beautiful, dangerous and vulnerable animals
  - a means of travel for hunters
  - the means of rescue and return to safety.
- Then explore the emotions that the sea engenders – fear, peacefulness, playfulness, security, etc.
- Use this information to write a Fast Poem (Corbett 2005:25) which requires one noun, two adjectives, three adverbs and four verbs. Use the sea or an associated noun for the first line. An example would be:

Sea
Jewelled, peaceful,
Gently, calmly, serenely,
Welcoming, playing, enfolding, providing.

If each writer focused on a different aspect of the sea, the collective poems would portray its contrasts as portrayed in *Kensuke's Kingdom*.

7   David Almond: *Skellig*

David Almond's 1998 debut novel is a modern classic. It tells the story of Michael, who is struggling with the combined stresses of moving away from his friends to live in a house in need of substantial renovation just as his sister is born prematurely. The baby hovers between life and death for much of the book, but in the dilapidated garage of his new home Michael finds an unorthodox angel. With the help of a new friend, Mina, he cares for the weak and dying angel, whose story and survival become inextricably linked with that of Michael's baby sister.

One of the many outstanding features of *Skellig* is its sensory appeal. Descriptions are so rich that the reader can feel the cobwebs, hear the creaking garage, smell Skellig's rancid breath and feel Mina's detailed clay models. Because of this, the novel lends itself to several possible Whooshes. The following Whoosh explores the development of Michael and Mina's relationship from their initial meeting until the point where they have formed a trusting friendship. It is written in the first person, showing Michael's perspective on the growing friendship.

Mina is first introduced into the story at the end of Chapter 7 and Michael and Mina are firm friends by the start of Chapter 20. This would be an effective point at which to use the following Whoosh, retrospectively considering how the relationship has grown and predicting future possibilities. Alternatively, use it as part of a study of the novel on completion of the story.

Objective

- to consider how an author develops a relationship between two characters.

Characters	Objects	Sounds
Michael	lane	clicking tongue
Mina	wall	thud
Dad	back garden	blackbird's warning call
baby	tree	opening door
Mum	front garden	owl hoots
Leaky	weeds	laughter
Coot	blackbird	birds singing
Monkey Mitford	nest	traffic
Miss Clart	hospital	rustling
Mrs McKee	house	breathing
Skellig	DANGER sign	squeaking
	gate	snap
	cat	Dad calling for Michael
	stairs	whispering
	windows	doorbell
	door	
	attic room	
	roof	
	tawny owls	
	window ledge	
	dawn	
	bird skeleton	
	blanket	
	books	
	garage	
	cobwebs	

There's a **lane** along the back of our **garden**. The first time I saw her, **she** was looking over the top of the **wall**, asking me if I was the new boy. Apparently her name is **Mina**. I wonder why she **clicks** her tongue like that? She didn't stay around for any longer than it took to find out that my name was Michael. And while **I** carried on brushing off the cobwebs, worried that **Dad** might see **me**, **I** heard a **thud** as she landed back on the path.

Later, **I** saw **her** sitting in a **tree**. **Dad** and **I** were in our **front garden** discussing the weeds and **Dad** was imagining what it was all going to look like when it was finished. **She** was drawing, but when **I** went to speak to her, she **clicked** her tongue and told me I'd scared away the **blackbird** she was sketching. **She** climbed down from the **tree** anyway though and showed me her sketchbook. She even explained that the blackbird's **call we** could both hear was a warning. There are babies in a **nest** in the **tree**, apparently. She might be OK, but she will keep clicking her tongue as though I've annoyed her. Talking of babies, **she** wants to meet my sister some time.

Not much hope of that, though. The **baby** had to go back into **hospital**, but almost as though she knew something was wrong, **Mina** just appeared, sitting on the **back wall**, watching me. She **sighed** when I told her about the baby, then asked me if I could keep a secret. **She** promised that it would only take five minutes and that Dad wouldn't even know I had gone.

WHOOSH

So I agreed to share her secret. **We** crept along the back **lane**, keeping low until we were out of **Dad**'s sight. Then another **lane**, until finally **Mina** stopped outside a **house** with a **DANGER sign** nailed across the **gate**. **She** unlocked the **gate** and led me in – **she** said it wasn't really dangerous; the sign was just there to keep people out. Her **cat**, Whisper, had appeared from somewhere. Then **she** wanted to know if I was brave, but while I was wondering, **she** seemed to decide the answer for herself and took me into the **house**.

We felt our way up a flight of **stairs**, but it was really hard to see anything because the **windows** were all boarded up and no daylight was getting in. **Mina** obviously knew the **house** well, because she led me up another two flights of wide **stairs** before the **stairs** went narrow and we got to what **Mina** called the attic.

Quietly opening a **door** and pulling me into a **room**, **she** told me to copy her and lie on the floor. As I looked around, I could see a **window** jutting out under the **roof**; the glass was broken and the last light of the day was trickling through the open space. As I watched and waited and wondered what we were looking for, a **bird** suddenly flew from inside the room to the **window ledge**. It hung on for a few seconds until its **mate** joined it on the **ledge**. Then, surveying the world outside, they **both** flew off into the gathering gloom.

Carefully locking the **gate**, we ran **home**. **Mina** told me that the birds were tawny owls which lived in the attic, caring for a nest full of chicks. Just before **she** left, **she** made me promise not to tell a soul about the **house**. As she ran off, I realised that I hadn't thought about the baby for a while.

WHOOSH

The next morning, I felt shaky and weird, so **Dad** phoned school to say that I wasn't well. I spent the morning cutting down **weeds** and the afternoon visiting the **baby**. It was good to see **Mum**, too. When we got home, there was **Mina** again, sitting on the **back wall**, reading a book. **She** seemed pleased to hear that the baby might not die. **She**'d noticed that I hadn't gone to school today. **She** doesn't go to school at all, because her Mum thinks that it shuts children's minds down instead of opening them up. I imagined myself playing **football** with **Leaky** and **Coot**. I conjured up images of **Monkey Mitford** losing his temper when we forgot fractions and **Miss Clart** crying over the story of Icarus. What was it like not to go to school? Would I mind?

But then the conversation took another turn. **We** were watching the **blackbird** taking worms to the **nest** to feed its chicks, when **Mina** started asking me if I believed that we were descended from apes. Something called evolution, apparently. I didn't really know, but **Mina** did seem impressed when I showed her how to mimic an owl's **hoot** by blowing between her hands. **She** practised a few times before **she** got it. I thought I might share my secret with her – it was just an idea that I mentioned. The trouble is, I don't know if it's true or just a dream. **She** didn't seem to mind, though; she thinks that facts and dreams can get muddled.

She laughed when I told her that our shoulder blades are where our angel wings used to be. I don't think she agreed; she seems to know quite a lot about skeletons. Then it was time for 27 and 53. **She** thinks I'm quiet – she called me mystery man as I left.

WHOOSH

She must have liked the idea of the owl **hoots**, because the next morning, when I went out at **dawn** and saw the **owls** returning from their night of hunting, I hooted three times. And I think an answer came from Mina's **window**. Later that morning, I wandered over to her **house**. **She** was lying on a blanket, spread out on the grass beneath the **tree**. For a while, **she** taught me how to listen. How to really listen. Until I could hear. And sure enough, I heard the birds **singing** beneath the **traffic** noise. I heard trees **rustling** beneath the birdsong. I heard my own **breathing** beneath the rustling. And then, finally, I heard the tiny sound of **squeaking** chicks.

Mina was looking at a bird **skeleton**. **She** picked up a bone and broke it with a sharp **snap**. **She** showed me how the inside of the bone was full of air pockets so that the bird was light enough to fly. **She** told me that she had dreamt about me last night. **She**'d seen me all covered in flies and cobwebs, hooting like an owl. **She** reminded me about my secret and **we** just stared at each other.

Then we heard **Dad calling**. Before I went home, I whispered a promise to share my secret later that day.

WHOOSH

When I went back later, the **blanket** and **books** were there, but Mina had gone. So I rang the **doorbell** and a **lady** who looked just like Mina answered. She introduced herself as **Mrs McKee**, Mina's Mum. **Mina** was busy modelling birds in clay. One shelf was full of detailed models of animals that Mina had made. I had a go, too, and found myself modelling the baby. But the clay dried out and the baby's face crumbled in my hands. Then I remembered what I had promised to do that afternoon.

I only needed to look at **Mina** for her to realise what I meant – she could read my eyes. **We** wrapped the clay to stop it drying out any more, then headed for the **garage**. **She** didn't seem to mind about the **cobwebs** or the fact that it was dangerous, but **she** stared and stared at me when I got the cod liver oil capsules out of my pocket. I didn't mind about any of that. I just wanted **Mina** to see what I saw. I asked her to trust me, and **she** obviously did, because even though **she** was trembling, **she** held my hand and let **me** lead her to **Skellig**.

Afterwards, as **we** sat with **Whisper** and picked out the flies and cobwebs from our hair and clothes, **we** decided how we were going to move Skellig. He wasn't going to die. **Mina** and I were going to save him. **We** stared at each other. **We** were going to save him together.

WHOOSH

Follow-up activities

- The friendship between Michael and Mina is carefully woven into the narrative. Working in groups, use the discussion cards provided as Resource 22 to consider how this friendship develops from the point at which they first meet to the afternoon when Michael introduces Mina to Skellig.
- When group discussions are completed, use the graph provided as Resource 23 to plot the growth of the friendship. The vertical axis represents relationship development. The horizontal axis represents events as the story unfolds – the first and last events of the Whoosh are provided. Pupils should select other incidents from the Whoosh to add to the horizontal axis and then plot a line graph to show how the friendship grows.
- Complete this activity by predicting what might happen next – will Michael and Mina continue to work together to save Skellig? What might happen to test their friendship? What might the outcomes of the novel therefore be?
- At one point in the story, Mina tells Michael that she writes about herself, Michael and Skellig in a diary. As an extension activity, ask pupils to write some diary entries, working in role as Mina and writing in the first person. This activity would encourage pupils to think about the friendship from a perspective other than that of Michael as the first person narrator of the story. Discuss how events can be viewed very differently by two people.
- At the end of the novel, explore how the friendship survived the teasing of Leaky and Coot, Mina's sarcasm and Michael's defensiveness. What does this tell the reader about their friendship?
- The graph could be extended to show the journey of the relationship through the latter stages of the novel.

Resource 22 **Discussion cards**
Michael and Mina

Mina is first introduced when she is seen looking over the wall at the end of Michael's back garden. Why does she do this? What does Michael think about her? **Card 1**	Michael goes to talk to Mina while she is sitting in a tree sketching. What does this tell the reader? He appears to annoy her, but she climbs down to show Michael her sketchbook. What does this indicate about Mina? **Card 2**
The day the baby has to go back to hospital Mina appears at the back wall. Why? She takes Michael to see the owls. What does this tell the reader about Mina's view of him? **Card 3**	When Michael arrives home from hospital, Mina is sitting on the wall waiting. What does this indicate about Mina and her intentions? Why does she appear so often when Michael is upset about the baby? **Card 4**
Mina starts a discussion about evolution. Michael changes the subject very suddenly. Why? This is the first time he has offered anything to the friendship. What effect does it have? **Card 5**	After Mina has finished teaching Michael to listen to the baby birds, she tells him that she dreamt about him. Was it a dream? Why does she tell Michael? What does this signify? **Card 6**
Michael cannot find Mina so he rings the door bell. What does this tell the reader? Mina is able to read his thoughts in his eyes. What does this indicate about the depth of their friendship? **Card 7**	Michael takes Mina to meet Skellig. What does this say about their trust in each other? Afterwards, they agree to work together to save Skellig. What does this signify? **Card 8**

Resource 23 **Michael and Mina – a friendship graph**

Trust

First
meeting

Mina appears
on back wall

Mina meets
Skellig

8   Robert Swindells: *Stone Cold*

Robert Swindells served in the Royal Air Force before training as a teacher, which is when he started writing young adult and children's fiction books. In 1984, his post-apocalyptic novel *Brother in the Land* won the Red House Children's Book Award, followed by further awards for *Room 13*, *Nightmare Stairs* and *Blitzed*, which were published between 1990 and 2003. *Stone Cold* (1993), a novel about homelessness, won the Carnegie medal.

Stone Cold is written in the first person, with the narrative alternating between the homeless sixteen-year-old Link (his street name) and the ironically named Shelter. He is an ex-army Sergeant Major who creates a one-man campaign to rid London of street people after being dismissed from his job on medical grounds after 29 years of service. He believes that he was really dismissed because a change in social ethos no longer permitted him to turn 'garbage' into real men. The two narratives run in parallel for most of the novel.

The novel is gritty and presents a realistic picture of life on the streets. Link becomes homeless after his mother's boyfriend throws him out. In search of anonymity, he travels to London where he is befriended by Ginger, an experienced dosser who teaches Link how to survive on the streets. Unknown to them, Shelter is forming the Camden Horizontals, his army of dead bodies which he lines up beneath his floorboards. He decides to recruit Link and Ginger after Ginger asks him for money, but they remain unaware that they have drawn the attention of a killer to themselves. One day, after leaving Link to visit some friends in Holborn, Ginger disappears.

The Whoosh explores the ending of the novel as the two narrative strands are brought together. Initially, there should be two positions for the action, with Shelter on one side of the space and the street scenes whooshed on the opposite side of the space, in order to reinforce the alternating narrative structure of the book. Combine the action centrally when Shelter and Link are brought together in the story.

The reader has been aware that Shelter is a serial killer since shortly after the novel begins, but the other characters do not become aware of it until the end of the book. At the point of the Whoosh, Ginger has just disappeared. Link has been searching for him and he knows that Ginger went somewhere with a man who said that Link had had an accident, but he has not been able to find out anything more. He has just met Gail, a new person on the streets, in a cafe.

Objective

* to write in role, demonstrating understanding of a social issue and its causes.

Characters	Objects	Sounds
Shelter Link Gail people in the cafe people with cold, hard looks old bloke market stall holders market shoppers people near the National Gallery people in Trafalgar Square seven recruits Toya's father Nick Toya DS Ireson Captain Hook two policemen Gavin	cafe cold, hard places market stalls doorway National Gallery pigeons phone box Shelter's house Camden Station police station three dustbins white front door darkened windows Shelter's lounge	ringing doorbell door slamming smashing doors

Commence the Whoosh with Shelter entering and standing silently to one side of the performance space watching Link and Gail.

Gail and I just sat in the busy **cafe** and talked. **We** hit it off straight away and suddenly I didn't feel like a freak any more. I forgot that I was dirty and that my clothes were worn out. I forgot about the **cold, hard places** that I had to sleep and the **cold, hard looks** that I got when I asked for money. It was just Gail and me. When **we** left, **we** sat on a wall in the sun holding hands. Some **old bloke** walked past us and glared, but I didn't care. I was falling in love.

'*Let's get some chips and eat them by the water*,' **she** suggested, so **we** did. **She** didn't seem to be too worried about making her money last. **She** just kept asking questions about life on the street and I answered them as though I had been there for years.

I didn't beg that day. Instead, **we** wandered around the **market** at Camden Lock, looking at all the **stalls**. They were full of hats, jewellery, tee shirts, mirrors, candles and ethnic stuff. It looked like rubbish, but **we** watched a lot of **people** spending a lot of money on it as we walked. **We** bought Cokes, ate for the second time that day and then found my favourite **doorway** to spend the night. I had hardly thought of Ginger at all.

We slept with our arms around each other and the next day **Gail** wanted to learn to beg. I did what Ginger had done for me – I left her asking **people** for money at the **National Gallery** while I went to Trafalgar Square. It was a very cold day; **people** just kept walking past me as though I was invisible and even the **pigeons** were doing better than me. But when I went back to find Gail, **she**'d gone. Panic set in as I searched for her, followed by relief when she appeared from a **phone box**. '*My sister in Glasgow*,' **she** said by way of explanation. '*She made me promise to keep in touch.*' **Gail** had made £2.30, so **we** ate again. Life was fantastic and it stayed that way until the spring.

WHOOSH

Shelter: '*I haven't got Link, but I haven't been idle. Seven recruits in the Camden Horizontals, all shiny boots and short hair. I've even got a black one, just to prove that there's no prejudice in my Army. They are volunteers, you know. Nobody forces 'em to come. All they want is an end to hunger and a roof over their heads. That's exactly what I give them. I spoil them really, they even get a floor.*'

Link: Even begging was easy with **Gail**. I began to get a bit possessive of her, frightened that someone with a job and a car was going to take her away. I really wished I had a job, so that I could offer her something, but **she** didn't seem to mind. I didn't think to ask why.

We were sitting in the sun on the towpath one afternoon when this **man** came up to us. '*Excuse me*,' he said anxiously. '*I'm trying to trace my daughter and I wondered if you might have seen her.*' **He** held out a photo – it was Toya.

'*I've seen her a couple of times. There. The market*,' I nodded. Apparently a man in a night watchman's hut (I knew him, he was called Captain Hook) had seen her about a week ago, going into a flat with an older man. **He** even had the address, but when he'd gone to the **house** and rung the **bell**, nobody had answered.

'*We'll look out for your daughter*,' I promised, '*and if we see her we'll say we saw you – get her to phone home. OK?*'

'*It's breaking her mother's heart*,' **he** sobbed. **He** was so grateful that he gave us a fiver before he shambled off. **Gail** and I pretended not to notice each other trying not to cry.

WHOOSH

Shelter: '*Someone rang the door bell last night. Middle aged chap, seemed anxious. He tried three times, but I wasn't going to answer – never give away your position. Never show a strong light after dusk either I thought, so I looked through the curtains. Eventually he went away. For some reason, I think he's related to one of my recruits. I'll be more careful for a few days.*'

Link: I probably wouldn't have thought any more about Toya if it hadn't been for **Nick** – he sells the Big Issue outside **Camden Station**. Funny thing is, **he**'d seen **Toya** walking away with the same **man** that he'd seen Ginger with. '*We could be talking about double murder*,' I pondered. For some reason, **Gail** chose that moment to go and ring her sister while **Nick** and I decided that we needed to watch this man's house for a bit. '*Cool chick*,' laughed **Nick**, punching my arm as we watched **Gail** walk away.

By the time **Gail** got back, I'd already decided to go the **police station** on Albany Street. It took a while, but I eventually managed to get past the front desk and **Detective Sergeant Ireson** showed me into a cubicle. **He** wasn't impressed, just like Gail had said. Apparently they'd already investigated a complaint and there was nothing wrong. '*The matter is officially closed*,' he said, showing me out.

WHOOSH

Shelter: '*Can you hear me having the last laugh? Two of them, there were, asking questions about the girl. Had I seen her? Well of course I had. I explained to them all about how I help these poor homeless kids, give them a meal, let them have a bath then send them on their way. I told them what a charming girl she was and how sorry I was to turn her back out on the streets. They ended up on my side. 'Do be careful who you bring into your home,' one of them warned as they left. I'm still laughing.*'

Link: I waited on the canal bridge while **Gail** went to ask **Captain Hook** for the man's address. While I was waiting, I thought about Gail. Somehow, she seemed too self-assured to be on the streets, but I pushed the thought away and forgot about it.

9, Mornington Place was a three storey Victorian house with a tiny front garden just big enough for three **dustbins**. A short path led to the white front **door**. There was no light showing from any of the **windows** – obviously nobody was home. **We** waited around for a while, then decided to try again the next day.

It was cold when **we** got back the next morning. The curtains were still pulled, but after about thirty minutes, the **door** opened and a cat was put outside, followed ten minutes later by the **owner** going to buy a paper. **We** gave up then – a man with a cat can't be a killer.

Gail and I had our first row later that day. I wanted to go back to Mornington Place, but it was raining and **Gail** said she had things to do. So I went on my own. I must have stood there for hours in the rain, thinking about Ginger and Toya and wishing that I hadn't had a row with Gail because I loved her. Then suddenly the **door** opened and there was the **man**, standing in the doorway, calling for the cat. When the cat didn't come, **he** shuffled down the path and started looking along the road, fiddling with a fork which he had in his hand. And that was when **he** spotted me.

WHOOSH

'*I say, excuse me*,' he called, '*you haven't by any chance seen a cat, have you?*' How could I be frightened of a man in his slippers looking for his cat? He couldn't really be a serial killer. I was more embarrassed than anything and I was about to walk away when the cat appeared. **He** picked it up, cradling it in his arms and called out, '*There's a coat, a good one, I don't use it any more. You're welcome to that if it'll help.*' It was that easy. I followed him into the **house**.

He was daft about the cat, wrapping it in a towel and asking me to fetch its bowl from the step. I went into the **lounge** to wait for him to finish feeding the cat. Everything was perfectly tidy, everything in its place. There was no way this soft noodle could be a murderer, I thought. That was when I spotted my watch, the one I had been mugged for, on the sideboard and my chest went tight.

Everything happened really suddenly. The **door** slammed, **he** was laughing as **he** showed me his **Army** under the floorboards, and then **he** was trying to kill me. I was gasping for breath when I heard doors being smashed in and two **policemen** pulling the man off of me. There was **Gail**, too, standing on the doorstep. '*How did you get the police to believe you?*' I was asking, just as some poncy looking **man** with a camera pranced up the path grinning, '*Louise, darling. You're a genius.*'

It took **me** a moment to realise that Louise and Gail were the same person. '*I'm Louise Bain*,' she said apologetically, '*I'm a journalist. This is Gavin,*' she went on, introducing the **man** with the camera. I was so angry and upset that I didn't want to listen to her explanations about how they had been on to this serial killer for months. '*Why don't you get some shots of the victims and send them to their parents?*' I shouted at Gavin.

Louise pushed some money into my hand before the **man** with the car and the job took her away. I should have thrown the money back in her face, but I didn't. I hope her story is truthful and makes people realise what it's like.

'Shelter? Well, he got life, so a bed, three meals a day and a roof over his head. Me? I'm still on the streets with the ghosts of Ginger and Toya for company. How is that justice?'

WHOOSH

Follow-up activities

- At one point in the story Shelter says, 'They *are* volunteers, you know – nobody forces 'em to come,' about the people that he has killed. This also reflects one view of homelessness – that people who live on the streets have chosen to be there. Ask students to review what they have learnt from *Stone Cold* about reasons for young people becoming homeless. Further research would expand their knowledge.
- As a whole class, list the information which has been derived from both the book and the research. Then conduct a class debate using the statement 'Homeless young people choose to live on the streets.'
- Next, focus students' attention on Gail. Link hopes that she tells the truth when she writes her article – what does he mean by 'the truth' and what does he hope she will say? Is it possible that she just used Link to get a sensationalist scoop about a serial killer and had little interest in the plight of the homeless?
- Finally, challenge students to write an article in role as a journalist. Ask them to choose an angle (ie sensationalist, factual, supportive, critical) and then demonstrate bias in their writing.
- Compare completed articles – how well do they show society's range of views about homelessness?

6   How to write a Whoosh

As this book demonstrates, any story can be whooshed, regardless of the complexity of the narrative. You can whoosh a complete story, just one scene or chapter, or selected sections of a text – the choice is yours, depending on the age, experience, confidence and learning needs of your pupils.

Step 1: Know your purpose. Define your outcome. Formulate a focused objective.

The Whoosh can fulfil a variety of purposes and it is important, if a Whoosh is to be effective, to define its purpose. With young children you can whoosh a complete story. In addition to enjoying the acting, pupils will also be internalising structure (if the Whoosh is written to reflect the main beginning/middle/end sections of the story), understanding characters and responding to settings.

With older pupils, use a Whoosh to introduce a new text – starting with a Whoosh to introduce key characters, initial plot line or the opening setting will hook students in. This is particularly valuable where the text for study is challenging or does not immediately lend itself to every student's interest.

You could choose to compare and contrast different characters, focus on the creation or development of a character or explore interactions between characters. Complex issues can be isolated for reflection or intricacies of elaborate plot and sub-plot can be examined. Individual setting can be considered, a range of settings across a text can be compared or the effect of setting can be investigated – this is particularly pertinent when studying historical, cultural or social context.

Deciding where to place Whooshes in a unit of work is also important – is your purpose to introduce, examine, reflect on or review a particular aspect of the text?

Step 2: Reflect on and decide the language focus.

Your purpose might be to introduce a text written in archaic language in which case the decision is whether to use brief extracts of the original text (as with Shakespearean dialogue) or whether to paraphrase. For other purposes, you can carefully select the dialogue and action which spotlights the particular aspects of text which you want pupils to focus on or you can take a broad sweep across a section of text to cover ground quickly – your use of language will be determined by your intention.

The use of a Whoosh can also focus attention on effective word selection. If a child acts out the sentence, 'The monster came through the door', decisions have to be made about how the monster entered. Did it creep, burst or smash through the door? Each word creates a different perception about the character of the monster and it is this detail which a Whoosh directs the actors to consider. When writing their own stories, pupils need to focus on word selection. Not only are they are more likely to do so after whooshing, they will also understand from their own active experience the power of words in shaping the reader's understanding of the story.

Step 3: Write the Whoosh and select highlighted content.

Writing an effective Whoosh requires you to be rigorously selective about content – everything must serve the objective. Not every object in the Whoosh needs to be highlighted. Focus on objects and sounds which are most important to your objective. Additionally, you could highlight objects, sounds or dialogue which you want to pick up on at a later point in the unit of work.

Step 4: Compose follow-up activities.

A Whoosh is an important part of text engagement and preparation for response to the text. All Whooshes should be followed up with discussion. This can take the form of paired, group or shared discussion and it can be exploratory, structured or guided – the important factor is that discussion aims to extend thinking and consolidate understanding.

Questioning is also important – pupils infer and deduce a great deal of information whilst they are whooshing and careful questioning is needed to help pupils articulate this and locate evidence. A video of the activity is particularly helpful for this.

Mapping, picture sequencing and retelling the story are all useful as follow-up activities for younger pupils. This helps pupils to understand narrative flow, sequencing, the rhythm of language and the need to imagine beyond the actual words which are being spoken. Retelling a story also requires the speaker to make immediate access to their vocabulary bank, making decisions about what words to choose in order to convey intended meaning to the audience.

All responses can then be used as a planning tool to scaffold writing. This could include writing in role, non-fiction or analytical writing, story writing or the writing of a Whoosh – the latter is particularly useful for revision purposes for older pupils.

Step 5: Perform, evaluate, assess and define next steps in learning.

Whooshing provides an excellent opportunity for formative assessment. Knowledge and understanding can be readily identified and next steps for individual pupils clearly defined. Peer- and self-assessment points can also form part of the follow-up discussion.

Although the greatest value of a Whoosh lies in its learning potential, it could also be extended to performance. Pupils could perform their Whoosh to a parallel class, older pupils could write and perform Whooshes of texts for younger pupils, and younger pupils themselves will always enjoy an opportunity to perform to parents.

Wherever a Whoosh is included in the English curriculum, if it is carefully written and thoughtfully used, it will provide a powerful learning experience for all pupils.

Bibliography

Almond, D. (1998) *Skellig*, London: Hodder Children's Books.

Bawden, N. (1973) *Carrie's War*, London: Puffin.

Booker, C. (2004) *The Seven Basic Plots: Why We Tell Stories*, London and New York: Continuum.

Boyce, F.C. (2008) *Cosmic*, London: Macmillan Children's Books.

Brontë, C. (2010) *Jane Eyre*, Kindle edition, downloaded 16 September 2012.

Coats, L. and Lewis, A. (2002) *Atticus the Storyteller's 100 Greek Myths*, London: Orion.

Conan Doyle, A. (2001) *The Hound of the Baskervilles*, London: Penguin Classics.

Corbett, P. (2005) *Jumpstart! Literacy Games and Activities for ages 7–14*, London: David Fulton.

Dickens, C. (2003) *A Christmas Carol and Other Christmas Writings*, London: Penguin Classics.

Dickens, C. (2007) *A Christmas Carol*, Stroud: Real Reads.

Dickens, C. (2004) *Great Expectations*, London: Penguin Classics.

Dickens, C. (2007) *Great Expectations*, Stroud: Real Reads.

Dickens, C. (2003) *Oliver Twist*, London: Penguin Classics.

Dickens, C. (2007) *Oliver Twist*, Stroud: Real Reads.

Dodge, M. M. (2003) *Hans Brinker, or the Silver Skates*, New York: Dover.

Eliot, G. (1996) *Silas Marner: The Weaver of Raveloe*, London: Penguin.

Grahame, K. (2012)*The Wind in the Willows*, Kindle edition, downloaded 4 August 2012.

Green, J. (2008) *Beowulf the Brave*, London: A & C Black.

Harris, J.C. (2006) *The Adventures of Brer Rabbit and Friends*, London: Dorling Kindersley.

Mackinnon, M. and Massari, A. (2010) *The Firebird*, London: Usborne.

Magorian, M. (1981) *Goodnight Mister Tom*, London: Puffin.

McCaughrean, G. and Chichester Clarke, E. (1992) *The Orchard Book of Greek Myths*, London: Orchard Books.

Milbourne, A. and Edwards, L. (2004) *Stories from India*, London: Usborne.

Milton, G. (1999) *Nathaniel's Nutmeg*, London: Hodder and Stoughton.

Morpurgo, M. and Chichester Clarke, E. (2004) *The Orchard Book of Aesop's Fables*, London: Orchard Books.

Morpurgo, M. and Foreman, M. (1999) *Kensuke's Kingdom*, London: Mammoth.

Morpurgo, M. and Foreman, M. (2005) *Sir Gawain and the Green Knight*, London: Walker Books.

Morpurgo, M. and Foreman, M. (2006) *Beowulf*, London: Walker Books.

Nesbit E. (2011) *Five Children and It*, Kindle Edition downloaded 4 August 2012.

Norriss, A. (2004) *The Touchstone*, London: Puffin.

Pirotta, S. and Hyde, C. (2010) *Firebird*, Dorking: Templar.

Priestley, J.B. (1992) *An Inspector Calls*, London: Heinemann.

Pullman, P. and others (2011) *Magic Beans: A Handful of Fairytales from the Storybag*, Oxford and New York: David Fickling Books.

Riordan J. and Foreman M. (1997) *The Songs my Paddle Sings*, London: Pavilion Books.

Sachar, L. (1998) *Holes*, London: Bloomsbury.

Shakespeare, W. (2011) *Complete Works of William Shakespeare*, Kindle edition, downloaded 20 August 2012.

Shaw, G. B. (2005) *Pygmalion*, Kindle edition, downloaded 28 September 2012.

Shelley, M. (2012) *Frankenstein*, Kindle Edition, downloaded 25 September 2012.

Stevenson, R. L. (2007) *Treasure Island*, London: Penguin Classics.

Sutcliff, R. (2005) *Beowulf: Dragonslayer*, London: Red Fox.

Swindells, R. (1995) *Stone Cold*, London: Puffin.

Wells, J.C. (1982) *Accents of English 1: An Introduction*, Cambridge: University Press.

Wilde, O. (2006) *Stories for Children*, London: Hodder Children's Books.

Williams, M. (2006) *Greek Myths*, London: Walker Books.

Winston, J. and Tandy, M. (2008) *Beginning Drama 4–11*, London: David Fulton Books.

Websites

www.aesops-fables.org.uk accessed 11 February 2012.
www.anansistories.com accessed 21 July 2012.
www.americanfolklore.net accessed 18 June 2012.
www.dollybay.com/flyingdutchmanstory.html accessed 17 July 2012.
www.essortment.com/flying-dutchman-legend-64877.html accessed 17 July 2012.
www.firstpeople.us accessed 18 June 2012.
www.greece.mrdonn.org accessed 26 June 2012.
www.gutenberg.org/files/2781/2781-h/2781-h.htm accessed 11 February 2012.
www.online-literature.com/george_bernard_shaw/pygmalion/1 accessed 19 July 2012.
www.panchatantra.org accessed 12 March 2012.
http://storynory.com/2006/01/24/the-elephants-child accessed 11 February 2012.
http://thelostdutchman.hubpages.com/hub/The-Flying-Dutchman accessed 17 July 2012.

Indexes

Alphabetical index by author (continued)

Title	Learning intention	Core skill	Page
Stories from the sea: *The Flying Dutchman*	character: viewpoint	speaking and listening	42
Swindells, Robert: *Stone Cold*	understanding social issues	writing/debate	143
The Panchatantra: *The Blue Jackal*	sequencing/text cohesion	writing: paragraphing	5
Uncle Remus tales: *Brer Rabbit and the Tar Baby*	character: humour	inference and deduction	44
Wilde, Oscar: *The Selfish Giant*	character: emotion	speaking and listening	36

Alphabetical index by title

Title	Learning intention	Core skill	Page
A Christmas Carol: Charles Dickens	create/develop a character	drama (2 activities)	92
A Midsummer Night's Dream: William Shakespeare	plot and character	drama	60
An Inspector Calls: J B Priestley	plot and character	speaking and listening/ group discussion/ writing	75
Anansi and the Sky God: Anansi stories	developing empathy	drama	20
Anansi and the Turtle: Anansi stories	moral meaning of a story	drama/writing	25
Beowulf: Grendel the Night Prowler: Anglo-Saxon epic tales	descriptive language	discussion/writing	34
Brer Rabbit and the Tar Baby: Uncle Remus tales	character: humour	inference and deduction	44
Carrie's War: Nina Bawden	historical and social context	discussion/writing	124
Cosmic: Frank Cottrell Boyce	character: relationships	group discussion	120
Five Children and It: E Nesbit	fantasy genre	discussion/writing	87
Frankenstein: Mary Shelley	narrative structure	writing	110
Goodnight Mister Tom: Michelle Magorian	character development	drama/writing	132
Great Expectations: Charles Dickens	character: values	drama/writing	102
Hamlet: William Shakespeare	exploring the central plot	group discussion	63
Holes: Louis Sachar	prediction/thinking skills	group discussion	130
How the Butterflies Came to Be: Native American legends	figurative language	drama	10
Jane Eyre: Charlotte Brontë	contrasts of setting	speaking and listening	105
Just So Stories: The Elephant's Child: Rudyard Kipling	key elements of a story	writing	8
Kensuke's Kingdom, Michael Morpurgo	understanding setting	writing/story mapping	135
King Midas: Greek myths	setting/characterisation	paired talk/writing	11
Mossycoat: English folk tales	character: viewpoint	speaking and listening	28
Oliver Twist: Charles Dickens	historical and social context	speaking and listening	97
Perseus and Medusa: Greek myths	conflict within a story	drama (2 activities)	15
Pygmalion: George Bernard Shaw	character interaction	writing: story mountain	77
Silas Marner: George Eliot	characterisation: parents	drama	113
Sir Gawain and the Green Knight: English legends	sequencing/story structure	group discussion	40
Skellig: David Almond	relationship development	oral storytelling group discussion/writing	138
Stone Cold: Robert Swindells	understanding social issues	writing/debate	143
The Blue Jackal: The Panchatantra	sequencing/text cohesion	writing: paragraphing	5
The Firebird: Russian folk tales	pace and structure	writing: story mapping	32
The Flying Dutchman: Stories from the sea	character: viewpoint	speaking and listening	42
The Hero of Haarlem: Legends across cultures	influence of setting on plot	discussion/writing	19
The Hound of the Baskervilles: Sir Arthur Conan Doyle	understanding language	writing	108
The Lion and the Mouse: Aesop's fables	story structure	writing: fable	4
The Merchant of Venice: William Shakespeare	understanding plot lines	drama	66
The Selfish Giant: Oscar Wilde	character: emotion	speaking and listening	36
The Taming of the Shrew: William Shakespeare	understanding plot/subplot	creative writing	70
The Tempest: William Shakespeare	understanding complex plot	drama	49
The Touchstone: Andrew Norriss	story opening	group discussion	118
The Wind in the Willows: Kenneth Grahame	character: behaviour	drama/writing	82
Treasure Island: Robert Louis Stevenson	introducing the text	discussion: prediction	89
Twelfth Night: William Shakespeare	character: comedy	speaking and listening	54

Index by learning intention

Index by learning intention (continued)

Learning intention	Title	Core skill	Page
Use of language			
to explore feelings generated by descriptive language	*Beowulf*	discussion/writing	34
to explore the use of figurative and expressive language	*How the Butterflies Came to Be*	speaking and listening	10
exploring imagery	*Carrie's War*	discussion/writing	124
to access archaic language in a classic text	*The Hound of the Baskervilles*	writing	108
Understanding meaning			
to develop empathy through reflecting on key events	*Anansi and the Sky God*	drama	20
to interpret and debate the moral meaning of a text	*Anansi and the Turtle*	drama/writing	25
to develop skills of prediction and open-minded thinking	*Holes*	group discussion	130
Genre			
to understand fantasy genre	*Five Children and It*	discussion/writing	87
to introduce the characters, setting and plot of an adventure story	*Treasure Island*	discussion: prediction	89
to explore the genre of comedy	*Twelfth Night*	speaking and listening	54

Index by core skill

Core skill	Title	Learning intention	Page
Speaking, listening and responding			
to locate and use evidence to support viewpoint	*An Inspector Calls*	plot and character	75
locate and respond to examples of figurative language	*How the Butterflies Came to Be*	figurative language	10
use paired talk to generate vocabulary	*Kensuke's Kingdom*	understanding setting	135
locate evidence of settings/defining interaction of characters with settings	*King Midas*	setting/character	11
find evidence of language which persuades the listener to adopt a particular view of the protagonist	*Mossycoat*	character: viewpoint	28
oral retelling of the story/ oral creation of a new story	*Sir Gawain and the Green Knight*	sequencing/story structure	40
conduct a class debate on the issue of homelessness	*Stone Cold*	social issues	143
define the viewpoint of the storyteller: consider alternatives	*The Flying Dutchman*	character: viewpoint	42
use emoticons to track a character's feelings	*The Selfish Giant*	character: emotion	36
analyse comic characterisation and create new characters	*Twelfth Night*	character: comedy	54
Group discussion and interaction			
to evaluate evidence and form a conclusion	*An Inspector Calls*	plot and character	75
analyse the use of language to portray feelings	*Beowulf*	descriptive language	34
inference and deduction of character	*Brer Rabbit and the Tar Baby*	character: humour	44
find textual evidence to explain context	*Carrie's War*	historical and social context	124
create a communication web to explore relationships	*Cosmic*	character	120
work in role as the main characters of the narrative	*Five Children and It*	fantasy genre	87
consider and select evidence to contribute to a debate	*Hamlet*	understanding plot	63
locate examples of foreshadowing to predict outcomes	*Holes*	prediction/thinking skills	130
card activity to consider parenting roles of two characters	*Silas Marner*	character: parents	113
discussion cards/friendship graph	*Skellig*	relationship development	138
define setting and discuss how this determines the plot	*The Hero of Haarlem*	influence of setting on plot	19
locate and plot the beginning/middle/end of a fable	*The Lion and the Mouse*	story structure	4
discuss characters, themes and plot as a basis for further study	*The Tempest*	understanding plot	49
formulate questions about character/plot. Predict possible outcomes for the narrative	*The Touchstone*	story opening	118
predict possible outcomes of the adventure	*Treasure Island*	introduction to text	89
Drama			
Role on the Wall (2 activities)	*A Christmas Carol*	character development	92
Freeze Frames	*A Midsummer Night's Dream*	plot and character	60
to work in role	*An Inspector Calls*	plot and character	75
Freeze Frames	*Anansi and the Sky God*	developing empathy	20
Sculptor and Sculpted/Thought Tracking	*Anansi and the Turtle*	moral meaning	25
talk in role to understand characters' feelings	*Beowulf*	descriptive language	34
Thought Tracking	*Goodnight Mister Tom*	character development	132
soliloquy	*Great Expectations*	character: values	102
Interview/Thought Collage	*Oliver Twist*	historical context	97
Freeze Frames	*Pygmalion*	character interaction	77
exploring disguise and confusion	*The Merchant of Venice*	understanding plot	66
Hot Seating to create a trial defence	*The Wind in the Willows*	character/behaviour	82
Writing			
to write persuasively	*An Inspector Calls*	plot and character	75
write thought bubbles to track a character's thoughts	*Anansi and the Turtle*	moral meaning	25

Index by core skill (continued)

Core skill	Title	Learning intention	Page
kennings/create a monster	*Beowulf*	descriptive language	34
information text/diary entry	*Carrie's War*	historical and social context	124
write a short story or make a film on a fantasy theme	*Five Children and It*	fantasy genre	87
write a Whoosh/write letters in role	*Frankenstein*	narrative structure	110
letter writing in role	*Goodnight Mister Tom*	character development	132
write a letter in role to future self	*Great Expectations*	character: values	102
storyboard/film creation, analytical writing about language	*Jane Eyre*	contrasts of setting	105
write a Fast Poem	*Kensuke's Kingdom*	understanding setting	135
create and annotate a story map to show key features	*The Elephant's Child*	key elements of a story	8
use a story mountain to track build up/resolution of conflict	*Perseus and Medusa*	conflict within a story	15
write a diary entry in role, demonstrating viewpoint	*Skellig*	relationship development	138
write in role as a journalist, adopting a viewpoint	*Stone Cold*	social issues	143
map a story, using the map as model for a new story	*The Firebird*	pace and structure	32
use a contemporary setting to create a new story plot	*The Hero of Haarlem*	influence of setting on plot	19
use a modelled story plan to write a new fable	*The Blue Jackal*	text cohesion	5
write a Whoosh to demonstrate understanding of plot, character and setting	*The Hound of the Baskervilles*	understanding language	108
use images to create a cohesive structure and explore paragraph structure	*The Lion and the Mouse*	story structure	4
write in prose to demonstrate viewpoint of a character	*The Taming of the Shrew*	understanding plot	70
report writing in role	*The Wind in the Willows*	character/behaviour	82